The New Investment Theory of Real Options and its Implication for Telecommunications Economics

Topics in Regulatory Economics and Policy Series

Michael A. Crew, Editor
Graduate School of Management, Rutgers University
Newark, New Jersey, U.S.A.

Previously published books in the series:

Gordon, R. L.:
Regulation and Economic Analysis: A Critique Over Two Centuries
Blackmon, G.:
Incentive Regulation and the Regulations of Incentives
Crew, M.:
Incentive Regulation for Public Utilities
Crew, M.:
Commercialization of Postal and Delivery Services
Abbott, T. A.:
Health Care Policy and Regulation
Goff, B.:
Regulation and Macroeconomic Performance
Coate, M.B. and A.N. Kleit:
The Economics of the Antitrust Process
Franz, R. S.:
X-Efficiency: Theory, Evidence and Applications (Second Edition)
Crew, M.:
Pricing and Regulatory Innovations Under Increasing Competition
Crew, M., and P. Kleindorfer:
Managing Change in the Postal Delivery Industries
Awerbuch, S. and A. Preston:
The Virtual Utility
Gabel, D. and D. Weiman:
Opening Networks to Competition: The Regulation and Pricing of Access
Zaccour, G.:
Deregulation of Electric Utilities
Young, W.:
Atomic Energy Costing
Crew, M.:
Regulation Under Increasing Competition
Crew, M.A. and P.R. Kleindorfer:
Emerging Competition in Postal and Delivery Services
Cherry, B.A.:
The Crisis in Telecommunications Carrier Liability: Historical Regulatory Flaws and Recommended Reform
Loomis, D.G. and L.D. Taylor
The Future of the Telecommunications Industry: Forecasting and Demand Analysis

The New Investment Theory of Real Options and its Implication for Telecommunications Economics

edited by

James Alleman
University of Colorado at Boulder and PHB Hagler Bailly

Eli Noam
Columbia University

Kluwer Academic Publishers
Boston/Dordrecht/London

Distributors for North, Central and South America:
Kluwer Academic Publishers
101 Philip Drive
Assinippi Park
Norwell, Massachusetts 02061 USA
Telephone (781) 871-6600
Fax (781) 871-6528
E-Mail <kluwer@wkap.com>

Distributors for all other countries:
Kluwer Academic Publishers Group
Distribution Centre
Post Office Box 322
3300 AH Dordrecht, THE NETHERLANDS
Telephone 31 78 6392 392
Fax 31 78 6546 474
E-Mail <orderdept@wkap.nl>

Electronic Services <http://www.wkap.nl>

Library of Congress Cataloging-in-Publication Data

Real options in telecommunications : the new investment theory and its implications for telecommunications economics / edited by James Alleman, Eli Noam.
p. cm.
Includes bibliographical references and index.
ISBN 0-7923-7734-6 (acid-free paper)
1. Telecommunication--Economic aspects. 2. Capital budget. 3. Options (Finance) I. Alleman, James H. II. Noam, Eli M.

HE7631 .R43 1999
384'.041--dc21

99-052725

Printed on acid-free paper.

Printed in the United States of America
This printing is a digital duplication of the original edition.

Contents

Preface

Randall B. Lowe
Piper & Marbury, L.L.P.

The issue of costing and pricing in the telecommunications industry has been hotly debated for the last twenty years. Indeed, we are still wrestling today over the cost of the local exchange for access by interexchange and competitive local exchange carriers, as well as for universal service funding.

The U.S. telecommunications world was a simple one before the emergence of competition, comprising only AT&T and independent local exchange carriers. Costs were allocated between intrastate and interstate jurisdictions and then again, between intrastate local and toll. The Bell System then divided those costs among itself (using a process referred to as the division of revenues) and independents (using a process called settlements). Tolls subsidized local calls to keep the politicians happy, and the firm, as a whole, covered its costs and made a fair return.

State regulators, however, lacked the wherewithal to audit this process. Their concerns centered generally on whether local rates, irrespective of costs, were at a politically acceptable level. Although federal regulators were better able to determine the reasonableness of the process and the resulting costs, they adopted an approach of "continuous surveillance" where, like the state regulator, the appearance of reasonableness was what mattered.

With the advent of competition, this historical costing predicate had to change. The Bell System, as well as the independents, were suddenly held accountable. Federal regulators wanted to ensure that monopoly rates did not subsidize competitive offerings. Otherwise, ratepayers would pay too much and competitors would be harmed by predatory prices.

As a result, various costing methodologies were devised by all sides to allocate costs among the dominant carriers' services. The FCC, for instance, came up with a number of fully distributed costing methodologies (FDC). AT&T proposed its version of marginal cost pricing, which it labeled long-run incremental costs (LRIC). FDC, of course, benefited competitors to AT&T because it attempted to spread costs among AT&T's services based on the historical reasons for incurring those costs. Under this method, AT&T's competitive services would be saddled with costs that were not incurred as part of the competitive enterprise, but were associated with more traditional offerings. Eventually, a compromise was reached: although LRIC was found to be unacceptable, a "pure" FDC method was used, as tracked by a more "incremental" FDC method, and was placed in a costing manual that AT&T was required to follow. Meanwhile, the states sat back and watched.

This approach did not work. On the assumption that "costs are as costs are defined," AT&T was able to use the manual in a manner that, strangely enough, resembled marginal costs. The FCC next tried structural separation, but that did not work either. Consequently, the FCC found itself before Judge Greene of the Washington, DC District Court arguing that divestment was the only solution. (Divestment was considered a solution because it separated monopoly services offered by what became the Regional Bell Operating Companies (RBOCs) from the now-competitive toll offerings of AT&T. Straightforward in theory, it was difficult to implement and failed to address the intraLATA toll that the RBOCs were allowed to offer and contained an escape clause that permitted exceptions to the separation.)

The FCC has relied more and more on market forces as the market shares of once-dominant companies fall. As new markets open up, such as the market for competitive local exchange services, the costing issue has gained strength. This issue is also now finding its way overseas as those markets open up to competition.

At the risk of oversimplifying, the issue of costs can be summarized as two-fold: the quantitative determination of the level of costs and the proper attribution of those costs. Both are fraught with questions. The amount of costs, for instance, can vary from book costs to marginal costs. The attribution of costs (i.e., incurred by whom for what service) can vary from those that are directly attributable to those that are joint and common. Hence, the need for costing theories and models.

Considering that, in the words of the FCC, costs are at the "heart" of just and reasonable rates and that such rates lead to universal service and a strong competitive environment, the industry is constantly in search of theories and models that more accurately reflect the underlying costs of service. It is in this light that the papers have been compiled for this book. Real options theory attempts to consider management's flexibility in valuation analysis and corrects the deficiencies of the traditional discounted present value and decision tree analyses. Drs. Alleman and Noam, as the editors of this compilation, have done a superb job by first setting forth an introduction and overview of the subject, and then providing the reader with a primer on real options in articles by Lenos Trigeorgis and Sanjai Bhagat. Other authors in the volume highlight the controversies that surround the application of real options in the telecommunications industry; however, the editors have effectively separated the issues of application from those of interpretation.

It is this type of work and inquiry that can illuminate the issue of costing and cost modeling for a more refined use in telecommunications. Although we should not, as one jurist put it, let perfection become the enemy of the good, we should constantly strive for a better way, especially in the constantly changing world of telecommunications. One can only hope that this book opens that door a little further.

Acknowledgements

This volume is the product of the encouragement and cooperation of many people and institutions. First, we would like to thank our home institutions, the Columbia Institute for Tele-Information (CITI) of Columbia University and the Interdisciplinary Telecommunications Program (ITP) of the University of Colorado – Boulder, which supported the workshop from which this proceeding was born. Columbia provided the facilities and venue. Both contributed funding, hosted web sites, supplied mailing lists, and in numerous other ways made the workshop a success.

The assistance of Hagler Bailly and Putnam, Hayes & Bartlett is also gratefully acknowledged (the firms have since merged and are now known as PHB Hagler Bailly). In addition to speakers and funding, it offered the support and guidance to ensure this volume was published.

Of course, it is not the institutions, but the people behind them who contribute time and effort. From CITI, Caterina Alvarez and later Lynette Mallett ensured that the workshop was well organized and smoothly run, while Kenneth Carter oversaw its planning and implementation.

From PHB Hagler Bailly, Lee Bauman added the drive and encouragement to see the workshop through to completion, championed these proceedings, and came through in emergencies. Mike Yokell and Bill Zarakas guided us through the process. A special thanks goes to Wynne Cougill, who edited this volume and Jane Enright, who laid out the text. They did an outstanding job under tremendous time pressure.

Last, we would like to acknowledge the speakers who gave generously of their time and talents to produce an excellent workshop and, as the reader can judge, a sound volume that initiates the debate on real options application to the telecommunications industry.

James Alleman and Eli Noam

Introduction and Overview

James Alleman
University of Colorado at Boulder and PHB Hagler Bailly

THE EPIPHANY

One of the editors had an epiphany after reading Dixit and Pindyck's book, *Investment under Uncertainty*. He had been teaching a course in engineering economics, which he had "inherited" when he joined the faculty of his university's telecommunications program. The text and syllabus were already in place. At about the same time, the arguments were beginning as to the cost of telephone services outside the bounds of traditional rate or revenue requirement proceedings. Although these costs had been debated before, the terms and stakes had become much higher due to the breakup of the Bell System and the inroads of competition. With the passage of the Telecommunications Act of 1996, the issue was joined. The Act required that interconnection prices, universal service, and unbundled network elements be based on cost, and directed the Federal Communications Commission to implement this legislation.

The parties developed engineering process models to estimate forward looking costs. To this editor, both the engineering economics and cost model approaches were unsatisfactory. Neither approach handled uncertainty or dynamics, or else did so clumsily.

The epiphany, as revealed in Dixit and Pindyck, was a method to handle uncertainty and dynamics in a satisfactory manner. Moreover, it linked the "real" market with the financial market. This had immediate implications for both engineering economics and cost modelling methodologies.

Engineering economics uses the tools of discounted present value with little or no emphasis on the financial side of the equation. Certainty is assumed – uncertainty is "handled," if at all, by raising the discount rate. This lowers the values in later periods, distorts the results, and gives incorrect conclusions. More sophisticated analysis may use a discount rate determined by the capital asset pricing model or the expected value based on decision tree analysis. Neither of these methods adequately deals with management's flexibility; hence, the entry of real options.

The insights garnered from the real options theory led to the workshop on the "New Investment Theory of Real Options and its Implications for the Cost Models in Telecommunications" (held at Columbia University on October 2, 1998) that resulted in this volume.

TENSIONS

At least three tensions manifest themselves in this volume:

- Incumbent local exchange carriers (ILECs) versus interexchange carriers (IXCs)
- Real options versus capital asset pricing model (CAPM) approaches
- Optimists versus pessimists.

ILEC/IXC. The ILECs would prefer that, *ceteris paribus*, cost estimates be higher, for these costs determine universal service support, interconnection prices, and the price of unbundled network elements. The higher the cost, the more the ILEC receives. Conversely, the IXCs prefer lower cost estimates because they are paying the ILECs. Thus, each commentator has a perspective on the direction of costs, depending on the position that he or she represents. Generally, they have, with a notable exception, the same framework within which to deal with estimates of costs. The exception is Jerry Hausman of MIT, who has suggested that the models have ignored the latest valuation techniques (i.e., real options). Both sides generally assume that the real options approach will raise costs, although the reader is cautioned that this is not axiomatic. This editor believes that corrections for other deficiencies in the models and the applications of real options techniques will most likely increase cost estimates, but the effect cannot be determined *a priori.*

Real Options/CAPM. Although it is not as obvious in this volume, the second tension is between the real options and CAPM approaches. This arises in part from a simple lack of understanding of the real options model. CAPM assumes that dynamics and uncertainty are incorporated into the models by applying the CAPM discount rate to the analysis – this editor believes that this assumption is incorrect. Real options incorporates elements of CAPM within its approach and explicitly addresses dynamics, uncertainty, and managerial flexibility. Moreover, the telecommunications cost models, as currently structured, cannot be manipulated to test the real options proposition, with or without CAPM.

Optimists/Pessimists. Finally, a tension exists between what might be termed the optimists and pessimists. The optimists represent the financial side of real options analysis, whereas the pessimists focus only on sunk or irreversible costs.

While *Investment under Uncertainty* consolidated over two decades' of research from the economist's point of view, work was proceeding on the financial side. *Real Options*, a book by this volume's lead author, Lenos Trigeorgis, was the financial analyst's equivalent to the Dixit and Pindyck book. It approaches valuation analysis from the financial side. It, too, consolidates decades of research, some of it overlapping with the Dixit and Pindyck approach. One difference, however, centers on the drivers of value. The emphasis in Dixit and Pindyck is on the value of deferring investment, particularly investments that are irreversible – sunk costs in the economist's terminology – versus management's flexibility in *all* aspects of the investment process, not only deferral.

ORGANIZATION

This volume is organized as follows. The first papers by Lenos Trigeorgis and Sanjai Bhagat introduce real options in greater detail. The first is a primer and the second, in addition to describing real options, demonstrates the approach's application to the telecommunications industry. Mark Jamison's paper develops a theoretical model that demonstrates some of real options' impacts without the complication of time within the analysis. While real options is new to the telecommunications industry, many other sectors have been using the approach for some time. Todd Strauss demonstrates that theory can move to practice. He presents various applications of the method in the energy field.

The next section explores the principles of properly constructed cost models. Richard Emmerson provides an overview, while an article by William Sharkey of the Federal Communications Commission addresses the design of forward looking cost models for exchange telecommunications networks. He initially addresses the principles. The criteria developed in this paper (and elaborated in the cited references) represent the hurdles that any cost model should be capable of clearing. The second half of his paper shows the detail with which the FCC approaches cost modelling. It indicates the specificity and the depth to which the process models can delve into the engineering features. Timothy Tardiff offers a critique of the FCC's approach.

In examining the implications of neglecting real options, Barbara Cherry, and Greg Hallman and Christopher McClain approach the issues from the ILEC's perspective. Cherry is concerned with the legal implications of not including real options in the estimation of cost for the ILECs. She views underestimating the cost as a more serious problem than overestimating it, not only because of the impact on investment but also because of the confiscatory nature of the underestimation, which is prohibited by the Takings Clause under the U.S. Constitution.

Real Options: An Overview

1

Real Options: A Primer[1]

Lenos Trigeorgis
University of Cyprus

Abstract – This paper serves to introduce the basic ideas and valuation principles for corporate real options, and basic concepts related to growth options, competition and strategy. It first uses an example to motivate the discussion of various real options and presents practical principles for valuing several common real options, such as the options to defer investment, expand capacity, abandon the project, or switch uses. It then presents a conceptual discussion of growth options, competition and strategy, proposing strategic questions and a new project classification scheme as a practical aid for option-based analysis. Finally, it discusses various applications and notes areas for future research.

Many academics and practicing managers now recognize that the net present value (NPV) rule and other discounted cash flow (DCF) approaches to capital budgeting are inadequate in that they cannot properly capture management's flexibility to adapt and revise future decisions in response to unexpected market developments. Traditional NPV makes implicit assumptions about an "expected scenario" of cash flows and presumes management's passive commitment to a certain "operating strategy" (for example, to initiate the project immediately and operate it continuously at base scale until the end of its pre-specified expected useful life).

The real-world marketplace, however, is characterized by change, uncertainty and competitive interactions, where the realization of cash flows will probably differ from what management expected initially. As new information arrives and uncertainty about market conditions and future cash flows is gradually resolved, management may have valuable flexibility to alter its operating strategy in order to capitalize on favorable future opportunities or mitigate downside losses. For example, management may be able to defer, expand, contract, abandon, or otherwise alter a project at different stages during its useful operating life.

Management's flexibility to adapt its future actions in response to altered future market conditions expands an investment opportunity's value by improving its upside potential. It can also limit downside losses relative to management's initial expectations under passive management. The resulting asymmetry (skewness) caused by managerial adaptability calls for an *expanded NPV* rule that reflects both value components: the traditional (static or passive) NPV of expected cash flows, and the option value of operating and strategic adaptability. This does not mean that traditional NPV should be scrapped; rather, it should be seen as a crucial and necessary input to an options-based *expanded NPV* analysis, i.e.:

$$\text{expanded (strategic) NPV} = \text{static (passive) NPV of expected cash flows} + \text{value of options from active management} \quad (1)$$

An options approach to capital budgeting has the potential to conceptualize, and even quantify, the value of options from active management. This value is manifest as a collection of corporate real (call or put) options embedded in capital investment opportunities, having as the underlying asset the gross project value of expected operating cash flows (ignoring capital costs and any embedded options). Many of these real options occur naturally (e.g., to defer, contract, shut down or abandon a project), while others may be planned and built-in at some cost (e.g., to expand capacity or build growth options, to abandon during construction when investment is staged sequentially, to switch between alternative inputs or outputs).

This paper provides an overview of real options, describing the basic principles for quantifying their value as well as thinking conceptually about the important competitive/strategic dimensions. An oil extraction and refinery project is used as an example to introduce the basic nature of various real options. The paper then presents, through simple numerical examples, useful principles for valuing various upside-potential operating options, such as to defer an investment or expand production, as well as various downside-protection options, such as to abandon for salvage value, switch among alternative uses (e.g., inputs or outputs), or abandon a project midstream during construction. Finally, a new options-based project classification scheme and strategic questions for capital budgeting analysis are proposed.

Section 1 of this paper uses an example to motivate the discussion of various real options and presents practical principles for valuing several such options. Section 2 presents a conceptual discussion of growth options, competition and strategy. Section 3 discusses applications and notes areas for future research. The paper's conclusions are presented in Section 4.

1. AN EXAMPLE AND BASIC VALUATION PRINCIPLES

This section discusses conceptually the basic nature and types of real options through a comprehensive example, and then illustrates some basic principles for valuing such options. A summary of the most common types of real options, the industries in which they are important, and related literature is provided in Table 1.

Table 1: Common Real Options

Category	Description	Important in	References
Option to defer	Management holds a lease on (or an option to buy) valuable land or resources. It can wait *x* years to see if output prices justify constructing a building or a plant or developing a field.	All natural-resource-extraction industries; real-estate development; farming; paper products.	McDonald and Siegel 1986; Paddock et al. 1988; Tourinho 1979; Titman 1985; Ingersoll and Ross 1992
Time-to-build option (staged investment)	Staging investment as a series of outlays creates the option to abandon the enterprise in midstream if new information is unfavorable. Each stage can be viewed as an option on the value of subsequent stages and valued as a compound option.	All R&D-intensive industries, especially pharmaceuticals; long-development capital-intensive projects (e.g., large-scale construction or energy-generating plants); startup ventures.	Majd and Pindyck 1987; Carr 1988; Trigeorgis 1993
Option to alter operating scale (e.g., to expand; to contract; to shut down and restart)	If market conditions are more favorable than expected, the firm can expand the scale of production or accelerate resource utilization. Conversely, if conditions are less favorable than expected, it can reduce the scale of operations. In extreme cases, production may be halted and restarted.	Natural-resource industries (e.g., mining); facilities planning and construction in cyclical industries; fashion apparel; consumer goods; commercial real estate.	Trigeorgis and Mason 1987; Pindyck 1988; Mcdonald and Siegel 1985; Brennan and Schwartz 1985
Option to abandon	If market conditions decline severely, management can abandon current operations permanently and realize the resale value of capital equipment and other assets on secondhand markets.	Capital-intensive industries (e.g., airlines, railroads); financial services; new-product introductions in uncertain markets.	Myers and Majd 1990
Option to switch (e.g., outputs or inputs)	If prices or demand change, management can change the output mix of the facility (product flexibility). Alternatively, the same outputs can be produced using different types of inputs (process flexibility).	*Output shifts:* Any good sought in small batches or subject to volatile demand (e.g., consumer electronics); toys; specialty paper; machine parts; autos. *Input shifts:* All feedstock-dependent facilities; electric power; chemicals; crop switching; sourcing.	Margrabe 1978; Kensinger 1987; Kulatilaka 1988; Kulatilaka and Trigeorgis 1994
Growth options	An early investment (e.g., R&D, lease on undeveloped land or oil reserves, strategic acquisition, information network) is a prerequisite or a link in a chain of interrelated projects, opening up future growth opportunities (e.g., new product or process, oil reserves, access to new market, strengthening of core capabilities). Like interproject compound options.	All infrastructure-based or strategic industries--esp. high tech, R&D, and industries with multiple product generations or applications (e.g., computers, pharmaceuticals); multinational operations; strategic acquisitions.	Myers 1977; Brealey and Myers 1991; Kester 1984, 1993; Trigeorgis 1988; Pindyck 1988; Chung and Charoenwong 1991
Multiple interacting options	Real-life projects often involve a collection of various options. Upward-potential-enhancing and downward-protection options are present in combination. Their combined value may differ from the sum of their separate values, i.e., they interact. They may also interact with financial flexibility options.	Real-life projects in most industries listed above.	Trigeorgis 1993; Brennan and Schwartz 1985; Kulatilaka 1994

1.1 An Oil Extraction and Refinery Project

A large oil company has a one-year lease to start drilling on undeveloped land with potential oil reserves. Initiating the project may require certain exploration costs, to be followed by the construction of roads and other infrastructure outlays, I_1. This would be followed by outlays for the construction of a new processing facility, I_2. Extraction can begin only after construction is completed, i.e., cash flows are generated only during the "operating stage" that follows the last outlay.

During construction, if market conditions deteriorate, management can choose to abandon the project midstream and forego any future planned outlays. It could also choose to reduce the scale of operation by c%, saving a portion of the last outlay, I_C, if the market is weak. Also, the processing plant can be designed up front so that, if oil prices turn out higher than expected, the rate of production can be enhanced by x% with a follow-up outlay of I_E. At any time, management may salvage a portion of its investment by selling the plant and equipment for their salvage value or switching them to an alternative use value, A. An associated refinery plant – which may be designed to operate with alternative sources of energy inputs – can convert crude oil into a variety of refined products. This type of project presents the following collection of *real options*:

- **The option to defer investment.** The lease enables management to defer investment for up to one year and benefit from the resolution of uncertainty about oil prices during this period. Management would invest I_1 (i.e., exercise its option to extract oil) *only if* oil prices increase sufficiently, but would not commit to the project, saving the planned outlays, if prices decline. Just before the lease expires, the value creation will be $\max(V - I_1, 0)$. The option to defer is thus analogous to a U.S. call option on the gross present value of the completed project's expected operating cash flows, V, with the exercise price being equal to the required outlay, I_1. Because early investment implies sacrificing the option to wait, this option value loss is like an additional investment opportunity cost, justifying investment only if the value of cash benefits, V, actually exceeds the initial outlay by a substantial premium. As noted in Table 1, the option to wait is particularly valuable in resource extraction industries, farming, paper products, and real estate development due to high uncertainties and long investment horizons.

- **The option to abandon during construction (or the time-to-build option).** In most real-life projects, the required investment is not incurred as a single up-front outlay. The staging of capital investment as a series of outlays over time creates valuable options to "default" at any given stage (e.g., after exploration if the reserves or oil prices are determined to be very low). Thus, each stage (e.g., building necessary infrastructure) can be viewed as an option on the value of subsequent stages by incurring the installment cost outlay (e.g., I_1) required to proceed to the next stage, and can therefore be valued in a manner similar to compound options. This option is valuable in all R&D-intensive industries, especially pharmaceuticals; in highly uncertain, long-development, capital-intensive industries, such as energy-generating plants or large-scale construction; and in venture capital.

- **The option to expand.** If oil prices or other market conditions turn out more favorable than expected, management can accelerate the rate or expand the scale of production (by x%) by incurring a follow-up cost outlay (I_E). This is similar to a call option to acquire an additional part (x%) of the base-scale project, paying I_E as the exercise price. The investment opportunity with the option to expand can be viewed as the base-scale project plus a call option on future investment, i.e., $V + \max(xV - I_E, 0)$. Given an initial design choice, management may deliberately favor a more expensive technology because of the built-in flexibility to expand production if and when it becomes desirable. As discussed further below, the option to expand may also be of strategic importance, especially if it enables the firm to capitalize on future growth opportunities. When the firm buys vacant undeveloped land, or when it builds a small plant in a new geographic location (domestic or overseas) to position itself to take advantage of a developing large market, it essentially installs an expansion/growth option. This option, which will be exercised only if future market developments turn out to be favorable, can make a seemingly unprofitable (based on static NPV) base-case investment worth undertaking.

- **The option to contract.** If market conditions are weaker than originally expected, management can operate below capacity or even reduce the scale of operations (by c%), thereby saving part of the planned investment outlays (I_C). This flexibility to mitigate loss is analogous to a put option on part (c%) of the base-scale project, with the exercise price equal to the potential cost savings (I_C), giving $\max(I_C - cV, 0)$. The option to contract, just as the option to expand, may be particularly valuable in the case of new product introductions in uncertain markets. This option may also be important, for example, in choosing among technologies or plants with a different construction-to-maintenance cost mix, where it may be preferable to build a plant with lower initial construction costs and higher maintenance expenditures in order to acquire the flexibility to contract operations by cutting down on maintenance if market conditions turn out to be unfavorable.

- **The option to shut down (and re-start) operations.** In real life, the plant does not have to operate (i.e., extract oil) in each and every period automatically. In fact, if oil prices are such that cash revenues are not sufficient to cover variable operating costs (e.g., maintenance), it might be better not to operate temporarily, especially if the costs of switching between the operating and idle modes are relatively small. If prices rise sufficiently, operations can start again. Thus, operation in each year can be seen as a call option to acquire that year's cash revenues (C) by paying the variable costs of operating (I_V) as the exercise price, i.e., $\max(C - I_V, 0)$.[2] Options to alter the operating scale (i.e., expand, contract, or shut down) are typically found in natural resource industries, such as mine operations, facilities planning and construction in cyclical industries, fashion apparel, consumer goods, and commercial real estate.

- **The option to abandon for salvage value.** If oil prices suffer a sustainable decline or the operation does poorly for some other reason, management does not have to continue incurring the fixed costs. It may instead have a valuable option to abandon the project permanently in exchange for its salvage value (i.e., the resale value of its capital equipment and other assets in second-hand markets). As noted, this option can be valued as a U.S. put option on current project value (V) with the exercise price being the salvage or best alternative use value (A), entitling management to receive $V + \max(A - V, 0)$ or $\max(V, A)$. Naturally, more general-purpose capital assets would have a higher salvage and option abandonment value than special-purpose assets. Valuable abandonment options are generally found in capital-intensive industries, such as in airlines and railroads, in financial services, and in new product introductions in uncertain markets.

- **The option to switch use (e.g., inputs or outputs).** Suppose the associated oil refinery operation can be designed to use alternative forms of energy inputs (e.g., fuel oil, gas, electricity) to convert crude oil into a variety of output products (e.g., gasoline, lubricants, polyester). This would provide valuable built-in flexibility to switch from the current input to the cheapest future input, or from the current output to the most profitable future product mix, as the relative prices of the inputs or outputs fluctuate over time. In fact, the firm should be willing to pay a certain positive premium for such a flexible technology over a rigid alternative that confers no or less choice. If the firm can in this way develop extra uses for its assets over its competitors, it may be at a significant advantage.

Generally, *process* flexibility can be achieved not only via technology (e.g., by building a flexible facility that can switch among alternative energy *inputs*) but also by maintaining relationships with a variety of suppliers and changing the mix as their relative prices change. Subcontracting policies may allow further flexibility to contract the scale of future operations at a low cost in case of unfavorable market developments. A multinational oil company may locate production facilities in various countries, allowing it to shift production to the lowest-cost producing facilities, as the relative costs, other local market conditions, or exchange rates change over time. Process flexibility is valuable in feedstock-dependent facilities, such as oil, electric power, chemicals, and crop switching. *Product* flexibility, which enables the firm to switch among alternative *outputs*, is more valuable in industries such as automobiles, consumer electronics, toys or pharmaceuticals, where product differentiation and diversity are important and/or product demand is volatile. In such cases, it may be worthwhile to install a more costly flexible capacity that gives the company the ability to alter product mix or production scale in response to changing market demands.

- **Corporate growth options.** Another version of the earlier option to expand that is of considerable strategic importance is *corporate growth options* that set the path of future opportunities. Suppose, in the above example, that the proposed refinery facility is based on a new, technologically superior *process* for oil refinement that has been developed and tested internally on a pilot plant basis. Although the proposed facility may appear unattractive in isolation, it could be only the first in a series of similar facilities if the process is successfully developed and commercialized, and may even lead to entirely new oil by-products. More generally, many early investments (e.g., R&D, a lease on undeveloped land or a tract with potential oil reserves, a strategic acquisition, an information technology network) can be seen as prerequisites or links in a chain of interrelated projects. The value of these projects may derive not so much from their expected directly measurable cash flows, but rather from unlocking future growth opportunities (e.g., a new-generation product or process, oil reserves, access to a new or expanding market, strengthening of the firm's core capabilities or strategic positioning). An opportunity to invest in a first generation high-tech product, for example, is analogous to an option on options (an inter-project compound option). Despite a seemingly negative NPV, the infrastructure, experience, and potential by-products generated during the development of the first-generation product may serve as spring-boards for developing lower-cost or improved-quality future generations of that product, or even for generating new applications into other areas. But unless the firm makes that initial investment, subsequent generations or other applications would not even be feasible. The infrastructure and experience gained can be proprietary and can place the firm at a competitive advantage, which may even reinforce itself if learning cost curve effects are present. Growth options are found in all infrastructure-based or strategic industries, especially in high-tech, R&D, or industries with multiple product generations or applications (e.g., semiconductors, computers, pharmaceuticals), in multi-national operations, and in strategic acquisitions.

In a more general context, the operating and strategic adaptability represented by corporate real options can be achieved at various stages during the value chain, from switching the factor input mix among various suppliers and subcontracting practices, to rapid product design (e.g., computer-aided design) and modularity in design, and to shifting production among various products rapidly and cost-efficiently in a flexible manufacturing system. The next section illustrates, through simple numerical examples, basic practical principles for valuing several of the above real options. For expositional simplicity, any return shortfall or other dividend-like effects are ignored.

1.2 Principles for Valuing Real Options

Consider, as in Trigeorgis and Mason (1987),[3] valuing a generic investment opportunity (e.g., similar to the above oil extraction project). Specifically, suppose a company is faced with an opportunity to invest I_0 = $104 (in millions) in an oil project whose (gross) value in each period will either move up by 80% or down by 40%, depending on oil price fluctuations: a year later, the project will have an expected value (from subsequent cash flows) of $180 (million) if the oil price moves up (C^+ = 180) or $60 if it moves down ($C^-$ = 60).[4] There is an equal probability (q = .5) that the price of oil will move up or down in any year. Let S be the price of oil, or generally of a *twin security* that is traded in the financial markets and has the same risk characteristics as (i.e., is perfectly correlated with) the real project under consideration (such as the stock price of a similar operating unlevered oil company). Both the project and its twin security (or oil prices) have an expected rate of return (or discount rate) of k = 20 percent, while the risk-free interest rate is r = 8 percent.

In what follows assume throughout that the value of the project (i.e., the value, in millions of dollars, in each year, t, of its subsequent expected cash flows appropriately discounted back to that year), V_t, and its twin security price (e.g., a twin oil stock price in \$ per share, or simply, the price of oil in \$ per barrel), S_t, move through time as follows:

```
                                        (324, 64.88)
                                       /
                      (180, 36)
                     /         \
        (100, 20)                       (108, 21.6)
                     \         /
                      (60, 12)
                                       \
                                          (36, 7.2)
   Year 0                1                   2
```

For example, the pair (V_0, S_0) above represents a current gross project value of \$100 million, and a spot oil price of \$20 a barrel (or a \$20 a share twin oil stock price). Under traditional (passive) NPV analysis, the current gross project value would be obtained first by discounting the project's end-of-period values (derived from subsequent cash flows), using the expected rate of return of the project's twin security (or, here, of oil prices) as the appropriate discount rate, i.e., $V_0 = (.5 \times 180 + .5 \times 60)/1.20 = 100$. Note that this gross project value is, in this case, exactly proportional to the twin security price (or the spot oil price). After subtracting the current investment costs, $I_0 = 104$, the project's NPV is finally given by:

$$NPV = V_0 - I_0 = 100 - 104 = -4 \ (< 0). \qquad (2)$$

In the absence of managerial flexibility or real options, traditional DCF analysis would have *rejected* this project based on its negative NPV. However, passive DCF cannot properly capture the value of embedded options because of their discretionary asymmetric nature and dependence on future events that are uncertain at the time of the initial decision. The fundamental problem, of course, lies in the valuation of investment opportunities whose claims are not symmetric or proportional and whose discount rates vary in a complex way over time.

Nevertheless, such real options can be properly valued using contingent claims analysis (CCA) within a backward risk-neutral valuation process.[5] Essentially, the same solution can be obtained in the actual risk-averse world as in a *risk-neutral* world in which the current value of any contingent claim could be obtained from its expected future values — with expectations taken over the *risk-neutral probabilities*, p, imputed from the twin security's (or oil) prices — discounted at the *riskless* rate, r. In such a risk-neutral world, the current (beginning of the period) value of the project (or of equityholders' claim), E, is given by:

$$E = [pE^{+} + (1 - p)E^{-}]/(1 + r),$$
$$\text{with } p = [(1 + r)S - S^{-}]/(S^{+} - S^{-}). \qquad (3)$$

The probability, p, can be estimated from the price dynamics of the twin security (or of oil prices):

$p = [1.08 \times 20 - 12]/(36 - 12) = 0.4$ (as distinct from the actual probability, $q = 0.5$),
and can then be used to determine "certainty-equivalent" values (or expected cash flows), which can be properly discounted at the risk-free rate. For example,

$$V_0 = [pC^{+} + (1 - p)C^{-}]/(1 + r) = [.4 \times 180 + .6 \times 60]/1.08 = 100.\text{[6]} \qquad (4)$$

In what follows, it is assumed that if any part of the required investment outlay (having a present value of $104 million) is not going to be spent immediately but in future installments, that amount is placed in an escrow account earning the riskless interest rate.[7] The next section illustrates how various kinds of both upside-potential options (such as to defer or expand) and downside-protection options (such as to abandon for salvage or default during construction) can enhance the value of the *opportunity* to invest (i.e., the value of equity or NPV) in the above generic project, under the standard assumption of all-equity financing. The focus here is on basic practical principles for valuing one kind of operating option at a time.

1.2.1 The Option to *Defer* Investment

The company has a one-year lease that gives it a proprietary right to defer undertaking the project (i.e., extracting the oil) for a year, thus benefiting from the resolution of uncertainty about oil prices over this period. Athough undertaking the project *immediately* has a negative NPV (of -4), the *opportunity* to invest afforded by the lease has a positive worth because management would invest *only* if oil prices and project value rise sufficiently, while it has no obligation to invest under unfavorable developments. Since the option to wait is analogous to a call option on project value, V, with an exercise price equal to the required outlay next year, $I_1 = 112.32$ ($= 104 \times 1.08$):

$$E^{+} = \max(V^{+} - I_1, 0) = \max(180 - 112.32, 0) = 67.68,$$
$$E^{-} = \max(V^{-} - I_1, 0) = \max(60 - 112.32, 0) = 0. \qquad (5)$$

The project's total value (i.e., the *expanded NPV,* which includes the value of the option to defer) from Equation (3) is:

$$E_0 = [pE^+ + (1 - p)E^-]/(1 + r) = [.4 \times 67.68 + .6 \times 0]/1.08 = 25.07. \quad (6)$$

From Equation (1), the value of the option to defer provided by the lease itself is thus given by:

$$\textit{Option to defer} = \text{expanded NPV} - \text{passive NPV} = 25.07 - (-4) = 29.07, \quad (7)$$

which, incidentally, is equal to almost one-third of the project's gross value.[8]

1.2.2 The Option to *Expand* (Growth Option)

Once the project is undertaken, any necessary infrastructure is completed, and the plant is operating, management may have the option to accelerate the rate or expand the scale of production by, say, 50% ($x = 0.50$) by incurring a follow-on investment outlay of $I_E = 40$, provided oil prices and general market conditions turn out better than originally expected. Thus, in year 1 management can choose either to maintain the base scale operation (i.e., receive project value, V, at no extra cost) or expand by 50% the scale and project value by incurring the extra outlay. That is, the original investment opportunity is seen as the initial-scale project plus a call option on a future opportunity, or $E = V + \max(xV - I_E, 0) = \max(V, (1+x)V - I_E)$:

$$E^+ = \max(V^+, 1.5V^+ - I_E) = \max(180, 270 - 40) = 230 \text{ (expand)};$$
$$E^- = \max(V^-, 1.5V^- - I_E) = \max(60, 90 - 40) = 60 \text{ (maintain base scale)}. \quad (8)$$

The value of the investment opportunity (including the value of the option to expand if market conditions turn out better than expected) then becomes:

$$E_0 = [pE^+ + (1 - p)E^-]/(1 + r) - I_0 = [.4 \times \mathbf{230} + .6 \times 60]/1.08 - 104 = 14.5, \quad (9)$$

and thus the value of the *option to expand* = 14.5 - (-4) = 18.5, (10)

or 18.5% of the gross project value.

1.2.3 Options to Abandon for *Salvage* Value or *Switch Use*

In terms of downside protection, management has the option to abandon the oil extraction project at any time in exchange for its *salvage value* or value in its best alternative use, if oil prices suffer a sustainable decline. The associated oil refinery plant also can use alternative energy inputs and has the flexibility to convert crude oil into a variety of products. As market conditions change and the relative prices of inputs, outputs or the plant resale value in a second-hand market fluctuate, equityholders may find it preferable to abandon the current project's use by switching to a cheaper input, a more profitable output, or simply selling the plant's assets to the second-hand market. Let the project's value in its best alternative use, A (or the *salvage value* for which it can be exchanged) fluctuate over time as:

```
                    230.4
                   /
             144
            /     \
      90            115.2
            \     /
              72
                  \
                    57.6
Year  0        1      2
```

Note that the project's current salvage or alternative use value (A_0 = 90) is below the project's value in its present use (V_0 = 100) – otherwise management would have switched use immediately – and has the same expected rate of return (20%). It nevertheless has a smaller variance so that if the market keeps moving up it would not be optimal to abandon the project early for its *salvage value*, but if it moves down management may find it desirable to *switch use* (e.g., in year 1 exchange the present use value of V_1 = 60 for a higher alternative use value of A_1 = 72).[9] Thus, equityholders can choose the maximum of the project's value in its present use, V, or its value in the best alternative use, A, i.e., E = max(V, A):

$$E^+ = \max(V^+, A^+) = \max(180, 144) = 180 = V^+ \text{ (continue)};$$
$$E^- = \max(V^-, A^-) = \max(60, 72) = 72 = A^- \text{ (switch use)}. \qquad (11)$$

The value of the investment (including the option to abandon early or switch use) is then:

$$E_0 = [pE^+ + (1 - p)E^-]/(1 + r) - I_0 = [.4 \times 180 + .6 \times 72]/1.08 - 104 = +2.67, \quad (12)$$

so that the project with the option to switch use is now desirable. The value of the option itself is:

$$\textit{Option to switch use} = 2.67 - (-4) = 6.67, \qquad (13)$$

or almost 7 percent of the project's gross value. This value is clearly dependent on the schedule of salvage or alternative use values.

1.2.4 The Option to *Default* During Construction

Even during the construction phase, management may abandon a project to save any subsequent investment outlays, if the coming required investment exceeds the value from continuing the project (including any future options). Suppose that the investment (of \$104 present value) necessary to implement the oil extraction project can be staged as a series of "installments:" I_0 = \$44 out of the \$104 allocated amount will need to be paid out immediately (in year 0) as a start-up cost for infrastructure, with the \$60 balance placed in an escrow account (earning the risk-free rate) planned to be paid as a I_1 = \$64.8 follow-up outlay for constructing the processing plant in year 1. Next year management will then pay the investment cost "installment" as planned only in return for a higher project value from continuing; otherwise, it will forego the investment and receive nothing. Thus, the option to default when investment is staged sequentially during construction translates into $E = \max(V - I_1, 0)$:

$$E^+ = \max(V^+ - I_1, 0) = \max(180 - 64.8, 0) = 115.2 \text{ (continue)};$$
$$E^- = \max(V^- - I_1, 0) = \max(60 - 64.8, 0) = 0 \text{ (default)}. \qquad (14)$$

The value of the investment opportunity (with the option to default on future outlays) is given by:

$$E_0 = [pE^+ + (1 - p)E^-]/(1 + r) - I_0 = [.4 \times 115.2 + .6 \times 0]/1.08 - 44 = -1.33, \quad (15)$$

and the *option to abandon by defaulting* during construction = -1.33 - (-4) = 2.67, (16)

or about 3 percent of project value. This value is, of course, dependent on the staged cost schedule.

For simplicity, the above examples were based on a one-period risk neutral, backward valuation procedure. This procedure can be easily extended to a discrete multi-period setting with any number of stages. Starting from the terminal values, the process would move backwards calculating option values one step earlier (using the up and down values obtained in the preceding step), and so on. As the number of steps increases, the discrete-time solution would approach its continuous (Black-Scholes type) equivalent (with appropriate adjustments).

2. GROWTH OPTIONS, COMPETITION AND STRATEGY

The most significant decisions in many cases, of course, are not so much the operating ones but those involving growth options, competition and strategy. For these dimensions to be properly captured, it must first be explicitly recognized that there are certain important differences between financial and real options. This section describes a general conceptual framework for viewing real investment opportunities as collections of real options (an *expanded or strategic NPV* framework) that integrates the important operating options (e.g., the options to defer or abandon a project early) with competitive/strategic interactions. Specifically, Section 2.1 presents an alternative, options-based project classification scheme, while Section 2.2 discusses strategic questions for capital budgeting analysis. To motivate the new options-based classification scheme, it is useful to first discuss some of the important differences between real and financial options. These include:

- **(Non)proprietary ownership/competitive impact.** A standard call option on common stock is "*proprietary*" in that it gives its owner an exclusive right of whether and when to exercise, i.e., the option holder does not have to worry about competition for the underlying investment. Similarly, some real options are proprietary in that they provide their holder with such exclusive rights of exercise, uninhibited by competitive threats. Investment opportunities with high barriers of entry for competitors such as a patent for developing a product having no close substitutes, or a unique knowhow of a technological process or market conditions that competitors are unable to duplicate for at least some time, are but a few examples of such real proprietary options.

  Other types of investment opportunities, however, may be jointly held by more than a single competitor. These real options are "*shared*" in that, as collective opportunities of the industry, they can be exercised by any one of the participants. Examples of such *shared real options* include the opportunity to introduce a new product unprotected by the possible introduction of close substitutes, or to penetrate a new geographic market without barriers to competitive entry. The nature of competitive reaction may, of course, be different if the investment opportunity is proprietary or shared.

- **Non-tradeability and preemption.** Standard call options on stocks, like stocks themselves, can be traded frequently in efficient financial markets at minimal costs. Real options, however, like most investment projects, are not generally tradeable.[10] Some proprietary real options – such as investment opportunities related to patents or licensing agreements – may be traded, although possibly at substantial costs in imperfect markets. Of course, certain proprietary projects may be abandoned before the end of their useful lives and traded for their *salvage value*.

Other real options may inseparably depend on other real or intangible assets with which they may be sold only as a package. On the other hand, shared real options may not be salable at all because they are already a collective or "public good" of the whole industry; a firm holding a real option shared by competitors cannot easily avoid even anticipated losses in value resulting from competitive entry by just turning around to sell the option. In many cases, the only available protection against such value losses is an early investment on its part, if it can, by so doing, preempt competitors from exercising their shared rights (e.g., see Spence 1979 and Dixit 1980 for various treatments of preemptive investments). For example, a firm anticipating an increase in demand – and hence subsequent competitive entry – may rush to expand its own production capacity early in order to preempt competition, whereas in the absence of such competition, it might have preferred to wait until the uncertainty surrounding future demand would resolve itself.

- **Across-time (strategic) interdependencies/compoundness.** Standard call options on common stock are *simple* in the sense that their value upon exercise derives entirely from the received shares of stock. Similarly, some real options (such as maintenance or standard replacement projects) are "*simple*" in that their value upon exercise is limited to the value of the underlying project's cash flows in themselves.

  Other real options, however, lead to further discretionary investment opportunities when exercised. In essence, they are options on options, or *compound options* (i.e., options whose payoff is another option).[11] Research and development (R&D) investments, a lease for an undeveloped tract with potential oil reserves, or an acquisition of an unrelated company are not undertaken just for the sake of the underlying asset alone, but also (or perhaps primarily) for the new opportunities that they may open up (a new technological breakthrough, large reserves of oil, or access to a new market).

  Real compound options may have a more *strategic* impact on a firm and are more complicated to analyze. They can no longer be looked at as independent investments, but rather as links in a chain of interrelated projects, the earlier of which may be prerequisites for the ones to follow. Again, the nature of compound real options that may invite competitive reaction (e.g., shared) may involve a more complicated (game-theoretic) analysis than proprietary ones.

2.1 Dimensions of Real Options Analysis: Toward a New Project Classification

In practice, firms often classify projects according to risk or functional characteristics (e.g., replacement or new product introduction) to simplify the capital budgeting process. These schemes are incomplete, however, in that they often overlook the option aspects of projects described earlier. To motivate a new options-based classification and be better able to appreciate the various dimensions that it encompasses, this discussion starts from simple NPV and gradually builds up the framework highlighting one aspect at a time. After discussing the flexibility to defer or abandon a project, it then focuses on the dimension of *compoundness* first within and later among projects, and finally highlights interactions introduced by competition.

2.1.1 Commitment to Invest: Static (Passive) NPV

Traditional NPV typically ignores strategic competitive interactions. But even in dealing with *games against nature*, naively applied NPV is further limited in that it implicitly presumes that management is *passive*, i.e., that all decisions are unequivocally taken upfront as if management does not have the flexibility to review its original plans in response to nature's deviation from its expected scenario of cash flows. As explained earlier, in the absence of such managerial flexibility, static or passive NPV would be correct: management would make an *immediate* investment outlay, I (considering for now the simplest case of a *single* one-time expenditure), only in return for a higher present value of expected cash inflows, V. The difference, i.e., NPV = V - I, is of course the current value of the *investment* (i.e., of an installed or completed project), provided the manager had no other choice but to "take it immediately, or leave it."

Note that mere delay in undertaking an investment does not *necessarily* confer flexibility to a project. Suppose that the firm has a *commitment* (e.g., due to environmental regulations) to make an investment, I, in the future (τ years from now). If the investment is traded and involves no intermediate cash flows, this delayed commitment value, as given by the value of a *forward contract* on a (non-dividend paying) asset of value V (assuming the investment cost does not escalate), would be: $V - I\,e^{-r\tau}$.

2.1.2 The *Opportunity* to Invest (Flexibility to Defer)

What is really of interest, however, is not the value of the immediate investment per se (or of the delayed commitment), but rather the value of the investment *opportunity*. As explained earlier, in a world of uncertainty where nature can "play games" (V may fluctuate randomly) the *opportunity to invest* can be more valuable than *immediate investment* (or a delayed commitment) because it gives management the *flexibility to defer* undertaking the investment until circumstances turn more favorable, or back out altogether if they become unsatisfactory.[12] The value of this opportunity to invest therefore exceeds the static NPV of cash flows from immediate investment (V - I) by the value of the flexibility to defer the investment. It also exceeds the value of a delayed commitment due to the future *choice* to avoid potentially unfavorable outcomes.

Such an investment opportunity may thus be economically desirable, even if the investment itself may have a *negative* NPV (i.e., V < I). It would therefore be very useful to distinguish between opportunities that allow management the *flexibility* to defer their undertaking and make the *choice* later after receiving additional information (such as projects with patents or leases), and projects that involve a *commitment* (such as an expiring offer to immediately expand capacity to meet extra demand by an impatient client or a required outlay to meet environmental regulations in the future).

Even if management lacks the flexibility to defer the undertaking of a project when faced with an immediate accept/reject decision, it may still have the flexibility to abandon a once-undertaken project for its *salvage value* before the end of its expected life if it turns out to perform worse than expected.[13] The flexibility to abandon a project early should therefore be explicitly accounted for in the investment decision whenever appropriate.

2.1.3 Multi-staged Projects (Intra-project Compoundness)

For now, assume that the flexibility to defer undertaking the project or abandon it for its salvage value is suppressed. Consider, however, the investment outlay, I, no longer as a single one-time expenditure at the outset, but rather as a sequence of investment cost "installments" starting immediately and extending throughout much of the life of the investment. In such a case the investment can actually be seen as a *compound option*, where an earlier investment cost installment represents the exercise price needed to acquire a subsequent option to continue operating the project until the next installment comes due, and so on. This is the idea of compoundness within the same multi-staged project – an intra-project interaction. If managerial flexibility is considered, intra-project compoundness highlights a series of distinct points in time (or *decision nodes*) – just before a subsequent investment installment comes due – when the project might be better discontinued if it turns out not to perform satisfactorily. DCF techniques, and particularly

NPV, that deal with the sequence of investment installments simply by subtracting their present value from that of the expected cash inflows (as if they were a commitment) or even by including all but the first investment installment costs in the so called "net cash flows," clearly undervalue such compound investments.

2.1.4 Project Interdependence (Inter-project Compoundness)

Return to the simple case of a single one-time investment outlay at the start of each project. Consider, however, the case of *contingent or interdependent projects* where undertaking the first is a prerequisite for the next, or provides the opportunity to acquire at maturity the benefits of the new investment by making a new investment. For example, a research project provides at completion the opportunity to acquire the revenues of the developed, commercialized product upon incurring a production outlay. This idea of *inter-project compoundness* is remarkably similar in structure when looking at a sequence of projects to the intra-project compoundness described above, with the difference that each investment "installment" now provides the opportunity to begin a new project rather than continue (another phase of) the same one. Compoundness between projects is an interaction of considerable *strategic* importance because it may justify the undertaking of projects with a *negative* NPV of direct cash flows on the basis of opening up subsequent future investment opportunities (or *growth options*).

2.1.5 Competition

Another dimension to the valuation of investment opportunities is introduced by competitive interaction. Here it is possible to distinguish between two forms of analysis depending on the type of interaction between competitors. If the impact of competitive entry can be considered *exogenous* and pertains basically to the threat of capturing part of the value of the investment away from the incumbent firm, then its management still faces an *optimization problem* – although a more complex one – in that it must incorporate the impact of competition in its own investment decision but can ignore any reciprocal effects of that decision on competitors' actions. If, however, each competitor's investment decisions are contingent upon and sensitive to the others' moves, as in most oligopolistic industries, then a more complex *game-theoretic* treatment becomes necessary. Investing earlier than one otherwise would to preempt competitive entry is a simple case of such *strategic games against competition*. Competitive strategy can be analyzed using a combination of option valuation principles with industrial organization (game-theoretic) concepts (e.g., see Smit and Trigeorgis, 1993).

2.2 Strategic Questions and an Options-based Project Classification

Based on the above dimensions of real options analysis, it is important for management to address a number of strategic questions in the investment evaluation process. The first refers to the *exclusiveness of option ownership* and the *effect of competition* on the firm's ability to fully appropriate the option value for itself. If the firm retains an exclusive right as to whether and when to invest, unaffected by competitive initiatives, then its investment opportunity is classified as a *proprietary option*. Investment opportunities with high barriers of entry for competitors such as a patent for developing a product having no close substitutes, or a unique knowhow of a technological process, or market conditions that competitors are unable to duplicate for at least some time, are just a few examples of such proprietary real options. In such cases, management may have the flexibility to abandon a project early (i.e., the project has additional *abandonment value*), or even temporarily interrupt the project's operation in certain "unprofitable" periods.[14] If, however, competitors share the right to exercise and may be able to take part (or all) of the project's value away from the firm, then the option is *shared*.[15] Shared real options can be seen as jointly held opportunities of a number of competing firms or of a whole industry, and can be exercised by any one of their collective owners. Such shared real options are, for example, the opportunity to introduce a new product unprotected by the possible introduction of close substitutes, or to penetrate a new geographic market without barriers to competitive entry. The loss in value suffered by a firm as a result of competitive interaction when a competitive firm exercises its shared rights is called *competitive loss*.[16]

The second strategic question concerns *inter- (or intra-) project interactions*, specifically compoundness.[17] Is an investment opportunity valuable in and by itself, or is it a prerequisite for subsequent investment opportunities? If the opportunity is a real option leading, upon exercise, to further discretionary investment opportunities, or an option whose payoff is another option, then it is classified as a *compound* option. Such real options on options may have a more *strategic* impact on a firm and are more complicated to analyze. They can no longer be looked at as *independent* investments, but rather as *links in a chain of interrelated projects*, the earlier of which are prerequisites for the ones to follow. An R&D investment, a lease for an undeveloped tract with potential oil reserves, or an acquisition of an unrelated company are just a few examples of such compound real options that may be undertaken, not just for their direct cash flows but also (or perhaps primarily) for the new opportunities that they may open up (a new technological breakthrough, large reserves of oil, or access to a new market). On the other hand, if the project can be evaluated as a *stand-alone* investment opportunity, it is referred to as a *simple* option. Such independent opportunities, whose value upon exercise is limited only to the underlying project in and of itself, are, for instance, standard replacement or maintenance projects.

The last *strategic question* refers to the committal or discretionary nature of the decision, focusing specifically on the *urgency of the decision.* Management must distinguish between those projects that need an immediate accept/reject decision (i.e., *expiring* investment opportunities) and those that can be deferred for future action (i.e., *deferrable* real options).[18] It would also be useful to further distinguish between deferrable investments that merely represent delayed commitments versus future decision (choice) opportunities. The value of the flexibility to defer undertaking a project is referred to here as the project's *deferrability value.* Discretionary deferrable projects require a more extensive analysis of the optimal timing of investment because management must compare the net value of taking the project today with the net value of taking it in all possible future years. Thus, management must analyze the relative benefits and costs of waiting in association with other strategic considerations (e.g., the threat of competitive entry in a shared-deferrable option may justify early capital commitment for preemptive purposes). This mode of analysis leads to the real options-based *classification scheme* shown in Figure 1.[19]

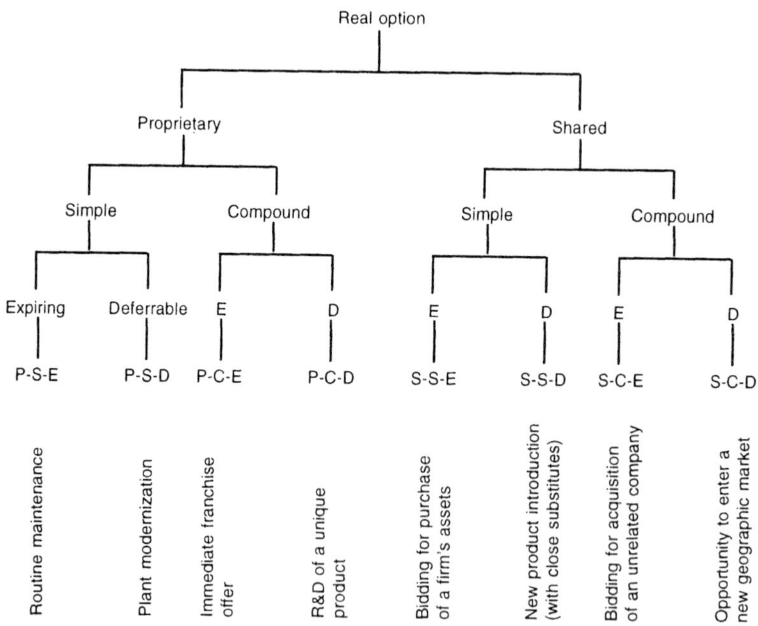

Figure 1: A Conceptual Options Framework for Capital Budgeting

This eight-fork classification scheme is intended to focus management's attention on the important characteristics of investment opportunities as options on real assets, as described above. Although the distinctions between the various categories may at times be more relative rather than absolute, most real investment opportunities, including strategic ones, can find a place in one of the eight branches of the options-based classification tree. For example, routine maintenance could be classified and analyzed as a proprietary-simple-expiring (P-S-E) option, plant modernization as proprietary-simple-deferrable (P-S-D), bidding for the purchase of assets as shared-simple-expiring (S-S-E), a new product introduction with close substitutes as shared-simple-deferrable (S-S-D), an immediate franchise offer as proprietary-compound-expiring (P-C-E), research and development of a unique product as proprietary-compound-deferrable (P-C-D), bidding for the acquisition of an unrelated company as shared-compound-expiring (S-C-E), and the opportunity to enter a new geographic market as shared-compound-deferrable (S-C-D).[20] It is clear that real options provides an intuitive way of thinking that is useful in most (especially the strategic) situations, as well as a way of quantifying the value of flexibility in specific (mostly operational) decision problems.

3. CURRENT AND FUTURE APPLICATIONS

Real options has been applied in a variety of contexts, such as in natural resource investments, land development, leasing, flexible manufacturing, government subsidies and regulation, R&D, new ventures and acquisitions, and foreign investment and strategy. Early applications naturally arose in the area of *natural resource investments* due to the availability of traded resource or commodity prices, high volatilities and long durations, resulting in higher and better option value estimates. Brennan and Schwartz (1985) first utilized the convenience yield derived from futures and spot prices of a commodity to value the options to shut down or abandon a mine. Paddock, Siegel and Smith (1988) valued options embedded in undeveloped oil reserves and provided the first empirical evidence that option values are better than actual DCF-based bids in valuing offshore oil leases. Trigeorgis (1990) values an actual minerals project considered by a major multinational company involving options to cancel during construction, expand production, and abandon for salvage. Bjerksund and Ekern (1990) value a Norwegian oil field with options to defer and abandon. Morck, Schwartz and Stangeland (1989) value forestry resources under stochastic inventories and prices. Laughton and Jacoby (1993) examine biases in the valuation of real options and long-term decision making when a mean-reversion price process is more appropriate. Kemna (1993) analyzes cases at Shell involving the timing of developing an offshore oil field, valuing a growth option in a manufacturing venture and the abandonment decision of a refining production unit.

In the area of *land development*, Titman (1985), Capozza and Sick (1994), and Quigg (1995) show that the value of vacant land should reflect not only its value based on its best immediate use (e.g., from constructing a building now) but also its option value if development is delayed and the land is converted into its best alternative use in the future. It may thus pay to hold land vacant for its option value, even in the presence of currently thriving real estate markets. Quigg (1993) reports empirical results indicating that option-based land valuation that incorporates the option to wait to develop land provides better approximations of actual market prices. In a different context, McLaughlin and Taggart (1992) view the opportunity cost of using excess capacity as the change in the value of the firm's options caused by diverting capacity to an alternative use. In *leasing*, Copeland and Weston (1982), McConnel and Schallheim (1983), Trigeorgis (1995b), and Grenadier and Weiss (1997) value various operating options embedded in leasing contracts.

In the area of *flexible manufacturing*, the flexibility provided by flexible manufacturing systems, flexible production technology or other machinery having multiple uses has been analyzed from an options perspective by Kulatilaka (1993, 1995), Triantis and Hodder (1990), and Kulatilaka and Trigeorgis (1994), among others. Baldwin and Clark (1993) study the flexibility created by modularity in design that connects components of a larger system through standard interfaces.

In the area of *government subsidies and regulation*, Mason and Baldwin (1988) value government subsidies to large-scale energy projects as put options, while Teisberg (1994) provides an option valuation analysis of investment choices by a regulated firm. In *research and development*, Kolbe, Morris and Teisberg (1991) discuss option elements embedded in R&D projects. Option elements involved in the staging of *start-up ventures* are discussed in Sahlman (1988) and Trigeorgis (1993b). Strategic *acquisitions* of other companies also often involve a number of growth, divestiture, and other flexibility options, as discussed by Smith and Triantis (1995). On the empirical side, Kester (1984) estimates that the value of a firm's growth options is more than half the market value of equity for many firms, even 70-80% for more volatile industries. Similarly, Pindyck (1988) suggests that growth options represent more than half of firm value if demand volatility exceeds 20%. In *foreign investment*, Baldwin (1987) discusses the various location, timing and staging options present when firms scan the global marketplace. Bell (1995) and Kogut and Kulatilaka (1994), among others, examine entry, capacity, and switching options for firms with multinational operations under exchange rate volatility. Hiraki (1995) suggests that the Japanese bank-oriented corporate governance system serves as the basic infrastructure that enables companies to jointly develop corporate real options. Various other option applications can be found in areas ranging from *shipping* (Bjerksund and Ekern, 1995) to *environmental pollution and global warming* (e.g., Hendricks, 1991). The potential for future applications itself seems like a growth option.

Other comprehensive treatments of real options can be found in articles by Mason and Merton (1985) and Trigeorgis and Mason (1987), a monograph by Sick (1989), an economics review article by Pindyck (1991), as well as edited volumes by Trigeorgis (1995a), Brennan and Trigeorgis (1999), and Trigeorgis (2000). The Spring 1987 issue of the *Midland Corporate Finance Journal*, a 1991 special issue of *Managerial Finance* (vol. 17, number 2/3), a special issue of *Financial Management* (Fall 1993), and a special issue of *The Quaterly Review of Economics and Finance* (vol. 38) have also been devoted to real options and capital budgeting. An Annual International Conference on Real Options also promotes current research and applications (www.realoptions.org). Clearly, an increased attention to application and implementation issues is the next stage in the evolution of real options.

Future applications are expected in the following areas:

- Focusing more on investments (such as in R&D, pilot or market tests, or excavations) that can *generate* information and learning (e.g., about the project's prospects) by extending/adjusting option pricing and risk-neutral valuation with Bayesian analysis or alternative (e.g., jump) processes.
- Exploring in more depth endogenous competitive counteractions and a variety of competitive/market structure and strategic issues using a combination of game theoretic industrial organization with option valuation tools.
- Modelling better the various strategic and growth options.
- Extending real options in an agency context, recognizing that the potential (theoretical) value of real options may not be realized in practice if managers, in pursuing their own agendas (e.g., expansion or growth, rather than firm value maximization), misuse their discretion and do not follow the optimal exercise policies implicit in option valuation. This raises the need for the firm to design proper corrective incentive contracts (taking also into account asymmetric information).
- Recognizing better that real options may interact not only among themselves but also with financial flexibility options, and understanding the resulting implications for the combined, interdependent corporate investment and financing decisions.
- On the practical side, applying real options to the valuation of flexibility in related areas, such as in competitive bidding, information technology or other

platform investments, energy and R&D problems, international finance options, and so on.

- Using real options to explain empirical phenomena that are amenable to observation or statistical testing, such as examining empirically whether the managements of firms that are targets for acquisition may sometimes turn down tender offers in part due to the option to wait in anticipation of receiving better future offers.
- Doing more field, survey, or empirical studies to test the conformity of theoretical real options valuation and its implications with management's intuition and experience, as well as with actual price data, when available.
- Revising current compensation and control systems to reflect the value of corporate real options and encouraging their proper exercise and management over time.
- Linking natural risk management through the exercise of the firm's real options in the capital budgeting area, with the broader risk management of the firm's other (financial) exposures in an holistic way as part of a total-enterprise package solution.

4. CONCLUSION

This paper provided a primer on real options, both describing the basic principles for quantifying their value as well as thinking conceptually about the important competitive/strategic dimensions. It described, through simple examples, practically useful principles for valuing various upside-potential operating options, such as to defer an investment or expand production, as well as various downside-protection options, such as to abandon for salvage value, switch among alternative uses (e.g., inputs or outputs), or abandon a project midstream during construction. It also sought to describe qualitatively a conceptual framework (an expanded or strategic NPV approach) for thinking about capital investment opportunities as collections of corporate real options, with emphasis on the important competitive/strategic dimensions that are typically left out of conventional DCF analyses. A new options-based project classification scheme and several strategic questions for capital budgeting analysis were proposed. This conceptual framework is intended as a practical aid in recognizing and understanding the frequently encountered collections of real options and the competitive/strategic dimensions of many investment opportunities.

NOTES

[1] This paper partly draws on work published by the author in *Financial Management, Advances in Options and Futures Research*, and elsewhere.

[2] Alternatively, management has an option to obtain project value V (net of fixed costs, I_F) minus variable costs (I_V), or shut down and receive the project value minus that year's foregone cash revenue (C), i.e., $\max(V - I_V, V - C) - I_F = (V - I_F) - \min(I_V, C)$. The latter expression implies that the option not to operate enables management to acquire project value (net of fixed costs) by paying the minimum of variable costs (if the project does well and management decides to operate) or the cash revenues (that would be sacrificed if the project does poorly and it chooses not to operate).

[3] Trigeorgis and Mason (1987) use a similar example to show how options-based valuation can be seen operationally as a special, although economically-corrected, version of decision tree analysis that recognizes open-market opportunities to trade and borrow.

[4] All project values are subsequently assumed to be in millions of dollars (with "millions" dropped).

[5] As noted, the basic idea is that management can replicate the payoff to equity by purchasing a specified number of shares of the "twin security" and financing the purchase in part by borrowing a specific amount at the riskless interest rate, r. This ability to construct a *synthetic* claim or an equivalent/replicating portfolio (from the "twin security" and riskless bonds) based on no arbitrage equilibrium principles enables the solution for the current value of the equity claim to be independent of the actual probabilities (in this case .5) or investors' risk attitudes (the twin security's expected rate of return or discount rate, $k = .20$).

[6] This confirms the gross project value, $V_0 = 100$, obtained earlier using traditional DCF with the actual probability ($q = 0.5$) and the risk-adjusted discount rate ($k = 0.20$).

[7] This assumption is intended to make the analysis somewhat more realistic and invariant to the cost structure make-up, and is not at all crucial to the analysis.

[8] The above example confirms that CCA is *operationally* identical to decision tree analysis (DTA), with the key difference that the probabilities are transformed so as to allow the use of a risk-free discount rate. Note, however, that the DCF/DTA value of waiting may differ from that given by CCA. The DCF/DTA approach in this case will overestimate the value of the option if it discounts at the constant 20% rate required of securities comparable in risk to the *naked* (passive) project:

$E_0 = [qE^+ + (1 - q)E^-]/(1 + k) = [.5 \times 67.68 + .5 \times 0]/1.20 = 28.20.$

Again, the error in the traditional DTA approach arises from the use of a single (or constant) risk-adjusted discount rate. Asymmetric claims on an asset do not have the same riskiness (and hence, expected rate of return) as the underlying asset itself. CCA corrects for this error by transforming the probabilities.

[9] For simplicity, it is assumed here that the project's value in its current use and in its best alternative use (or salvage value) are perfectly positively correlated. Of course, the option to switch use would be even more valuable when the correlation between V and A is lower.

[10] The possibility that the option to take a project may not be tradable may necessitate dividend-like adjustments and justify preemptive investments, thus indirectly affecting the timing of exercise and value of a real option.

[11] There are, of course, examples of compound options in traded financial securities as well, such as callable convertible bonds.

[12] The *opportunity to invest* is thus formally equivalent to a *call option* on the value of a completed project, V, with exercise price the one-time investment outlay, I.

[13] "*Salvage value,*" or value in the best alternative use, may come from the value of expected cash flows from switching use (or inputs/outputs), a market price for which the project may sell in a second-hand market or, in situations where subsequent expenditures are due, the value of subsequent cost savings from discontinuing the project.

[14] To simplify exposition, the rest of this section ignores the option (not) to operate, as well as the options to expand or contract the scale of operation and various other options.

[15] As pointed out earlier, shared options can be differentiated further depending on whether the impact of competition is taken as exogenous or causes endogenous strategic counteractions. The latter can be further differentiated depending on the nature of competitive reaction (contrarian or reciprocating).

[16] Normally, "competitive loss" has a negative value (i.e., it is a loss), especially if competitors enter after the firm has undertaken the project. In some cases, however, it may actually be a gain (i.e., a negative "loss"). One example is an R&D investment that develops a new technology that competitors can easily imitate, resulting in lower production costs and higher profits for all competitors. Another example is when a competitor's investment, such as advertising expenditures, promotes the whole product category and not just the competitor's particular brand (e.g., "buy liquid soap," rather than "Jergen's Liquid Soap is the Best"), thus increasing the total "market pie" for all, or reducing the need for advertising expenditures by the particular firm. In this case, a competitor's investment is like a public service benefiting all (a shared investment). As a third example, consider the effect of competition on the value of the option to introduce a new product when acceptance by the market is highly uncertain. An introduction of a substitute product by a competitor may on the one hand take some market share away from the firm, while on the other it may resolve uncertainty about the market's reception of that type of product. It is conceivable that the "*learning effect*" for the firm may be more valuable than the direct market share loss, so that the firm may obtain a net gain from such competitive entry.

[17] There are, of course, other forms of interproject dependence such as "mutually exclusive" projects where undertaking one project precludes undertaking the other, or "synergistic" projects that enhance each other's cash flows when taken together. These interactions are ignored here; compoundness is the focus instead.

[18] The distinction between "expiring" and "deferrable" investment opportunities is one of degree. It is also in a sense related to the distinction between shared and proprietary options, in that in a shared option the threat of competition may, for preemptive reasons, effectively turn a "deferrable" option into an "expiring" one (although, in this case, management still has a choice as to whether or not to make an immediate preemptive investment, whereas in a strictly expiring option such a choice is precluded entirely).

Also, the horizon of a deferrable real option is a relative notion compared to contractual financial options. In the case of real options, it may be useful to analyze whether the expiration of the option (end of the waiting horizon) is brought about by abrupt versus incremental changes. An abrupt event such as the termination of a patent for producing a new product or of a lease for oil drilling can be treated as an exogenously determined point in time when the deferrable option expires. On the other hand, incremental changes in value resulting from the introduction of substitute products in a shared-deferrable option can be treated as endogenous effects analogous to dividends in call options (although in the extreme case where the substitute product is a technological breakthrough causing an abrupt project value drop to zero, its introduction may effectively be treated as the expiration time for the horizon of the incumbent firm's real option).

[19] The basic form of this classification is similar to that first proposed by Kester (1984).

[20] It is worth noting that, under this real options classification scheme, conventional (static) NPV investments are properly seen as a special case under the leftmost branch of proprietary-simple-expiring options because such investments are typically evaluated as if they were exclusively owned (i.e., ignoring competitive interaction, hence *proprietary*), independent (hence *simple*), and immediate (hence *expiring*) opportunities.

REFERENCES

Baldwin, C. 1987. "Competing for Capital in a Global Environment." *Midland Corporate Finance Journal* 5, no. 1: 43-64.

Baldwin, C. and K. Clark. 1993. Modularity and Real Options. Working paper, Harvard Business School.

Baldwin, C. and L. Trigeorgis. 1993. *Real Options, Capabilities, TQM, and Competitiveness.* Working paper 93-025, Harvard Business School.

Bell, G. 1995. "Volatile Exchange Rates and the Multinational Firm: Entry, Exit, and Capacity Options." *Real Options in Capital Investment: Models, Strategies, and Applications*, ed. L. Trigeorgis. Praeger.

Bjerksund, P. and S. Ekern. 1990. "Managing Investment Opportunities Under Price Uncertainty: From 'Last Chance' to 'Wait and See' Strategies." *Financial Management* 19, no. 3: 65-83.

Bjerksund, P. and S. Ekern. 1995. "Contingent Claims Evaluation of Mean-Reverting Cash Flows in Shipping." In *Real Options in Capital Investment: Models, Strategies, and Applications*, ed. L. Trigeorgis. Praeger.

Black, F. and M. Scholes. 1973. "The Pricing of Options and Corporate Liabilities." *Journal of Political Economy* 81 (May-June): 637-659.

Brennan, M. and E. Schwartz. 1985. "Evaluating Natural Resource Investments." *Journal of Business* 58, no. 2: 135-157.

Brennan, M. and L. Trigeorgis. 1999. *Project Flexibility, Agency, and Product Market Competition.* Oxford University Press.

Capozza, D. and G. Sick. 1994. "The Risk Structure of Land Markets." *Journal of Urban Economics* 35: 297-319.

Carr, P. 1988. "The Valuation of Sequential Exchange Opportunities." *Journal of Finance* 43, no. 5: 1235-1256.

Childs, P., S. Ott and A. Triantis. 1998. "Capital Budgeting for Interrelated Projects: A Real Options Approach." *Journal of Financial and Quantitative Analysis* 33, no. 3: 305-334.

Copeland T. and J.F. Weston. 1982. "A Note on the Evaluation of Cancellable Operating Leases." *Financial Management* 11, no. 2: 60-67.

Dixit, A. 1980. "The Role of Investment in Entry Deterrence." *Economic Journal* 90 (March): 95-106.

Dixit, A. 1992. "Investment and Hysteresis." *Journal of Economic Perspectives* 6 (Winter): 107-132.

Dixit, A. and R. S. Pindyck. 1994. *Investment Under Uncertainty*. Princeton University Press.

Geske, R. 1979. "The Valuation of Compound Options." *Journal of Financial Economics* 7, no. 1: 63-81.

Grenadier, S. and A.M. Weiss. 1997. "Investment in Technological Innovations: An Option Pricing Approach." *Journal of Financial Economics* 44: 397-416.

Hendricks, D. 1991. Optimal Policy Responses to an Uncertain Threat: The Case of Global Warming. Working paper, Kennedy School of Government, Harvard University.

Hiraki, T. 1995. "Corporate Governance, Long-term Investment Orientation, and Real Options in Japan." *Real Options in Capital Investment: Models, Strategies, and Applications*, ed. L. Trigeorgis. Praeger.

Ingersoll, J. and S. Ross. 1992. "Waiting to Invest: Investment and Uncertainty." *Journal of Business* 65, no. 1: 1-29.

Kemna, A. 1993. "Case Studies on Real Options." *Financial Management* 22, no. 3: 259-270.

Kester, W.C. 1984. "Today's Options for Tomorrow's Growth." *Harvard Business Review* 62, no. 2: 153-160.

Kogut, B. and N. Kulatilaka. 1994. "Operating Flexibility, Global Manufacturing, and the Option Value of a Multinational Network." *Management Science* 40, no. 1: 123-139.

Kolbe, A.L., P. A. Morris, and E. O. Teisberg. 1991. "When Choosing R&D Projects, Go with Long Shots." *Research-Technology Management* (January-February).

Kulatilaka, N. 1993. "The Value of Flexibility: The Case of a Dual-Fuel Industrial Steam Boiler." *Financial Management* 22, no. 3: 271-279.

Kulatilaka, N. 1995. "The Value of Flexibility: A General Model of Real Options." In *Real Options in Capital Investment: Models, Strategies, and Applications*, ed. L. Trigeorgis. Praeger.

Kulatilaka, N. and L. Trigeorgis. 1994. "The General Flexibility to Switch: Real Options Revisited." *International Journal of Finance* 6, no. 2.

Laughton, D.G. and H.D. Jacoby. 1993. "Reversion, Timing Options, and Long-term Decision-Making." *Financial Management* 22, no. 3: 225-240.

Luehrman, T. 1998. "Strategy as a Portfolio of Real Options." *Harvard Business Review* (Sept.-Oct.): 89-99.

Martzoukos, S. and L. Trigeorgis. 1998. General Multi-stage Capital Investment Problems with Multiple Uncertainties. Working paper, University of Chicago.

Mason, S.P. and C. Baldwin. 1988. "Evaluation of Government Subsidies to Large-scale Energy Projects: A Contingent Claims Approach." *Advances in Futures and Options Research* 3: 169-181.

Mason, S.P. and R.C. Merton. 1985. "The Role of Contingent Claims Analysis in Corporate Finance." *Recent Advances in Corporate Finance*, ed. E. Altman and M. Subrahmanyam. Irwin.

McConnel, J. and J. Schallheim. 1983. "Valuation of Asset Leasing Contracts." *Journal of Financial Economics* 12, no. 2: 237-261.

McDonald, R. and D. Siegel. 1985. "Investment and the Valuation of Firms When There is an Option to Shut Down." *International Economic Review* 26, no. 2: 331-349.

McDonald, R. and D. Siegel. 1986. "The Value of Waiting to Invest." *Quarterly Journal of Economics* 101, no. 4: 707-727.

McLaughlin, R. and R. Taggart. 1992. "The Opportunity Cost of Using Excess Capacity." *Financial Management* 21, no. 2: 12-23.

Merton, R.C. 1973. "Theory of Rational Option Pricing." *Bell Journal of Economics and Management Science* 4, no. 1: 141-183.

Merton, R.C. 1998. "Applications of Option-Pricing Theory: Twenty-Five Years Later." *American Economic Review* 88, no. 3: 336-340.

Morck, R., E. Schwartz, and D. Stangeland. 1989. "The Valuation of Forestry Resources under Stochastic Prices and Inventories." *Journal of Financial and Quantitative Analysis* 24, no. 4: 473-487.

Myers, S.C. 1987. "Finance Theory and Financial Strategy." *Midland Corporate Finance Journal* 5, no. 1: 6-13.

Myers, S.C. and S. Majd. 1990. "Abandonment Value and Project Life." *Advances in Futures and Options Research* 4: 1-21.

Paddock, J., D. Siegel, and J. Smith. 1988. "Option Valuation of Claims on Physical Assets: The Case of Offshore Petroleum Leases." *Quarterly Journal of Economics* 103, no. 3: 479-508.

Panayi, S. and L. Trigeorgis. 1998. "Multi-stage Real Options: The Cases of Information Technology Infrastructure and International Bank Expansion." *Quarterly Review of Economics and Finance* 38: 675-692.

Pindyck, R. 1988. "Irreversible Investment, Capacity Choice, and the Value of the Firm." *American Economic Review* 78, no. 5: 969-985.

Pindyck, R. 1991. "Irreversibility, Uncertainty, and Investment." *Journal of Economic Literature* 29, no. 3: 1110-1148.

Quigg, L. 1993. "Empirical Testing of Real Option-Pricing Models." *Journal of Finance* 48, no. 2: 621-640.

Quigg, L. 1995. "Optimal Land Development." *Real Options in Capital Investment: Models, Strategies, and Applications*, ed. L. Trigeorgis. Praeger.

Sahlman, W. 1988. "Aspects of Financial Contracting in Venture Capital." *Journal of Applied Corporate Finance* 1: 23-36.

Schwartz, E. and L. Trigeorgis. 2000. *Real Options and Investment under Uncertainty: Classical Readings and Recent Contributions.* MIT Press.

Sick, G. 1989. *Capital Budgeting with Real Options.* Monograph, Salomon Brothers Center, New York University.

Smit, H.T.J. and L.A. Ankum. 1993. "A Real Options and Game-Theoretic Approach to Corporate Investment Strategy under Competition." *Financial Management* 22, no. 3: 241-250.

Smit, H.T.J. and L. Trigeorgis. 1993. Flexibility and Commitment in Strategic Investment. Working paper, Tinbergen Institute, Erasmus University, Rotterdam.

Smit, H.T.J. and L. Trigeorgis. 1997. R&D Option Strategies. Working paper, University of Chicago.

Smit, H.T.J. and L. Trigeorgis. 1999. "Flexibility, Strategic Options and Dynamic Competition in Technology Investments." *Real Options Applications*, ed. A. Micalizzi and L. Trigeorgis. Egea.

Smith, K.W. and A. Triantis. 1995. "The Value of Options in Strategic Acquisitions." In *Real Options in Capital Investment: Models, Strategies, and Applications*, ed. L. Trigeorgis. Praeger.

Spence, M. 1979. "Investment Strategy and Growth in a New Market." *Bell Journal of Economics* 10 (Spring): 1-19.

Teisberg, E. 1994. "An Option Valuation Analysis of Investment Choices by a Regulated Firm." *Management Science* 40, no. 4: 535-548.

Titman, S. 1985. "Urban Land Prices Under Uncertainty." *American Economic Review* 75, no. 3: 505-514.

Triantis A. and J. Hodder. 1990. "Valuing Flexibility as a Complex Option." *Journal of Finance* 45, no. 2: 549-565.

Trigeorgis, L. 1988. "A Conceptual Options Framework for Capital Budgeting." *Advances in Futures and Options Research* 3: 145-167.

Trigeorgis, L. 1990. "A Real Options Application in Natural Resource Investments." *Advances in Futures and Options Research* 4: 153-164.

Trigeorgis, L. 1991a. "Anticipated Competitive Entry and Early Preemptive Investment in Deferrable Projects." *Journal of Economics and Business* 43, no. 2: 143-156.

Trigeorgis, L. 1991b. "A Log-Transformed Binomial Numerical Analysis Method for Valuing Complex Multi-Option Investments." *Journal of Financial and Quantitative Analysis* 26, no. 3: 309-326.

Trigeorgis, L. 1993a. "The Nature of Option Interactions and the Valuation of Investments with Multiple Real Options." *Journal of Financial and Quantitative Analysis* 28, no. 1: 1-20.

Trigeorgis, L. 1993b. "Real Options and Interactions with Financial Flexibility." *Financial Management* 22, no. 3: 202-224.

Trigeorgis, L., ed. 1995a. *Real Options in Capital Investment: Models, Strategies, and Applications*. Praeger.

Trigeorgis, L. 1995b. "Evaluating Leases with Complex Operating Options." *European Journal of Operational Research* (Special Issue on Financial Modelling) 75.

Trigeorgis, L. 1996. *Real Options: Managerial Flexibility and Strategy in Resource Allocation*. MIT Press.

Trigeorgis, L. 2000. *Innovation and Strategy, Flexibility, Natural Resources and Foreign Investment: New Developments and Applications in Real Options*. Oxford University Press.

Trigeorgis, L. and S.P. Mason. 1987. "Valuing Managerial Flexibility." *Midland Corporate Finance Journal* 5, no. 1: 14-21.

2 Real Options Applications in the Telecommunications Industry

Sanjai Bhagat
Graduate School of Business,
University of Colorado at Boulder

Two examples of the application of real options to the telecommunications industry are suggested in this paper. These applications move beyond the traditional capital budgeting procedures, which cannot properly capture management's flexibility to adapt and later revise decisions in response to unexpected regulatory/technological/market developments. Real options techniques can conceptualize and value managerial flexibility to alter initial operating strategy in order to capitalize on favorable future opportunities or to react to mitigate losses. Recognizing a particular capital budgeting project as a real option has value, particularly as the business environment becomes more uncertain.

1. CAPITAL BUDGETING AND REAL OPTIONS

Capital budgeting is the process by which businesses allocate capital. There are three dimensions of allocation decisions: Which project to invest in, how much to invest, and when to invest? Traditional approaches assume an expected scenario of cashflows and presume management's passive commitment to a certain static operating strategy. Such a strategy might be appropriate when the business environment is stable or predictable. However, the current business world is characterized by change, uncertainty and competitive interactions. As new information arrives and uncertainty about market conditions is resolved, management may have valuable flexibility to alter its initial operating strategy in order to capitalize on favorable future opportunities or to react so as to mitigate losses. This managerial operating flexibility is like financial options, and is known as strategic options or real options.

> *We will maintain our highly disciplined approach to capital spending. Our objective remains to maximize return on every dollar we invest — and to invest where we find the very best growth opportunities.*
>
> Richard C. Notebaert,
> Chairman and CEO
> Ameritech (1997 Annual Report)
>
> *Finance theory properly applied, is critical to managing in an increasingly complex and risky business climate. Option analysis provides a more flexible approach to valuing our investments. To me all kinds of business decisions are options.*
>
> Judy Lewent, CFO
> Merck (1992 Annual Report)

Traditional discounted cashflow approaches such as the net present value (NPV) rule cannot properly capture management's flexibility to adapt and later revise decisions in response to unexpected market developments. Considering real options in the capital budgeting process is the appropriate way to incorporate the value of managerial flexibility in the decision-making process.

2. SOURCE OF VALUE IN AN OPTION

Option pricing theory was first developed in the context of financial options, such as call options and put options. Conceptually, financial and real options are quite similar with one exception: The underlying asset for a financial option is a financial asset, like a common stock, while the underlying asset for a real option is a business project.

A call option gives the owner the right, with no obligation, to acquire the underlying asset by paying a prespecified amount (the exercise price, X) on or before the maturity date. Figure 1 illustrates the payoff (on the maturity date) from owning a call option.

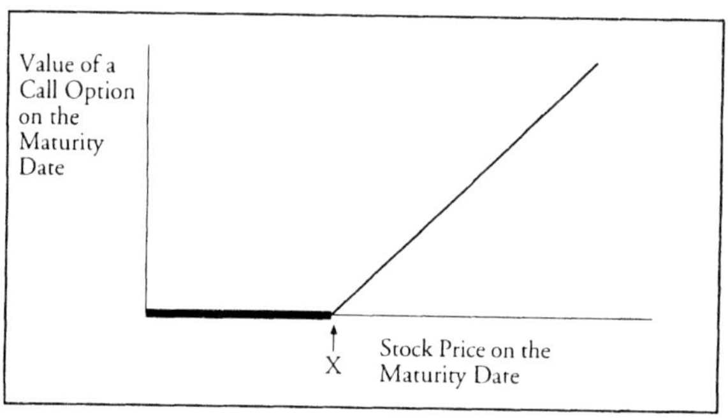

Figure 1

The source of value in an option is the asymmetry from having the right, but not the obligation, to exercise the option (notice the asymmetric nature of payoffs in the above graph). While the source of value in an option is the asymmetric nature of payoffs, this payoff profile makes the valuation of options through traditional methods, such as the discounted cashflow analysis, inappropriate.

3. TRADITIONAL APPROACHES TO DEALING WITH UNCERTAINTY AND COMPLEXITY IN CAPITAL BUDGETING

Real options is a relatively new addition to the tool-kit of capital budgeting decision makers. Traditionally there have been three approaches to dealing with uncertainty and complexity in capital budgeting:

3.1 Sensitivity Analysis

Sensitivity analysis considers the effect on the NPV of varying one variable at a time. It is useful in identifying key drivers in a project. It indicates how large the forecast error on a key driver can before the project becomes unacceptable.

Pro: Sensitivity analysis is easy to implement and understand.

Con: This approach ignores interdependencies among variables (at a point in time) and over time. For example, usually there is an inverse relationship between market share and the price charged; such a relationship is not modeled in this analysis.

3.2 Simulation

There are four steps in implementing the simulation process:

1. Equations specify relationships among variables.
2. Probability distributions of underlying variables are specified.
3. Random draws from above distributions. NPV is computed.
4. Steps 1, 2, and 3 are repeated many times.

Pro: Simulation takes into account interdependencies among variables.

Cons: A. This approach makes it difficult to interpret a distribution of NPVs. The traditional view of NPV as an "increase in shareholder wealth from accepting the project" is not applicable.

Solution: Use simulation to assess the distribution of the net cashflows.

B. Step 1 presents problems in specifying interdependencies. For example, while the relationship between market share and the price charged is inverse, the functional form of such a relationship is unclear.

C. This approach cannot handle well asymmetries in the distributions introduced by management's flexibility to revise its prior operating strategy as more information about project cashflows becomes available over time.

3.3 Decision Tree Analysis

The decision tree analysis helps structure the managerial decision problem by mapping out feasible managerial alternatives in response to future events.

Pro: Decision tree analysis forces management to recognize its implied operating strategy and the interdependencies between the initial and subsequent decisions. For example, investment in an R&D project today could give managers an opportunity to invest in an attractive project in the future if the R&D effort were successful.

Cons: A. The number of different paths on the tree increases geometrically. This makes it increasingly difficult to determine the probability of being on a certain branch, and the cashflows associated with the branch.

B. Choice of discount rate: The risk of the project may change over time.

Table 1 summarizes the three approaches to dealing with uncertainty and complexity in capital budgeting and their pros and cons:

Table 1

Traditional Approaches	Description	Pros	Cons
Sensitivity Analysis	Varies one variable at a time	Identifies key drivers Easy to implement and understand	Ignores interdependencies among variables
Simulation	1. Equations specify relationships among variables. 2. Specify probability distribution of underlying variables. 3. Random draws from distributions; compute NPV. 4. Repeat steps 1, 2, and 3 many times.	Interdependencies considered.	Interpretation of a distribution of NPVs is problematic. Traditional view of NPV not applicable. Specifying interdependencies among variables is difficult. Management's flexibility is not easily incorporated.
Decision-tree analysis	Maps future managerial alternatives.	Structures managerial decisions. Recognizes management's: • Implied operating strategy and • Interdependencies between initial and subsequent decisions.	Branches on the tree increase geometrically with a corresponding increase in the difficulty of implementing this procedure. Correct discount rate may change over time.

4. EXAMPLE OF REAL OPTIONS

The following discussion based on Trigeorgis (1996, pp 9 ff.) provides a set of stylized examples of real options.

The SuperCom Project: A large telecommunications company faces an opportunity to invest in an R&D project that will revolutionize the way consumers use telephones, internet, and TV. R&D would be conducted for the first three years. If this R&D effort were successful, commercialization would be initiated. The following diagram notes the real options associated with the SuperCom Project.

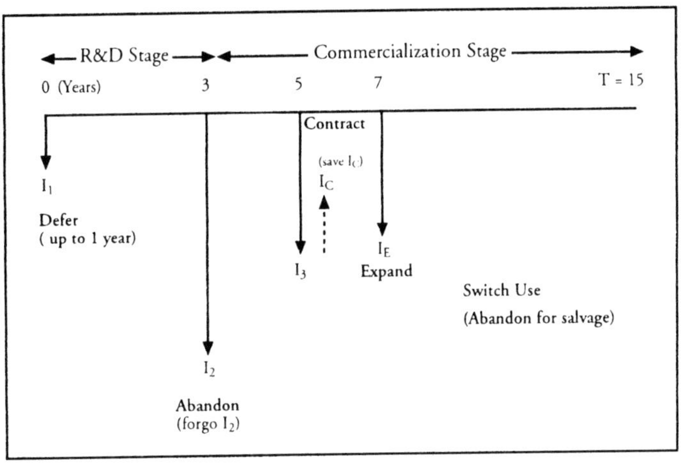

Figure 2. *Real Options* in the SuperCom Project

SuperCom's cash outflows and inflows are:

I_1: Required investment in the R&D project.

I_2: Required investment in the commercial-scale plant, marketing, and distribution, if the R&D effort is successful and if market conditions are favorable.

I_3: Final investment in the project can be decreased by I_c if the market is weak.

I_E: Flexibility in the design of the production process allows for output expansion with an outlay of I_E.

V: Gross present value of the completed project's expected operating cashflows.

Before citing examples of real options associated with SuperCom, it should be noted that while conceptually the above cashflows are easy to describe, in practice, they might be quite difficult to estimate. For example, V incorporates cashflows over *many years* in the future *if* the R&D effort were successful.

1. Option to Defer Investment. Congress is currently debating the viability and the process by which to allocate or auction the airwaves that are crucial to the commercial success of SuperCom. If Congress passes legislation unfavorable to our company, then SuperCom would not be commercially viable. Our lobbyist in Washington advises us that the debate would be resolved within a year. We could initiate the R&D project immediately, or wait a year to see what Congress does. The option to defer investing in the R&D project is similar to a call option whose value is $max\ (V - I_I,\ 0)$.

2. Option to Expand. Given an initial design choice, management may deliberately favor a more expensive technology for the built-in flexibility to expand production/sales if and when it becomes desirable. If the market's response to SuperCom is better than expected, management can accelerate the rate or expand the scale of production by x% by incurring a follow-on cost I_E. The option to expand has value $max\ (xV - I_E,\ 0)$.

The option to expand also applies to complementary markets: Investing in SuperCom in a new geographical area allows for the possibility to expand to other similar markets. For example, besides local and long-distance telecommunication, the market for telephone-via-internet could be explored in the new geographical area.

3. Option to Default during Staged Construction (Time-to-Build-Option). Investing in the R&D project, or investing I_1, provides the opportunity to invest in the commercial stage by investing I_2 or to abandon the project if the R&D and initial test marketing are unsatisfactory.

4. Option to Contract. If the market does not respond to SuperCom as expected, management can reduce the scale of operations by c%, thereby saving I_c of the planned investment outlays. This option to mitigate loss has value $max\ (I_c - cV,\ 0)$.

5. Option to Abandon for Salvage Value. If SuperCom does significantly worse than expected in the market, management may choose to abandon the project permanently in exchange for its salvage value: the resale value of the capital equipment, license, etc. for A. This flexibility to abandon the project has value $max\ (V,\ A)$.

Table 2 describes and notes examples of various types of real options commonly encountered:

Table 2

Real Option	Description	Examples
Defer	To wait before taking an action until more is known or timing is expected to be more favorable	When to introduce a new product or replace an existing piece of equipment
Expand or contract	To increase or decrease the scale of an operation in response to demand	Adding to or subtracting from a service offering, or adding memory to a computer
Abandon	To discontinue an operation and liquidate the assets	Discontinuation of a research project or product/service line
Stage investment	To commit investment in stages, giving rise to a series of valuations and abandonment options	Staging of research and development projects or financial commitments to a new venture
Switch inputs or outputs	To alter the mix of inputs or outputs of a production process in response to market prices	The output mix of telephony/internet/ cellular services for a telecommunications company
Grow	To expand the scope of activities to capitalize on perceived new opportunities	Extension of brand names to new products or marketing through existing distribution channels

5. LIMITATIONS OF THE OPTIONS ANALOGY

While the real options technique has the potential to improve capital budgeting decisions, the conceptualization and valuation of such real options presents some issues and limitations:

1. Valuation Techniques. The standard techniques of valuing options are based on a no-arbitrage equilibrium, using portfolios of traded securities to replicate the payoff to options. Can this valuation technique be justifiably applied to capital budgeting where projects may not be traded? Answer: Yes. The computation of NPV requires the calculation of a discount rate - the weighted average cost-of-capital or the required return on an asset that is traded in the capital markets of similar risk as the project. Hence, the non-tradability of the project is no more problematic for the real options framework than it is for the standard NPV analysis.

2. Exclusiveness of Ownership and Competitive Interaction. The financial call option on a common stock is proprietary; only the owner can exercise it without worrying about competition for the underlying security. Some real options (patents, licenses) are also proprietary. Other real options are shared and can be exercised by any firm in the particular industry. Examples: opportunity to penetrate a new geographic market or to introduce a new product unprotected by the possible introduction of close substitutes.

3. Nontradability and Preemption. Financial call options are traded with minimal transaction costs. Real options are not generally traded. The non-tradability of real options may lead to their early exercise. For example, a firm anticipating an increase in industry demand - and hence subsequent competitive entry - may rush in early to expand its own production/sales capacity to preempt competition. In the absence of such competition, it might have preferred to wait for the uncertainty surrounding future demand to resolve itself.

4. Strategic Interdependencies and Option Compoundness. Financial call options are simple: their value derives entirely from the received shares of the stock. Some real options (such as maintenance or standard replacement projects) are simple. Others are compound: R&D investments are like an option on an option (the second option being the opportunity to invest in the commercial venture generated by the R&D project). Compound real options may have a more strategic impact on firm value than simple real options, and are more complicated to analyze. Compound real options must be looked at not as independent projects but rather as links in a chain of interrelated projects, the earlier of which may be prerequisites for those to follow.

6. THE BOTTOM LINE

Traditional capital budgeting procedures cannot properly capture management's flexibility to adapt and revise later decisions in response to unexpected regulatory/technological/market developments. The real options technique can conceptualize and value managerial flexibility to alter its initial operating strategy in order to capitalize on favorable future opportunities or to react to mitigate losses.

6.1 The Real Value in Real Options!

In option pricing theory, the value of a call option increases with:

- Increase in variance of the underlying asset
- Increase in the value of the underlying asset
- Increase in the time to expiration
- Increase in the risk-free rate
- Decrease in the exercise price.

While the valuation of real options might be non-trivial, *recognizing* a particular capital budgeting project as a real option has value. The above comparative static results from option pricing theory suggest that recognizing and valuing real options becomes more valuable as the business environment becomes more uncertain!

As noted above, the actual valuation of real options is non-trivial. However, real options can be valued! The following numerical example illustrates how real options can be identified, modeled, and valued.

6.2 An Example: LaserTalk

A large telecommunications company, TCOM Inc., is considering the real/strategic options associated with investing in a project in a new country: *The LaserTalk Investment Opportunity (LaserTalk).*

The real options associated with *LaserTalk* are business opportunities that will become available to TCOM only if *LaserTalk* were to be invested in now. What might be the nature of these business opportunities? From an economic and strategic viewpoint, these opportunities would be in TCOM's areas of core competencies. If TCOM has a comparative advantage at doing something in their existing market, they probably enjoy a similar advantage at doing it elsewhere. Additionally, these business opportunities may arise as a result of TCOM's R&D success in the United States, or legal/regulatory changes in the new country.

How are the real options associated with *LaserTalk* valued? Below, a modification of the Black-Scholes call option valuation equation is used to value the real options associated with *LaserTalk.*

$$\text{Value of Call option} = V\, e^{-yt}\, N(d_1) - X\, e^{-rt}\, N(d_2)$$

Where, $d_1 = [\ \ln (V/X) + (r - y + (\sigma^2)/2)\ t\ ] \ /\ \sigma(t)^{1/2}$
$d_2 = d_1 - \sigma\,(t)^{1/2}$. $N(.)$ = cumulative normal density function.

The other variables are described below.

Table 3

Variable	(Financial) Call Option	Real Option
V: Underlying asset	Stock	Business project
Value of V	Stock price	Present value of project's net cashflows
X	Exercise price	Present value of project's cash outflows
t	Time to maturity	Time over which the project decision may be made
r	Risk-free rate	Risk-free rate
σ^2	Variance of the stock price	Variance of the present value of project's net cashflows

Table 3 above also notes the corresponding variables between the call option and real option equations. From this, the following equation for the real option's value is derived:

$$\text{Value of real option} = V\, e^{-yt}\, N(d_1) - X\, e^{-rt}\, N(d_2)$$

Where, $d_1 = [\, \ln (V/X) + (r - y + (\sigma^2)/2)\, t\,] \,/\, \sigma(t)^{1/2}$, and $d_2 = d_1 - \sigma\, (t)^{1/2}$

N (.) = Cumulative normal density function.

V = Present value of expected cash inflows from investing in future projects in the new country. Obviously, V will depend on the size and scope of such future business opportunities in the new country. The following assumptions can be made (considering the sensitivity of the value of the real options associated with *LaserTalk* to these assumptions):

Price charged as % of price in existing market	=	90%
TCOM's weighted-average cost of capital	=	12.63%
Life of project (years)	=	10
New country market size (fraction of TCOM's current market)	=	0.3
Operating costs (as a % of operating costs in existing market)	=	120%
Capital expenditure (as a % of cap. exp. in existing market)	=	110%

Given the above assumptions and the present value of TCOM's future cashflows, V = \$2.5 billion.

X = Present value of the costs of investing in future projects in the new country. Again, X will depend on the size and scope of such future business opportunities in the new country. Given the above assumptions and the present value of TCOM's future cashflows, X = \$3.0 billion.

σ^2 = Variance in the expected net cashflows over time from investing in future projects in the new country, allowing for technological, legal, and market changes. The estimation of this variable has been quite prominent in the empirical option pricing regarding financial options. All the caveats and problems associated with estimating the variance in the empirical option pricing literature regarding financial options are equally applicable here. The problem is further complicated by the fact that even the underlying asset is not known at this time. The underlying assets are the future projects in the new country; the exact specifics of such projects are not known at this time. For illustrative purposes, the historical variability in cashflows in the U.S. telecommunications industry can be considered as the starting point for this analysis; $\sigma^2 = (40\%)^2$. The sensitivity of the value of the real options (associated with *LaserTalk*) to this assumption can also be considered.

t = Number of years during which the real option can be exercised, that is, the number of years during which investments could be made in future projects in the new country. For illustrative purposes, assume that t = 4 years. The sensitivity of the value of the real options (associated with *LaserTalk*) to this assumption is also considered.

$$y = 1 / t.$$

r = Risk-free interest rate for t years. For illustrative purposes, it is assumed that r = 6.40%. The sensitivity of the value of the real options (associated with *LaserTalk*) to this assumption is also considered.

The NPV of the future projects in the new country = V – X = -\$500 million. Hence, this project would be rejected on the basis of simply considering the traditional NPV. However, using the above real option valuation equation and the parameter estimates, the real option value of investing in the new country is \$800 million!

Below, the sensitivity of the value of the real options (associated with *LaserTalk*) to this assumption is analyzed graphically. As a result, for example, the value of the real option associated with *LaserTalk* is quite sensitive to the price that can be charged in the new country, but not very sensitive to the variability in the expected net cashflows over time from investing in future projects in the new country.

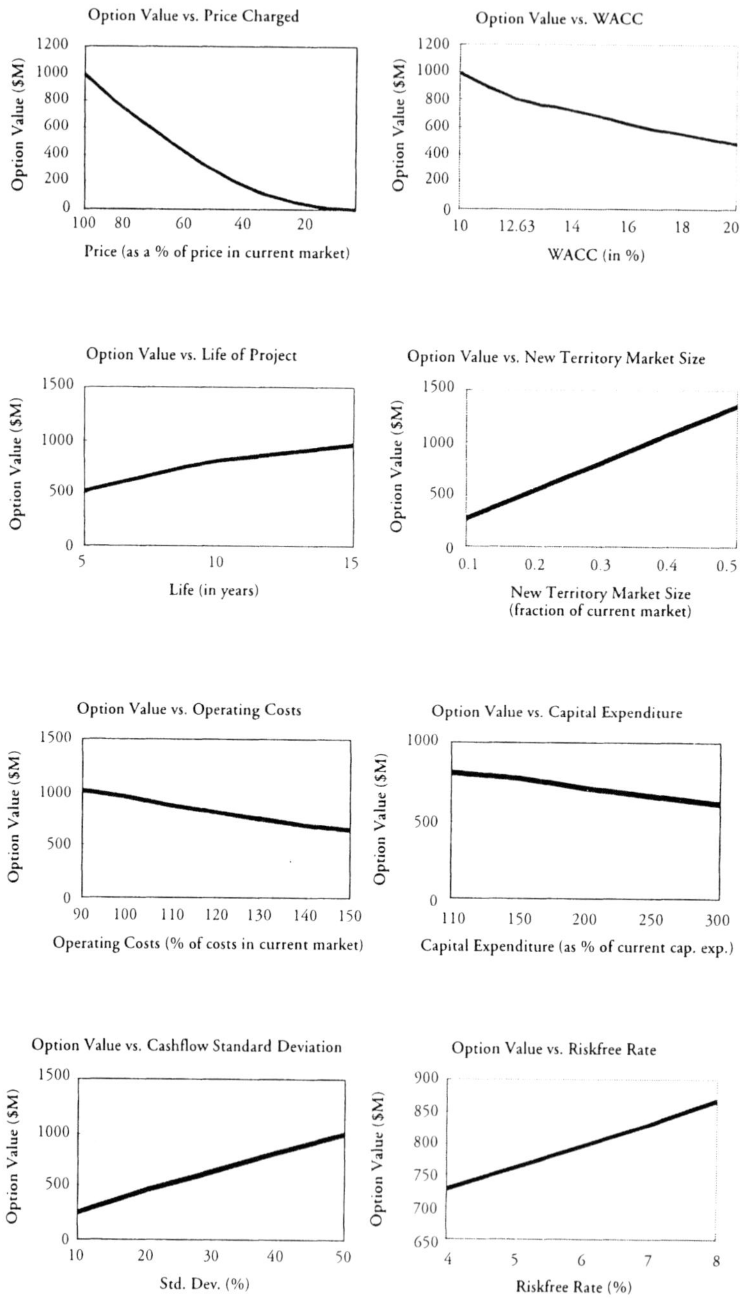

Figure 3. Sensitivity Analysis of Real Option Value of Investing in LaserTalk

7. SUMMARY

Traditional capital budgeting procedures cannot properly capture management's flexibility to adapt and revise later decisions in response to unexpected regulatory/technological/market developments. The real options techniques can conceptualize and value managerial flexibility to alter its initial operating strategy in order to capitalize on favorable future opportunities or to react to mitigate losses. While the valuation of real options might be non-trivial, *recognizing* a particular capital budgeting project as a real option has value, especially as the business environment becomes more uncertain.

REFERENCES

Baldwin, C., and L. Trigeorgis. 1995. "Real Options, Capabilities, TQM, and Competitiveness," Harvard Business School Working Paper.

Capozza, D., and Y. Li. 1994. "The Intensity and Timing of Investment: The Case of Land," *American Economic Review*.

Dixit, A., and R.S. Pindyck. 1994. *Investment Under Uncertainty*. Princeton, NJ: Princeton University Press.

Kogut, B., and N. Kulatilaka. 1994. "Operating Flexibility, Global Manufacturing, and the Option Value of a Multinational Network," *Management Science*.

Kulatilaka, N. 1995. "The Value of Flexibility: A General Model of Real Options," *Real Options in Capital Investments*. Westport, CT: Praeger.

Trigeorgis, L. 1996. *Real Options: Management Flexibility and Strategy in Resource Allocation*. Cambridge, MA: MIT Press.

3 Does Practice Follow Principle? Applying Real Options Principles to Proxy Costs in U.S. Telecommunications

Mark A. Jamison[1]
University of Florida

Abstract - This paper analyzes whether current practices in estimating incremental costs for regulated telecommunications companies provide them with efficient investment incentives. In implementing the Telecommunications Act of 1996, regulators are using incremental cost studies, with some markup for shared costs, to establish prices for interconnection, reciprocal compensation, unbundled network elements, and universal service. Regulators use these incremental cost estimates, which come from proxy cost models, to set upper bounds on these prices. This is a significant change from past practices, where incremental cost studies were used for setting price floors for competitive or potentially competitive services.

This new application of incremental costs has prompted new debates about cost studies. The applicability of real options investment analysis is one of these debates. The use of real options is analyzed by considering a model in which the regulator affects ILEC investment decisions and market outcomes through price controls. It shows that existing TELRIC models tend to discourage efficient ILEC investment by understating incremental costs and that the inefficiency is not as great as the real options proponents claim.

This paper analyzes whether current U.S. practices to estimate incremental costs for telecommunications companies provide efficient investment incentives to regulated incumbent local exchange companies (ILECs). The implementation of the Telecommunications Act of 1996 (Act) has raised this issue.[2] In implementing the Act, the Federal Communications Commission (FCC) and many state public utility commissions (PUCs) are using incremental cost studies, with some mark-up for shared costs, to establish prices for interconnection, reciprocal compensation, unbundled network elements (UNEs),[3] and universal service.[4] Regulators use these incremental cost estimates, which come from proxy cost models,[5] to set ceilings on these prices. This is a significant change in regulatory practice. Before the Act, regulators used incremental cost studies to set price floors for competitive or potentially competitive services.

This change in the use of incremental cost studies has affected stakeholder interest. Previously, ILECs had an incentive to keep the cost estimates low in order to obtain more flexibility to lower their prices in competitive markets. Now these companies' interests are to keep the estimates high to obtain greater flexibility in protecting revenue streams and affecting competitors' costs. This does not mean that ILECs would always choose to price at the ceiling if the ceiling were high. ILECs may price below the ceiling to discourage the development of competitive networks or simply to meet competition for UNEs. Even if the price ceiling were higher than the price the ILEC actually charged, the higher ceiling still has value to the ILEC because it gives the ILEC the option to raise prices should the market situation change. Also, when incremental cost studies formed the basis for price floors, some ILEC competitors wanted high cost estimates to secure price umbrellas in competitive markets. Now competitors want to keep the estimates low to decrease the payments that they have to make to their competitors, the ILECs.

This new stakeholder dynamic has prompted new investigations into the appropriateness of how regulators perform and apply incremental cost studies. The current debate focuses on total element long-run incremental cost (TELRIC) studies because the FCC and many PUCs are adopting them (Jamison, 1998b; Salinger, 1998). One element of this debate has concerned the applicability of real options investment analysis.[6] This debate has raised concerns that TELRIC-based prices do not induce efficient investments on the part of ILECs because TELRIC studies do not reflect the economic depreciation of ILEC investments, uncertainty in demand, and inter-temporal opportunity costs.

This paper analyzes these issues by considering a model in which the regulator affects ILEC investment decisions and market outcomes through price controls. By comparing this model to TELRIC practice, this analysis shows that prices based on existing TELRIC models could discourage efficient ILEC investment by understating incremental costs. These models understate ILECs' incremental costs by inappropriately updating input prices without adjusting depreciation and by overstating expected demand. This paper also shows that the inefficiency is not as great as some claim. For example, Hausman (1996) states that TELRIC models omit depreciation, demand uncertainty, and real options. The first two claims are incorrect and the effect of omitting real options is ambiguous.

The remainder of the paper is organized as follows. Section 1 describes the economic model. The term "model" is used to characterize this paper's stylized assumptions about how regulators regulate ILECs, how ILECs make investment decisions, and how ILEC competitors buy UNEs. This is a non-technical explanation that non-economists should find readable. The Appendix contains the technical explanation. Section 2 examines how various properties of TELRIC models affect the efficiency of ILECs' investment decisions. Section 3 is the conclusion.

1. THE MODEL

This section describes the model and applies it to identify efficient prices.

1.1 Description of the Model

This paper's model considers an ILEC that produces multiple products and that makes investment decisions subject to regulatory price controls and uncertain demand.[7] It assumes that the ILEC enjoys economies of joint production from producing multiple products, but makes no assumptions about whether the ILEC is a natural monopoly; i.e., it does not assume that a single ILEC could serve the entire market demand more efficiently than two or more other firms (Baumol, 1977; Jamison, 1998a), although it does not preclude it. The ILEC produces both retail products and UNEs. Some of the ILEC's retail products are subject to universal service obligations (USOs). A product subject to USOs is defined as a product where the regulator requires the ILEC to charge a price that is lower than what would be found in a perfectly competitive market. In other words, the ILEC cannot charge the regulator's mandated price without an external source of funding or without charging supercompetitive prices for other products. If demands are independent, then by definition, the per-unit funding needed to allow the ILEC to charge the mandated price and earn its cost of capital is the difference between the competitive market price and the mandated price.

The model assumes that the ILEC's prices and investment affect demand, that demand is stochastic, and that buyers buy less at higher prices than they do at lower prices, all other things being equal. ILEC investment affects demand because higher levels of investment improve the quality of the UNEs and retail products, making customers of either type of product more willing to buy from the ILEC.

This paper further assumes that the quantity produced and ILEC investment determine the ILEC's production costs.[8] Increases in the quantities produced will increase costs. Investment is also a cost, but one that lowers other production costs. In effect, this assumption means that the ILEC can trade sunk investments for variable costs and vice versa, although the trade may not be one-for-one.

The ILEC's decision to produce or not produce a product, even if the regulator makes the choice for the ILEC, changes the ILEC's costs and revenues. The change in costs is called the incremental cost of the product. The incremental cost covers the ILEC's entire production of this product. For example, if the ILEC produces ten thousand unbundled loops in a market and this causes the ILEC's total cost for all products to increase from $900 million per month to $900.2 million per month, then the incremental cost of providing unbundled loops in this market is $200,000 per month. Likewise, this model considers the ILEC's change in revenues from providing a product to be the incremental revenues for the product. As in the case of incremental cost, it is the change in the company's total revenue that is important. So the incremental revenue from the product is the change that it causes in the ILEC's total revenues. To simplify discussion, this section generally assumes that adding or dropping a product does not affect demand for other ILEC products. This assumption allows a discussion of prices rather than incremental revenues. The discussion on real options drops this assumption.

The model has the regulator, the ILEC, and the customers make decisions in sequence. The regulator makes the first decision. She selects the prices for UNEs and USOs using TELRIC models. Because the regulator uses these models, prices are tied to neither the ILEC's actual economic costs nor its earnings as in rate of return regulation. It is assumed that, properly applied, it is technically feasible for the TELRIC model to reliably estimate the ILEC's incremental cost.[9] Also, the regulator enforces her other price requirements by setting maximum prices and not by rate of return regulation.

The ILEC makes the second decision. It chooses whether and how much to invest and executes its investment choice. The ILEC knows the regulators' price ceilings, but does not know the quantities that UNE and USO customers will buy. It is assumed that the ILEC and the regulator know the minimum and maximum amounts that these buyers could purchase and the probabilities of them buying any particular amount between the minimum and maximum. The regulator requires the ILEC to supply all that customers want to buy from the ILEC. It is further assumed that the ILEC wants to maximize expected profits and is risk neutral.

Customers make the last decisions. They make their buying decisions based upon the prices the ILEC charges, the investment-induced quality of the ILEC's products, and other factors. These other factors were unknown at the time that the ILEC made its investment decision. This gives demand its stochastic properties. Once these buyers make their purchasing decisions, the ILEC incurs the remainder of its costs for providing the products and receives its revenues.

To simplify the analysis, the model assumes that the demand and supply effects of investment are such that the ILEC sells no products and incurs no incremental costs if it chooses to make no investment.

This model is a reasonable approximation of what is happening in telecommunications in the United States. Regulators are setting UNE and USO prices using TELRIC models, generally with contributions to shared costs. Even though these prices apply to ILECs' existing networks and not just new investments, the prices signal how much profit the ILEC can expect from new investments that may be used for UNEs and USO products. Also, investment can increase quality and lower other production costs. Furthermore, ILECs do not know demand with certainty when they invest. ILECs invest to replace facilities serving current demand and to serve projected new demand. In the case of existing demand, ILECs can have a reasonable amount of certainty that demand in the near future will be similar to what they are experiencing today. However, it is always possible that demand will decrease if competitors place facilities that eventually serve existing demand, or if customers move to other locations.[10] Projected new demand is also uncertain. Population shifts, housing developments that do not live up to forecasts, and slowdowns in economic growth can all result in realized demand being less than forecasted demand. Also, new demand may not last for the entire average economic life[11] of the facilities for the same reasons that current demand may decline.

1.2 Application of the Model

Assume that the regulator wants the ILEC to choose an investment level, I^*, that maximizes the total benefit that ILEC investment can bring to the economy. The benefits of I^* are the decrease in ILEC unit production costs and the increase in the value of ILEC products brought about by the increase in ILEC product quality. The cost of I^* is simply the cost of the investment. If the regulator had complete and perfect information, as well as complete control over the ILEC and customers, the regulator would choose I^* and the optimal quantity, q^*, by equating marginal benefits with marginal costs and requiring the ILEC to make the investment I^* and customers to buy q^*. But in the real world, the regulator does not have complete and perfect information and does not have complete control over the other players. Instead, the regulator must use incentive mechanisms to induce the ILEC to choose I^* and customers to buy q^*, or at least to induce them to choose amounts close to I^* and q^*.[12]

To determine which price ceilings will induce the most efficient investment, the regulator uses backwards induction; in other words, she starts at the end of the sequence of decisions that will take place in response to her price controls and works backwards through the decisions to determine which price control will give her the most desirable outcome. She begins by considering the ILEC's customers' situations. These customers will choose quantities of ILEC products based upon the prices the ILEC charges and I. However, because there is a stochastic element to demand, the regulator does not know with certainty how much customers will purchase at particular price and investment levels. Instead, like the ILEC, she knows how prices and investment affect demand and has expectations about the stochastic effects. She bases her expectation on her knowledge of the range of possible quantities demanded and the likelihood of each potential level of demand.

Having formed her expectations about how customers will respond to the ILEC's prices and investments, and knowing that the ILEC shares these expectations,[13] the regulator considers how the ILEC will respond to her price controls and their shared expectations about customer demand. From the ILEC's perspective, once the regulator establishes her price ceilings, which are called $\mathbf{p}_0^M$, where M represents all of the ILEC's products, the ILEC chooses its investment level, I_0, to maximize its profits. The prices that relate to UNEs and USOs are called $\mathbf{p}_0^S$ where S represents the UNEs and USO products. The ILEC's actual profits will be the difference between its realized revenues and the sum of its realized production costs and investment. However, at the time the ILEC makes its investment decision, it does not know what its actual profits will be because it does not know how much customers will buy. So the ILEC bases its investment decision on its expected profits, which are equal to expected revenues minus the investment and the expected production costs.

Next the regulator attempts to choose the price that induces I^* and q^*. Unfortunately, there is no price that does this because the regulator has only one tool and is trying to determine two outcomes. The tool is the price per unit sold.[14] The two outcomes are the investment made and quantity sold. If the regulator had a two-dimensional price – one dimension that reflected quantity sold and another that reflected quality – then she might be able to achieve her efficient outcome. This paper does not model this possibility because no regulators appear to do this in practice (Jamison, 1998b).

What the regulator does instead is choose a price that maximizes total social surplus subject to the ILEC's and customers' decision-making processes. Total social surplus is the difference between the value customers place on UNEs and USO products and the cost of providing them. The amounts they choose are I_0^* and q_0^*. As the next subsection explains in more detail, the regulator chooses a price that covers the ILEC's expected incremental cost. The effects that price changes have on investment determine whether the price is above or below the ILEC's marginal cost. If price increases lead to increased investment, then the optimal price is above marginal cost. The reverse is true if the price increases decrease investment. The Appendix describes this in more detail.

1.3 Cost-Based Prices

Now consider how the regulator's efficient price control compares with the ILEC's costs. Recall that the ILEC chooses I_0 by equating the investment's marginal effect on expected revenues with its marginal effect on expected cost. The marginal effect on revenues is simply $\mathbf{p}_0^S$ times the expected marginal effect on demand. The marginal effect on cost is simply the marginal effect on expected production costs (including effects on demand) plus the marginal investment. This means that $\mathbf{p}_0^S$ must reflect the expected marginal cost. Because the ILEC cannot charge directly for quality, it chooses investment levels that cause marginal costs to be either above or below $\mathbf{p}_0^S$. The direction and magnitude of the deviation from marginal cost depends on how investments affect demand and costs. The interactions among demand, costs, and investment are complex, but in general, large investment-induced changes in demand cause the ILEC to keep marginal costs below $\mathbf{p}_0^S$, especially if investment causes the demand curve to become steeper.[15] Both of these conditions might occur if quality is important to customers, especially at higher prices. This necessary relationship between prices and marginal costs is called the *optimization constraint.*

The optimization constraint induces the ILEC to make an efficient investment only if the ILEC is willing to invest. The regulator ensures that the ILEC is willing to invest by applying the same process that she used to develop her optimization criteria, but with two slight differences. The first difference is that she must consider the total effect of the investment, and not just the marginal effect. In other words, she must consider the investment's total effect on the ILEC's expected revenues and the investment's total effect on the ILEC's costs to induce the ILEC to invest. The second difference is that she does not need to concern herself with equating the effects. She only needs to ensure that the revenue effect is at least as great as the cost effect. As long as this is true, the ILEC is willing to participate in the regulator's mechanism. This is called the *participation constraint.* With a small amount of algebraic manipulation, which the Appendix shows, the participation constraint can be expressed as $\mathbf{p}_0^S$ being greater than or equal to the expected incremental cost of the ILEC choosing $I_0 = I_0^*$ over $I_0 = 0$, divided by the expected demand. In other words, the regulator's price ceiling must be greater than or equal to the ILEC's expected TELRIC (which may be different from the regulator's estimated TELRIC) divided by expected demand.

Salinger (1998) applies a dynamic model to provide a useful explanation of the ILEC's incremental costs. He explains that the incremental cost is a current price that makes the current value of the incremental revenues just equal to the current values of the incremental operating costs and incremental investment, given that these values will continue to be equal in all future periods. In other words, the optimization constraint and the participation constraint should be understood to imply present values of prices to be charged, expected quantities to be sold, and expected production costs over the life of the investment.[16] He also shows that the assumption that the expected life is known (which is the typical assumption in TELRIC studies) understates incremental cost. He further demonstrates the possibility that technology improvements will increase the capacity of assets and decrease incremental cost.

1.4 Real Options

Now consider the effect of real options on the optimization and participation constraints. Real options theory states that, if investing at the current time creates or destroys future opportunities, the foregone or gained value of these opportunities should be considered in estimating the value of the investment decision (Trigeorgis, 1996). To examine this effect, let ψ represent the products associated with the ILEC's alternative investment, which the ILEC cannot make because it is investing for *S*. ψ could be another set of products or simply a change in the timing of an investment to provide *S*. That is to say, ψ could represent the same products as *S*, but the products are provided on a different time schedule or in a different way. ψ might also include retail products that other firms sell in competition with the ILEC.[17] Regardless of whether ψ represents a temporal or intertemporal difference from *S*, or both, it is possible to re-express the optimization and participation constraints to explicitly include real options. Doing so changes the optimization constraint to the requirement that $\mathbf{p}_0^S$ must equal the expected marginal cost, plus the adjustment for the ILEC not being able to charge directly for quality, plus the expected marginal unit value of the foregone options. The participation constraint becomes the requirement that $\mathbf{p}_0^S$ be greater than or equal to the expected incremental cost of the ILEC choosing $I_0 = I_0^*$ over $I_0 = 0$, plus the value of the options that are foregone by increasing investment from 0 to I^*, divided by the expected demand. In other words, the regulator's price ceiling must be greater than or equal to the ILEC's expected TELRIC plus the change in option values, divided by expected demand.

Incorporating real options improves ILEC incentives to invest efficiently, but the effect on the optimization and participation constraints is ambiguous. Hausman (1996) argues that real options values are positive, meaning that investments always foreclose options (Salinger, 1998). If this is the case, TELRIC-based prices induce ILECs to invest too little. Other writers (Trigeorgis, 1996) point out that real options values can be positive or negative. In the context of pricing UNEs, real options might be negative if the investment creates opportunities. For example, the investment might be necessary to maintain a market presence and avoid costs of re-entering a market. Because the direction of the effect on $\mathbf{p}_0^S$ is ambiguous, regulators would need to assess the effects of real options on a case-by-case basis if they choose to consider real options in regulating UNE and USO prices.

1.5 Real Options as ECPR

Incorporating real options into UNE and USO pricing is effectively an application of the efficient component pricing rule (ECPR), which was developed in the context of contestable market theory. The ECPR, which is also called the Baumol-Willig rule, recommends that competitors pay ILECs their opportunity costs. In other words, the prices an ILEC would charge to competitors would ensure that the ILEC would make the same amount of profit regardless of whether it succeeds in the competitive portion of the market. The ECPR formula for setting UNE prices (called wholesale prices in the formula) is (Baumol and Sidak, 1994):

$$\textit{Wholesale price} = \textit{Retail price} - [\textit{Retail IC} - \textit{Wholesale IC}]$$

Or alternatively,

$$\textit{Wholesale price} = \textit{Retail markup} + \textit{Wholesale IC} \qquad (1)$$

Where *IC* is the acronym for incremental cost and *Retail markup* = *Retail price* – *Retail IC*. Comparing Equation 1 to the participation constraint with real options, *Wholesale price* represents $\mathbf{p}_0^S$ (setting aside USO products for the moment), *Wholesale IC* represents the incremental cost of *S*, and *Retail markup* represents the real option value of ψ.

Because real options is an application of the ECPR, several conclusions from the ECPR literature may applicable to real options. Examples that may need to be considered include:

- The underlying model assumes that competitors are fringe competitors that can offer only some subset of what the ILEC produces (Willig, 1979)
- *Retail markup* should contain no monopoly profits (Tye, 1994; Baumol and Sidak, 1994)

- The retail market should be homogeneous, or the *Retail markup* should be adjusted for the differences in value to customers (Willig, 1979; Armstrong and Doyle, undated)
- The ILEC is less likely to try to protect markets from competition and discriminate against competitors than with a lower *Wholesale price* (Ordover, Sykes, and Willig, 1985).

2. HOW TELRIC PRICES AFFECT INVESTMENT INCENTIVES

This section describes how various properties of TELRIC studies affect ILEC investment incentives. It describes the relevant features of TELRIC studies first. It then discusses the concerns with economic depreciation, demand uncertainty, and real options.

2.1 TELRIC Studies

The basic TELRIC formula begins by estimating the incremental capital expense (CAPEX) that $\mathbf{q}^S$ causes. The formula then multiplies an annual carrying charge by the incremental CAPEX. This carrying charge consists of the cost of capital, investment-related taxes, and depreciation expense. The result is an annual carrying cost of the CAPEX. The formula then adds annual operating expenses to this annual carrying cost and expresses the result on a relevant unit basis (for example, per unit per month).

Traditionally, CAPEX has been the main driver in incremental cost studies. This was because analysts assumed that CAPEX drove almost all carrying costs and expenses, or at least that there was a strong positive correlation. Critical assumptions for CAPEX calculations have been:

1. *Technology* – By necessity, a TELRIC study assumes a particular technology is used to provide the network elements. Assumptions can vary, but the FCC prefers to assume that studies assume the most efficient or least-cost technology that is generally available.
2. *Network architecture* – TELRIC studies tend to assume a scorched node; i.e., existing central office locations and cable routes are assumed to be fixed, but technologies can change.
3. *Utilization or fill factor* – "Utilization" or "fill factor" refers to the percent of the capacity of a facility that the study assumes will be used. For example, an

assumption of 50% utilization of a 200-pair cable means that it is assumed that 100 pairs are used. The FCC appears to favor average fill. However, calculating average fill is very difficult because, in practice, every node and link has a different fill and the fills change on a regular basis. The last time the author examined TELRIC models, the HAI (formerly Hatfield) TELRIC model interpreted average fill to mean that the scorched-node network would be optimized with respect to fill, but with the constraint that network facilities must be purchased in standard sizes. So, for example, if a cable route needed 202 copper pairs, the model would use the next size cable above 200 pair for estimating TELRIC.[18]

4. *Depreciation* – The models use whatever depreciation rates the regulator sets.
5. *Cost of capital* – The models use whatever cost of capital the regulator sets.
6. *Operating expenses* – Traditionally, incremental cost studies estimated operating expenses by multiplying CAPEX by an expense/asset ratio calculated from ILECs' accounting records. This appears to be the method used by the TELRIC models that the FCC is considering. Recently, some ILECs have begun using activity-based costing.

2.2 Comparison of Economic Principles with TELRIC Practice: Depreciation

Hausman (1996) argues that TELRIC studies do not include depreciation, or at least include too little depreciation. The previous subsection described how TELRIC studies incorporate depreciation on assets. With respect to the amount of depreciation, Hausman (1996) is correct that TELRIC studies should include economic depreciation and the effects of decreases in input prices. These effects are part of incremental cost. It is unlikely that the studies do this because, even if they use appropriate depreciation lives and depreciation methods, the studies' technology assumptions continually update the investment amounts according to technology and price improvements. As technology becomes more efficient and unit prices decline, updating the technology assumptions lowers depreciation expenses, all other things being equal. Unless this effect is incorporated into the depreciation, this updating causes TELRIC models to understate depreciation. Regulatory depreciation practices do not appear to consider this dynamic of using depreciation in TELRIC models. As a result, there is a risk that prices will be too low.

2.3 Comparison of Economic Principles with TELRIC Practice: Demand Uncertainty

Hausman (1996) also argues that TELRIC studies do not adequately reflect the effects of demand uncertainty on ILECs' irreversible investments. This appears to be at least partially true, but not to the extent claimed.

This paper's model incorporates demand uncertainty and irreversible investments. In the model, the ILEC makes the investment before it knows demand and is unable to reverse the investment. The participation constraint states that the price must be greater than or equal to expected average incremental cost. The numerator for the average incremental cost includes all of the costs the ILEC incurs to provide q^S, including costs incurred for demand that does not materialize or that does not remain for the entire economic life of the plant. The denominator is the expected sales. As a result, average incremental cost represents an average over projects that live up to their demand expectations, projects that exceed their demand expectations, and projects that fail to live up to their demand expectations. All irreversible investments are covered in the participation constraint.[19] Likewise, the optimization constraint incorporates expected demand and costs over all projects incorporating the UNE or USO.

Unfortunately, it appears that the TELRIC models that the FCC is considering do not live up to the optimization and participation constraints with respect to uncertain demand. As Section 1.1 above explains, the FCC has determined that TELRIC studies should assume an average utilization amount. This results in per-unit TELRICs that are equal to average incremental costs. However, the implementation of this decision in the HAI model does not take into account all factors that cause utilization to be less than optimal.[20] Specifically, by optimizing the network based on current demand and future growth, the studies do not consider projects that fail to live up to the investors' demand expectations. As a result, the application of the TELRIC models understates average incremental cost and marginal cost.

Hausman (1996) also states in the context of uncertain demand that TELRIC-based prices truncate the amount of profits that ILECs can expect from innovation, thus discouraging innovation-related investments. His assertion is correct. In fact, any regulation that limits the amount of profit that an ILEC receives from an investment has this effect. TELRIC-based prices are more onerous than, for example, regular price cap constraints in that normal price caps allow companies to adjust prices and so earn extra profits on a particular service should market conditions permit. However, the problem is with price limits on innovations, not with demand uncertainty. At least in theory, the proper remedy for this problem would be to have few, if any, price constraints on innovations. In practice, it is difficult to determine when something is an actual innovation and not just an opportunistic use of regulatory rules.

2.4 Comparison of Economic Principles with TELRIC Practice: Real Options

Hausman (1996) also asserts that TELRIC studies understate incremental cost because they fail to reflect the value of real options – inter-temporal investment options foreclosed when the ILEC chooses I. This may be true in some instances, but it is difficult to imagine that the effect is large.

The ECPR equations in Section 1 illustrate that an ILEC's choice to make UNE and USO product investments, I_0^S, must provide more profit than the ILEC's best alternative investment, I_0^Ψ, that I_0^S forecloses for the ILEC to choose I_0^S. The ECPR equations also illustrate how real options created by I_0^S lower the profit needed from I^S to induce the ILEC to make the investment. To foreclose investments, I_0^S must occupy some space that I_0^Ψ requires. This space could be:

1. *Physical.* This would be space in, for example, conduit, buildings, or radio spectrum, that I_0^Ψ could occupy in the future. If this is the only available space for $I_0^{\Psi\varpi}$, then the full value of I_0^Ψ is in the real option. "Value of I_0^Ψ" means the net present value of cash and options from I_0^Ψ. If there are other spaces that I_0^Ψ could occupy, then only the incremental loss of I_0^Ψ's full value would be included.
2. *Capital.* This would include the consumption of capital that could not be replaced in the future except at a higher cost.
3. *Demand.* The investment I_0^S might supply some consumer demand that could be served with higher-valued investment sometime in the future.
4. *Cost.* The investment I_0^S might supply consumer demand that could be served with lower-cost investment sometime in the future.
5. *Rights.* The investment I_0^S might cause the ILEC to lose some legal right that has value. For example, if a rural ILEC purchased other exchanges in its state, it might become sufficiently large to lose its rural ILEC status. As a non-rural ILEC, the ILEC would be subject to the unbundling and other local exchange competition requirements of the Act.

An investment creates an option when it presents an opportunity that did not exist previously. For example, an investment in opening local exchange markets to competition creates a long distance option for Regional Bell Operating Companies, which are currently prohibited from providing this service. If I_0^S does foreclose or open a profitable investment I^Ψ, it may be necessary to apply something like the ECPR to give the ILEC an incentive to make the investment.[21]

If it is necessary to consider the opportunity cost of a foreclosed investment in pricing interconnection or USOs, it is also necessary to incorporate all of the cost and revenue effects of taking the foreclosed investment. For example, if the alternative investment is a delayed investment in cable used to serve a particular market, then the cost of re-entering the market should be incorporated, as should the revenue loss from helping competitors increase their market penetration.

Also because the inter-temporal opportunity cost applies only to certain conditions and can be positive or negative, it should be modeled separately from the TELRIC cost. A general adjustment to all TELRIC estimates would not necessarily improve investment incentives. Also, making the inter-temporal opportunity cost a separate model makes it easier for regulators to assess the validity of the cost and the assumptions made when estimating it.

2.5 Comparison of Economic Principles with TELRIC Practice: Other Factors

There are other factors that affect the appropriateness of TELRIC practices. These may also decrease investment incentives below an optimal level.

One factor is the application of the markup above TELRIC. Some regulators omit the markups. Others provide markups only to cover shared costs. The first practice provides an inefficient incentive to decrease investment and the second practice might also do this. Recall that TELRIC is the sum of all marginal costs. The common assumption in telecommunications is that marginal costs are constant as production increases. In local exchanges, production economies come from density and scope rather than scale. If higher prices induce greater investment, which is also a common assumption, then the efficient price is above marginal cost and, therefore, above TELRIC, expressed on a per-unit basis. Contributions to shared costs might provide the appropriate markup, but this would only occur by accident because the formulas for spreading shared costs do not consider an investment's effects on quality.

Another factor is the omission of the effects of rivalry on appropriate prices. If ILECs are subject to general multilateral rivalry, the rivalry forces ILECs to price below stand-alone cost for individual products and for groups of products. This, in turn, means that ILEC prices for individual products and for groups of products must exceed TELRIC for the ILEC to remain financially viable. Also, the lack of opportunity to charge for quality may lower the quality of services customers ultimately receive because ILECs benefit from investing in quality only through increased demand. This increased demand passes along to the ILEC only a portion of the value that the investment creates. This may provide companies with an uneconomic incentive to merge in areas with large amounts of network interconnection because the merger allows the merged company to internalize some of the benefits of investment in quality.

The last factor is that the regulatory process for using TELRIC models affects risk. This paper assumes that the regulator commits to a price schedule that the ILEC is certain will hold over the entire life of the investment. This is unlikely to be true. U.S. and international experience with such models indicates that regulators can cause wide swings in cost study results by changing a few critical assumptions. In the days of rate of return regulation, assumptions in fully distributed cost studies and rate cases primarily affected when costs would be recovered and from what service. While these issues were important to market efficiency, they did not rise to the level of today's use of cost studies where changes in assumptions determine total revenues without a clear remedy for inter-temporal errors, except to seek stranded cost recovery. If ILECs believe that regulators will act arbitrarily or opportunistically with the TELRIC models, then the ILECs will underinvest.

3. CONCLUSION

This paper considers issues that the real options debate has raised regarding the estimation and application of incremental costs. It shows that current TELRIC models underestimate incremental costs, but not to the extent that some claim. It also shows that concerns with inter-temporal opportunity costs are effectively an application of the ECPR. This means that some of the literature about the ECPR should be applicable to this issue.

There are other issues that this paper has not discussed or modeled that also influence the effects of using current TELRIC models for pricing UNEs and USO products. One such issue is the effect of stranded cost remedies on ILEC investment decisions. Economic literature on contract breach remedies appears to imply that some stranded cost remedies would alleviate underinvestment concerns and may actually encourage overinvestment. Customer contributions for line extensions and contributions by real estate developers may also have these effects.

This paper's model does not consider rivalry in the ILEC's markets. As the previous section mentions, multilateral rivalry would provide alternatives for both the ILECs and customers. This would generally create additional pricing constraints. Also, customers' opportunities to self-provide UNEs affect outcomes. Reciprocal compensation also affects the economics of buying and selling UNEs.

Also, this paper's assumption about the nature of investment is quite specific. It assumes that investment both produces quality and reduces costs. This may be true for some investments, but not for all. A more thorough study is needed that considers both specific and joint investments.

Last, this paper does not address whether the regulator should try to estimate TELRIC accurately, or try to overestimate or underestimate TELRIC. This paper assumes that the regulator can come fairly close. It may be that the regulator, knowing that she has a probability of error, should seek to overstate TELRIC or understate TELRIC because one has less of a negative effect on efficiency.

APPENDIX

This model considers a multiproduct ILEC that makes investment decisions subject to regulatory pricing constraints and uncertain demand. The ILEC produces products $M \subset N$, where N is the set of all products in the economy. The ILEC's products $S \subset M$ are products that fall either into the category of UNEs or into the category of products subject to USOs. A product i is subject to a USO if the regulator requires the ILEC to charge a price $p_0^i < \phi^i$, where ϕ^i is the price the ILEC would charge in a perfectly competitive market.

Demand is given by $\mathbf{q}(\mathbf{p}, \theta, I)$, where nature determines θ and I represents investments that the ILEC can undertake. Investment improves quality, so $\mathbf{q}_I(\mathbf{p}, \theta, I) > 0$, where subscripts denote first derivatives. Also, $\partial q^i(\mathbf{p}, \theta, I)/\partial p^i < 0,\ \forall\, i \in M$.

$C(\mathbf{q}^M, I)$ is the ILEC's cost function and $\Delta C(\mathbf{q}^S, I) = C(\mathbf{q}^M, I) - C(\mathbf{q}^{M \setminus S}, I) < C(\mathbf{q}^S, I)$ is the incremental cost of producing $\mathbf{q}^S$. Assume that $C_I < 0$, $\Delta C_I < 0$, $\partial C(\mathbf{q}^M, I)/\partial q^i > 0$, and $\partial^2 C(\mathbf{q}^M, I)/\partial q^i\, \partial I < 0,\ \forall\, i \in M$. The incremental revenue effect of producing $\mathbf{q}^s$ is:

$$\Delta R^S(\mathbf{p}^M, \theta, I) = \mathbf{q}^M(\mathbf{p}^M, \theta, I) \cdot \mathbf{p}^M - \mathbf{q}^{M \setminus S}(\mathbf{p}^M, \theta, I) \cdot \mathbf{p}^{M \setminus S}$$

Assume there are no demand cross-elastic effects between S and $M\backslash S$, so $\Delta R^S(\mathbf{p}^M, \theta, I) = \mathbf{q}^S(\mathbf{p}^S, \theta, I) \cdot \mathbf{p}^S$.

Assume that if the ILEC makes no investment, it produces no UNEs and USO products because customers would not buy them. In other words, $\mathbf{q}^S(\mathbf{p}^S, \theta, 0) = 0$ and $\Delta C(0, 0) = 0$.

Competitors' profits are suppressed here by assuming that they operate in perfectly competitive markets. Also assume that the regulator wants to maximize weighted surplus

$$Z \equiv \int_{\theta^{min}}^{\theta^{max}} \left[w^C V(\mathbf{q}^S, \theta, I) - w^{ILEC} \left(\Delta C(\mathbf{q}^S, I) + I \right) + \left(w^{ILEC} - w^C \right) \bullet \mathbf{q}^S(\mathbf{p}^S, \theta, I) \bullet \mathbf{p}^S \right] dF \geq 0$$

where w^{ILEC} and w^C are the weights given to ILEC profits and customer surplus, respectively, and $V(\mathbf{q}^S, \theta, I)$ is the customer's gross surplus. For simplicity, assume that these weights are equal. This simplifies the regulator's problem to maximizing

$$Z \equiv \int_{\theta^{min}}^{\theta^{max}} \left(V(\mathbf{q}^S, \theta, I) - \Delta C(\mathbf{q}^S, I) - I \right) dF \geq 0 \qquad (2)$$

There are three time periods. In the first, the regulator selects the price vector $\mathbf{p}_0^S$ for UNEs and USOs using TELRIC models. The regulator does not know I or θ. However, the regulator knows that $\theta \in [\theta^{min}, \theta^{max}]$ and is distributed according to the cumulative density function $F(\theta)$. The regulator also knows that the ILEC is profit maximizing and risk neutral, so the regulator can accurately estimate the ILEC's best response function to customer demand and the regulator's price controls. The regulator also selects the price vector $\mathbf{p}_0^{M\backslash S}$ using some price capping mechanism and not rate of return regulation. The purpose of this assumption is to remove opportunities for cost shifting and incentives for padding the rate base.

In the second period, the ILEC chooses I_0. The ILEC knows $\mathbf{p}_0^S$. The ILEC does not know q, but knows the range and density function just as the regulator does. In the third period, nature chooses θ_0, customers buy $\mathbf{q}^S(\mathbf{p}_0^M, \theta_0, I_0)$, and the ILEC receives incremental revenues of $\mathbf{q}^S(\mathbf{p}_0^S, \theta_0, I_0) \cdot \mathbf{p}_0^S$.

To solve Equation 2, the regulator chooses the optimal price vector, $\mathbf{p}_0^{S*}$, by backwards induction. For simplicity, the model represents the group of customers as a single customer. The regulator calculates that in the last stage of the game, this customer maximizes utility according to

$$\max_{\mathbf{q}^S \in [0, \mathbf{q}^{S\max}]} \left\{ V\left(\mathbf{q}^S, \theta_0, I\right) - \mathbf{p}_0^S \bullet \mathbf{q}\left(\mathbf{p}_0^S, \bar{\theta}, I\right) \right\} \geq 0$$

The customer's first order conditions are

$$V_{q^i}\left(\mathbf{q}^S, \theta_0, I\right) = p_0^i \quad \forall\, i \in S \tag{3}$$

Assume that second order conditions are satisfied. Equation 3 implies an optimal quantity choice $\mathbf{q}^{S*}(\mathbf{p}, \theta, I)$.

The regulator then calculates the ILEC's best response function to the customer's choice. The ILEC maximizes profits according to

$$\max_{I \in [0, I^{\max}]} \pi\left(\mathbf{q}^M, \theta, I\right) \equiv \int_{\theta^{\min}}^{\theta^{\max}} \left[\mathbf{q}^{M*}\left(\mathbf{p}_0^M, \theta, I\right) \bullet \mathbf{p}_0^M - C\left(\mathbf{q}^{M*}\left(\mathbf{p}_0^M, \theta, I\right), I\right) \right] dF - I \geq 0$$

Isolating S gives

$$\max_{I \in [0, I^{\max}]} \pi\left(\mathbf{q}^S, \theta, I\right) \equiv \int_{\theta^{\min}}^{\theta^{\max}} \left[\mathbf{q}^{S*}\left(\mathbf{p}_0^S, \theta, I\right) \bullet \mathbf{p}_0^S - \Delta C\left(\mathbf{q}^{S*}\left(\mathbf{p}_0^S, \theta, I\right), I\right) \right] dF - I \geq 0$$

because of the assumption that demands are independent.

This gives the first order conditions

$$0 \equiv \int_{\theta^{\min}}^{\theta^{\max}} \begin{bmatrix} q_I^{i*}\left(\mathbf{p}_0^S, \theta, I^*\right) \cdot p_0^i - \Delta C_{q^i}\left(q^{i*}\left(\mathbf{p}_0^S, \theta, I^*\right), I^*\right) \cdot q_I^{i*}\left(\mathbf{p}_0^S, \theta, I^*\right) \\ - \Delta C_I\left(q^{i*}\left(\mathbf{p}_0^S, \theta, I^*\right), I^*\right) \end{bmatrix} dF - 1 \quad \forall\, i \in S \tag{4a}$$

or

$$p_0^i \equiv \frac{\mathbb{E}\left(\Delta C_{q^i}\left(q^{i*}\left(\mathbf{p}_0^S, I^*\right), I^*\right) \cdot q_I^{i*}\left(\mathbf{p}_0^S, I^*\right)\right) + \mathbb{E}\Delta C_I\left(q^{i*}\left(\mathbf{p}_0^S, I^*\right), I^*\right) + 1}{\mathbb{E} q_I^{i*}\left(\mathbf{p}_0^S, I^*\right)} \quad \forall\, i \in S \tag{4b}$$

where $\mathbb{E}(arg)$ is the expected value of *arg*. Equations 4a and 4b are the optimization constraints and imply an optimal investment $I^*(\mathbf{p}^S)$. The ILEC is willing to make the optimal investment as long as these hold and

$$p_0^i \geq \frac{\mathbb{E}\Delta C\left(q^{i*}\left(\mathbf{p}_0^S, I^*\right), I^*\right) + I^*}{\mathbb{E} q^{i*}\left(\mathbf{p}_0^S, I^*\right)} \quad \forall\, i \in S \tag{5a}$$

which is the participation constraint.

If the regulator were able to choose investment directly, the regulator's choice would be to optimize Equation 2 with respect to quantity and investment. This would give the first order conditions

$$0 = \int_{\theta^{min}}^{\theta^{max}} \left[V_{q'}\left(\mathbf{q}^S, \theta, I\right) - \Delta C_{q'}\left(\mathbf{q}^S, I\right) \right] dF \tag{6}$$

$$0 = \int_{\theta^{min}}^{\theta^{max}} \left[V_I\left(\mathbf{q}^S, \theta, I\right) - \Delta C_I\left(\mathbf{q}^S, I\right) \right] dF - 1 \tag{7}$$

The regulator is unable to satisfy these conditions in this model. This is shown by combining the regulator's first order conditions with the customer's and ILEC's first order conditions. Combining Equations 3 and 4a gives

$$0 \equiv \int_{\theta^{min}}^{\theta^{max}} \left[\begin{array}{l} q_I^{i*}\left(\mathbf{p}_0^S, \theta, I^*\right) \cdot \left(V_{q'}\left(\mathbf{q}^S, \theta, I\right) - \Delta C_{q'}\left(q^{i*}\left(\mathbf{p}_0^S, \theta, I^*\right), I^*\right)\right) \\ - \Delta C_I\left(q^{i*}\left(\mathbf{p}_0^S, \theta, I^*\right), I^*\right) \end{array} \right] dF - 1 \quad \forall i \in S \tag{8}$$

From Equation 6

$$V_{q'}\left(\mathbf{q}^S, \theta, I\right) - \Delta C_{q'}\left(q^{i*}\left(\mathbf{p}_0^S, \theta, I^*\right), I^*\right) = 0$$

so Equation 8 becomes

$$-\mathrm{E}\Delta C_I\left(q^{i*}\left(\mathbf{p}_0^S, \theta, I^*\right), I^*\right) = 1 \quad \forall i \in S$$

which means Equation 7 becomes $V_I(\mathbf{q}, I) = 0$. So the regulator can satisfy her first order conditions only in the special case where the customer's marginal value of investment is zero and investment's marginal effect on the ILEC is to decrease cost dollar for dollar.

Because the regulator cannot dictate quantity and investment, the best the regulator can do is maximize the following

$$\max_{\mathbf{p}} \int_{\theta^{min}}^{\theta^{max}} \left[V\left(\mathbf{q}^{S*}\left(\mathbf{p}^S, \theta, I^*\left(\mathbf{p}^S\right)\right), I^*\left(\mathbf{p}^S\right)\right) - \Delta C\left(\mathbf{q}^{S*}\left(\mathbf{p}^S, \theta, I^*\left(\mathbf{p}^S\right)\right), I^*\left(\mathbf{p}^S\right)\right) \right] dF - I^*\left(\mathbf{p}^S\right) \geq 0$$

which gives the following first order conditions

$$\int_{\theta^{min}}^{\theta^{max}} \left[V_{q^i} \cdot q^{i*}_{p^i} + V_{q^i} \cdot q^{i*}_{I} \cdot I^*_{p^i} + V_I \cdot I^*_{p^i} - \Delta C_{q^i} \cdot q^{i*}_{p^i} - \Delta C_{q^i} \cdot q^{i*}_{I} \cdot I^*_{p^i} - \Delta C_I \cdot I^*_{p^i} \right] dF - I^*_{p^i} = 0 \quad \forall i \in S \quad (9a)$$

Assume that second order conditions are satisfied.

To isolate price, the customer's first order conditions from Equation 3 are used to obtain

$$\int_{\theta^{min}}^{\theta^{max}} \left(p^i \cdot q^{i*}_{p^i} - \Delta C_{q^i} \cdot q^{i*}_{p^i} + V_I \cdot I^*_{p^i} \right) dF + I^*_{p^i} \left\{ \int_{\theta^{min}}^{\theta^{max}} \left(p^i \cdot q^{i*}_{I} - \Delta C_{q^i} \cdot q^{i*}_{I} - \Delta C_I \right) dF - 1 \right\} = 0 \quad \forall i \in S$$

From the ILEC's first order conditions in Equation 4a, the value inside the {} is zero, so the regulator's first order conditions become

$$\int_{\theta^{min}}^{\theta^{max}} \left(q^{i*}_{p^i} \left(p^i - \Delta C_{q^i} \right) + V_I \cdot I^*_{p^i} \right) dF = 0 \quad \forall i \in S \qquad (10a)$$

or

$$\bar{p}^i = \frac{\mathrm{E}\left(\Delta C_{q^i} \cdot q^{i*}_{p^i} \right) - \mathrm{E} V_I \cdot I^*_{p^i}}{\mathrm{E} q^{i*}_{p^i}} \quad \forall i \in S \qquad (10b)$$

Equation 10a shows that the regulator's optimal price ceiling will equal marginal cost only if the customer's marginal value of investment is zero. By assumption, $V_I > 0$ and $q^{i*}_{pi} < 0$, so the sign of I^*_{pi} determines whether the optimal price ceiling is above or below marginal cost. The regulator's optimal price ceiling is above marginal cost if an increase in price increases investment, and the regulator's optimal price ceiling is below the marginal cost if an increase in price decreases investment. To determine the sign of I^*_{pi}, divide the total derivative of the ILEC's first order conditions (Equation 4a) with respect to price by the total derivative of its first order conditions with respect to investment. In other words,

$$I^*_{p^i} = -\frac{\pi_{I p^i}}{\pi_{II}}$$

From second order conditions, $\pi_{II} < 0$, so the sign of π_{Ipi} determines the sign of I^*_{pi}. π_{Ipi} and is

$$\int_{\theta^{min}}^{\theta^{max}} \left[q^{i*}_{I p^i} \cdot p^i_0 + q^{i*}_{I} - \Delta C_{q^i q^i} \cdot q^{i*}_{I} \cdot q^{i*}_{p^i} - \Delta C_{q^i} \cdot q^{i*}_{I p^i} - \Delta C_{I q^i} \cdot q^{i*}_{p^i} \right] dF \quad \forall i \in S$$

Rearranging terms and reversing signs to get rid of the negative sign in front of the quotient gives

$$\int_{\theta^{min}}^{\theta^{max}} \left(q^{i*}_{p^i} \left(\Delta C_{I q^i} - \Delta C_{q^i q^i} \cdot q^{i*}_I \right) + q^{i*}_{I p^i} \left(\Delta C_{q^i} - p^i_0 \right) - q^{i*}_I \right) dF \quad \forall i \in S$$

The sign of the first expression depends upon the sign of the expression inside the parentheses because $q^{i*}_{pi} < 0$. The second expression's sign depends upon the sign of q^{i*}_{Ipi} because the sign of the expression inside the parentheses depends upon the sign of Γ_{pi}. If $\Gamma_{pi} > 0$, then the regulator's price is above marginal cost and the expression is negative. If $\Gamma_{pi} < 0$, the reverse is true. q^{i*}_I is positive by assumption. So sufficient conditions for $\Gamma_{pi} > 0$ are

$$\left.\begin{aligned} &\Delta C_{q^i q^i} \cdot q^{i*}_I > -\Delta C_{I q^i} \\ &q^{i*}_{I p^i} > 0 \end{aligned}\right\} \qquad (11)$$

$$\left.\begin{aligned} &\Delta C_{q^i q^i} \cdot q^{i*}_I < -\Delta C_{I q^i} \\ &q^{i*}_{I p^i} > 0 \\ &q^{i*}_{p^i} \left(\Delta C_{I q^i} - \Delta C_{q^i q^i} \cdot q^{i*}_I \right) - q^{i*}_I < -q^{i*}_{I p^i} \left(\Delta C_{q^i} - p^i_0 \right) \end{aligned}\right\} \qquad (12)$$

$$\left.\begin{aligned} &\Delta C_{q^i q^i} \cdot q^{i*}_I > -\Delta C_{I q^i} \\ &q^{i*}_{I p^i} < 0 \\ &q^{i*}_{I p^i} \left(\Delta C_{q^i} - p^i_0 \right) - q^{i*}_I < -q^{i*}_{p^i} \left(\Delta C_{I q^i} - \Delta C_{q^i q^i} \cdot q^{i*}_I \right) \end{aligned}\right\} \qquad (13)$$

Conditions 11 hold if the extra marginal costs caused by the investment-induced demand growth dominate the investment-induced decrease in marginal costs, and if investment causes the inverse demand curve to be steeper. Conditions 12 hold if the investment-induced decrease in marginal costs dominates the extra marginal costs caused by the investment-induced demand growth, if investment causes the inverse demand curve to be steeper, and if the combined effects of the steeper inverse demand curve and price exceeding marginal cost dominate the other effects. Conditions 13 hold if the costs caused by the investment-induced demand growth dominate the investment-induced decrease in marginal costs, if investment causes the inverse demand curve to flatten, and if the combined effects of the marginal cost decrease and demand changing with price increases and investment increases dominate the other effects.

Sufficient conditions for $\Gamma_{pi} < 0$ are

$$\left.\begin{array}{l} \Delta C_{q'q'} \cdot q_I^{i^*} < -\Delta C_{Iq'} \\ q^{i^*}_{Ip'} > 0 \\ q^{i^*}_{p'}\left(\Delta C_{Iq'} - \Delta C_{q'q'} \cdot q_I^{i^*}\right) + q^{i^*}_{Ip'}\left(\Delta C_{q'} - p_0^i\right) > q_I^{i^*} \end{array}\right\} \quad (14)$$

$$\left.\begin{array}{l} \Delta C_{q'q'} \cdot q_I^{i^*} > -\Delta C_{Iq'} \\ q^{i^*}_{Ip'} > 0 \\ -q^{i^*}_{p'}\left(\Delta C_{Iq'} - \Delta C_{q'q'} \cdot q_I^{i^*}\right) + q_I^{i^*} < q^{i^*}_{Ip'}\left(\Delta C_{q'} - p_0^i\right) \end{array}\right\} \quad (15)$$

$$\left.\begin{array}{l} \Delta C_{q'q'} \cdot q_I^{i^*} < -\Delta C_{Iq'} \\ q^{i^*}_{Ip'} < 0 \\ -q^{i^*}_{Ip'}\left(\Delta C_{q'} - p_0^i\right) + q_I^{i^*} < q^{i^*}_{p'}\left(\Delta C_{Iq'} - \Delta C_{q'q'} \cdot q_I^{i^*}\right) \end{array}\right\} \quad (16)$$

Conditions 14 hold if the investment-induced decrease in marginal costs dominates the extra marginal costs caused by the investment-induced demand growth, investment causes the inverse demand curve to be steeper, and investment's effect on demand is dominated by all other effects. Conditions 15 hold if the extra marginal costs caused by the investment-induced demand growth dominate the investment-induced decrease in marginal costs, investment causes the inverse demand curve to be steeper, and the combined effects of the steepening inverse demand curve and price exceeding marginal cost dominate the other effects. Conditions 16 hold if the costs caused by the investment-induced demand growth are dominated by the investment-induced decrease in marginal costs, investment causes the inverse demand curve to flatten, and the combined effects of the marginal cost decrease and demand changing with price increases and, investment increases dominate the other effects.

Now consider the effects of real options. The customer's first order conditions in Equation 3 still hold. However, the ILEC's maximization problem and first order conditions become

$$\max_{I\in[0,I^{\max}]} \pi\left(\mathbf{q}^S,\theta,I\right)\equiv\int_{\theta^{\min}}^{\theta^{\max}}\left[\mathbf{q}^{S*}\left(\mathbf{p}_0^S,\theta,I\right)\bullet\mathbf{p}_0^S-\Delta C\left(\mathbf{q}^{S*}\left(\mathbf{p}_0^S,\theta,I\right),I\right)\right]dF-I\pm\rho\geq 0$$

$$0\equiv\int_{\theta^{\min}}^{\theta^{\max}}\begin{bmatrix}q_I^{i*}\left(\mathbf{p}_0^S,\theta,I^*\right)\cdot p_0^i-\Delta C_{q^i}\left(q^{i*}\left(\mathbf{p}_0^S,\theta,I^*\right),I^*\right)\cdot q_I^i\left(\mathbf{p}_0^S,\theta,I^*\right)\\-\Delta C_I\left(q^{i*}\left(\mathbf{p}_0^S,\theta,I^*\right),I^*\right)\end{bmatrix}dF-1\pm\rho_I\quad\forall i\in S\quad(4c)$$

where ρ is the net absolute value of the real options foreclosed or opened by I_0^S. Give ρ a plus sign if the net value of the real options is positive and give ρ a negative sign if the net value of the real options is negative.

Assume that some portion $\alpha\in[0,1]$ of r is a social benefit or cost, so 1-α of ρ is private to the ILEC. The regulator's maximization problem and first order conditions are now

$$\max_{\mathbf{p}}\int_{\theta^{\min}}^{\theta^{\max}}\left[V\left(\mathbf{q}^{S*}\left(\mathbf{p}^S,\theta,I^*\left(\mathbf{p}^S\right)\right),I^*\left(\mathbf{p}^S\right)\right)-\Delta C\left(\mathbf{q}^{S*}\left(\mathbf{p}^S,\theta,I^*\left(\mathbf{p}^S\right)\right),I^*\left(\mathbf{p}^S\right)\right)\right]dF-I^*\left(\mathbf{p}^S\right)\pm\alpha\cdot\rho\geq 0$$

$$\int_{\theta^{\min}}^{\theta^{\max}}\begin{bmatrix}V_{q^i}\cdot q_{p^i}^{i*}+V_{q^i}\cdot q_I^{i*}\cdot I_{p^i}^*+V_I\cdot I_{p^i}^*-\Delta C_{q^i}\cdot q_{p^i}^{i*}\\-\Delta C_{q^i}\cdot q_I^{i*}\cdot I_{p^i}^*-\Delta C_I\cdot I_{p^i}^*\end{bmatrix}dF-I_{p^i}^*\pm\alpha\cdot\rho_I\cdot I_{p^i}^*=0\quad\forall i\in S\quad(9b)$$

where the first order condition solves to

$$\int_{\theta^{\min}}^{\theta^{\max}}\left(q_{p^i}^{i*}\left(p^i-\Delta C_{q^i}\right)+I_{p^i}^*\left(V_I\pm(\alpha-1)\rho_I\right)\right)dF$$

$$+I_{p^i}^*\left\{\int_{\theta^{\min}}^{\theta^{\max}}\left(p^i\cdot q_I^{i*}-\Delta C_{q^i}\cdot q_I^{i*}-\Delta C_I\right)dF-1\pm\rho\right\}=0\quad\forall i\in S$$

which, when combined with the ILEC's first order conditions, becomes

$$\int_{\theta^{\min}}^{\theta^{\max}}\left(q_{p^i}^{i*}\left(p^i-\Delta C_{q^i}\right)+I_{p^i}^*\left(V_I\pm(\alpha-1)\rho_I\right)\right)dF=0\quad\forall i\in S$$

or

$$p^i=\frac{\mathbb{E}\left(\Delta C_{q^i}\cdot q_{p^i}^{i*}\right)-I_{p^i}^*\left(\mathbb{E}V_I\pm(\alpha-1)\rho_I\right)}{\mathbb{E}q_{p^i}^{i*}}\quad\forall i\in S$$

Because $\rho_I > 0$ and $\alpha - 1 < 0$, the effect of real options is to decrease the mark-up above marginal cost if the real option is opened by investment, and to increase the mark-up above marginal cost if the real option is foreclosed by investment. Real options do not affect the sign of I^*_{pi}.

The participation constraint becomes

$$p_0^i \geq \frac{E\Delta C\left(q^{i*}\left(\mathbf{p}_0^S, I^*\right), I^*\right) + I \pm \rho}{Eq^{i*}\left(\mathbf{p}_0^S, I^*\right)} \quad \forall i \in S \tag{5b}$$

which is the ECPR.

NOTES

1 The author would like to thank David Sappington, Tracy Lewis, James Alleman, William Sharkey, Steve Slutsky, and William Baumol for their helpful comments and suggestions. Any errors are my own responsibility.

2 Telecommunications Act of 1996, P.L. No. 104-104, 110 Stat. 56 (1996).

3 Interconnection, reciprocal compensation, and UNEs all involve a competitor connecting to the ILEC's network. This paper addresses UNE pricing. Models for reciprocal compensation are more complex than this paper's model because both ILECs and new entrants pay for and receive reciprocal compensation.

4 In this paper, "price" for universal service means the compensation that the regulator allows the service provider to receive in exchange for charging subcompetitive prices. Section 1 explains this in more detail.

5 A proxy cost model is a cost model that computes cost for a non-existent representative company rather than for a specific company, which used to be the practice.

6 For examples of this debate, see Hausman (1996) and Hubbard and Lehr (1996). The issues this paper addresses are based on the issues raised in these documents.

7 In this paper, the term "product" is used to infer a product being sold in a particular market. So, for example, a UNE in one market would be considered a separate product from the same UNE sold in another market. Defining products this way segregates products along the dimensions of technical characteristics, geographic market, customer type, and distribution channel.

8 For simplicity, this paper assumes that investment both improves quality and decreases operating costs. An example of such an investment might be the purchase of a digital switch, which offers a higher-quality signal than older technologies and also has lower prices for spare parts. Not all investments do both.

9 Without this assumption, the effects of miscalculating incremental cost would be ambiguous. Regulated prices cause overinvestment or underinvestment in specific regions. Miscalculating incremental cost provides incentives for inefficiency if and only if the miscalculation prompts the regulator to move regulated prices from one region to another.

10 Telecommunications plant has only limited potential for serving demand in more than one geographic location. The most fungible equipment is circuit equipment. Technicians can remove this equipment from one location and place it in any other location that uses the same technology. Some switching equipment can also be moved to another location that uses the same technology. Feeder cable can be

used to serve any demand that occurs in the feeder planning area. As a result, if demand decreases along part of the feeder cable's route, the idled portion of the feeder cable becomes available to serve demand in another part of the route. However, feeder cable in one route cannot be moved to serve demand in another feeder route. Distribution cable has limited fungibility.

11 Regulatory accounting applies one depreciation life to all telecommunications of a particular type. Even if this depreciation life is correct on average, it may be too long for some locations and too short for others.

12 There may be constraints that keep the regulator from inducing the ILEC to choose I^*. For example, the ILEC may possess private information about how much I lowers operating costs. Also, the Act requires regulators to base prices on cost. In certain situations, such as when cost-based prices provide ILEC customers with surplus at the margin, this restriction may cause the ILEC to underinvest.

13 In practice, the regulator may have less information about customers than the ILEC. In such a case, the regulator will have to allow the ILEC to earn extra profits in order to induce efficient investment decisions. But even with this, the ILEC will underinvest.

14 According to Jamison's (1998b) international survey results, prices for interconnection and network elements are generally linear, but not always. This paper assumes linear prices for simplicity.

15 The Appendix provides sufficient conditions for when the ILEC would choose to keep marginal cost above price and for when it would choose to keep marginal cost below price.

16 This does not mean that prices have to be constant. Rather, it means that the regulator and the company view the regulator's price control decision as establishing current prices and prices for each period over the life of the asset, allowing that the prices may change from period to period.

17 This is effectively a static treatment of a timing issue. While this has been a standard approach in investment analysis in telecommunications for a number of years, it is unclear whether it captures the full effect of the timing issues in real options.

18 In a dynamic sense, this creates a simultaneity problem because price affects quantity demanded. TELRIC models are static and so ignore this problem.

19 Even though using average fill would remedy the irreversibility of investments for individual projects, it does not remedy irreversibility for the ILEC's investment as a whole. This irreversibility should be reflected in the cost of capital. Henry Ergas (1998) argues that traditional cost of capital tools such as CAPM do not adequately reflect this irreversibility. Hubbard and Lehr (1996) argue that they do. Not being an expert on cost of capital, the author leaves this debate to others.

20 According to an FCC staff report, the BCPM2 model uses similar fill factors.

21 However, as has been shown in the ECPR literature, it is inappropriate to consider any portion of these higher profits that represent monopoly profits.

REFERENCES

Armstrong, M. and C. Doyle. No date. *Access Pricing, Entry and the Baumol-Willig Rule,* Discussion Paper No. 9422, University of Southampton.

Baumol, William J. 1977. "On the Proper Cost Tests for Natural Monopoly in a Multiproduct Industry," *American Economic Review,* 67: 809-822.

Baumol, William J., and J. Gregory Sidak. 1994. *Toward Competition in Local Telephony.* Cambridge, Massachusetts: MIT Press.

Dixit, A. K. 1990. *Optimization in Economic Theory.* Oxford: Oxford University Press.

Ergas, Henry. 1998. "Valuation and Costing Issues in Access Pricing with Specific Applications to Telecommunications," *Infrastructure Regulation and Market Reform: Principles and Practice,* M. Arblaster and M. Jamison, eds. Melbourne, Australia: Competition and Consumer Commission, 91-112.

Hausman, Jerry. April 7, 1996. Testimony before the California Public Utilities Commission.

Hubbard, R. Glenn and William H. Lehr. July 18, 1996. "Capital Recovery Issues in TSLRIC Pricing: Response to Professor Jerry A. Hausman," In the Matter of Implementation of Local Competition Provisions of the Telecommunications Act of 1996, CC Docket No. 96-98.

Jamison, Mark A. 1998a. "A Further Look at Proper Cost Tests for Natural Monopoly" (unpublished).

Jamison, Mark A. 1996. "General Conditions for Subsidy-Free Prices." *Journal of Economics and Business,* no. 4 (October): 371-385.

Jamison, Mark A. 1998b. "International Survey of Interconnection Policies: Final Report" (unpublished).

Jamison, Mark A. 1998c. "Regulatory Techniques for Addressing Interconnection, Access, and Cross-subsidy in Telecommunications," *Infrastructure Regulation and Market Reform: Principles and Practice,* M. Arblaster and M. Jamison, eds., Melbourne, Australia: Competition and Consumer Commission. 113-127.

Kahn, Alfred and William Taylor. 1994. "The Pricing of Inputs Sold to Competitors: A Comment," *Yale Journal on Regulation,* 11: 225-240.

Mitchell, Mitchell, Werner Neu, et al. 1995. "The Regulation of Pricing of Interconnection Services" (unpublished).

Ordover, J.A., A.O. Sykes, and R.D. Willig. 1985. "Nonprice Anticompetitive Behavior by Dominant Firms toward the Producers of Complementary Products," *Antitrust and Regulation: Essays in Memory of John J. McGowan,* F. M. Fisher, ed. Cambridge, Massachusetts: MIT Press.

Salinger, Michael A. 1998. "Regulating Prices to Equal Forward-Looking Costs: Cost-Based Prices or Price-Based Costs?" *Journal of Regulatory Economics,* 14:149-163.

Trigeorgis, Lenos. 1996. *Real Options: Managerial Flexibility and Strategy in Resource Allocation.* Cambridge, Massachusetts: MIT Press.

Tye, William. 1994. "The Pricing of Inputs Sold to Competitors: A Response," *Yale Journal on Regulation,* 11: 203-224.

Willig, Robert. 1979. "The Theory of Network Access Pricing," *Issues in Public Utility Regulation,* H. Trebing, ed. East Lansing, Michigan: Michigan State University Press, 109–152.

4 Real Options: What Telecommunications Can Learn from Electric Power

Todd Strauss
PHB Hagler Bailly, Inc.

Abstract - An example of an option associated with operating flexibility in electric power production and a real options approach to valuing the option are presented. This approach is contrasted with the standard discounted cash flow approach and a pure financial option valuation approach. Some connections between electric power and telecommunications are drawn, and lessons for the telecommunications industry are highlighted.

This paper describes a real options approach to assessing the value of a power plant. On face, it might seem odd to include a paper describing an electric power application in an edited volume on real options in the telecommunications industry. But the industries are not all that dissimilar. Both are capital-intensive, technologically-oriented industries with a long history of regulation. And both are undergoing rapid transformation in an age of globalization and deregulation.

Also, an understanding of the modeling process illustrated here will bear fruit for those interested in applying real options to the telecommunications industry. Much of the real options literature focuses on investment options – options to expand, delay, or abandon investments in capital assets. The application described here focuses on an option associated with operating flexibility in a network industry.

Last, much of the literature on the real options approach contrasts it with the standard discounted cash flow approach. This paper also illustrates the distinctions between a real options approach and a pure financial option valuation approach.

1. APPLICATION: ASSESSING THE VALUE OF A POWER PLANT

There is much regulatory interest in answering the question: What is the value of a power plant? There is also a substantial business need for answers to this question. The answers are used in formulating bids for plant auctions and in the syndication of debt financing of power plant acquisitions.

For this discussion, only the broadest outlines of electricity generation need be mentioned. For one, power plants are like refineries for electricity. A commodity fuel goes in, and out comes electricity. Also, there are constraints on production. Some constraints are associated with the physical characteristics of boilers, turbines and generators. Others are associated with regulatory requirements, such as environmental restrictions. That's all we really need to know about power plants for right now.

The usual approach to valuing a power plant is to perform a discounted cash flow analysis. The first step is to forecast each year's revenues and costs. Annual net revenues are then computed. Next, each year's net revenues are discounted using some risk-adjusted discount rate. Finally, the discounted annual net revenues are summed to yield a net present value. Market prices, gross revenues, and annual net cash flows are determined using production cost models.

Production cost models for electric power have features that are similar to those of the cost models used in telecommunications. The models are purported to focus on economic fundamentals. However, while the models have detailed engineering representations on the supply side, they have very poor representation on the demand side. Neither the uncertainty of demand nor the elasticity of demand is represented. It is assumed that price equals marginal cost. Modelers are clever, in electricity as in telecommunications, and so they try to jigger the inputs so that the prices output by the models represent market competition, perhaps even ability to exercise market power. The most striking similarity between the telecommunications and electric power cost models is that they are legacy models coming out of the regulatory contexts of the 1970s and 1980s.

In particular, both types of model exclude real options. For example, the electric power models do not include the value of possible site expansion. An old, inefficient power plant has infrastructure – electric transmission connections, gas pipeline connections, operating permits – making it easy to upgrade to a new, highly-efficient power plant in several years. This opportunity to upgrade may be worth a lot, particularly in areas where it is very difficult to obtain a new, "greenfield" site for a power plant. However, possible site expansion is not captured in the standard discounted cash flow analysis. This is broadly recognized. Many analysts attempt to include the value of possible site expansion by using a subjective probability of site expansion and a projected net cash flow for the site expansion, then computing an expected value for the site expansion possibility, and finally adding the expected value to the base case NPV. As discussed elsewhere in this book and in the literature, the real options approach is a superior way to value possible site expansion.

The most commonly cited examples for applications of the real options approach tend to be investment options – options to expand, delay, or abandon investments in capital assets. Included in this category is the above-mentioned option for site expansion. Investment options are rather generic in nature, with applicability across a broad spectrum of industries and organizations. A growing literature maps out how to identify and value investment options, and there is no special insight the telecommunications industry can glean from an application in electric power.

Examples of options associated with operating flexibility appear much less frequently in discussions of the real options approach. An example of such an option and an approach to valuing it is presented next. To tailor the lesson to the telecommunications industry, some connections are drawn between electric power and telecommunications, and the lessons that may be applied to the telecommunications industry are highlighted.

Now, more on electricity markets and power plants. Across the country and around the world, there are wholesale electricity markets for production, specified in intervals as short as one hour. Such markets are one of the hallmarks of the global trend toward electricity deregulation, or as insiders put it, "restructuring." Electric power is becoming a commodity. Because electric power is difficult or expensive to store, and because the regulatory transition leaves many retail customers insensitive to short-term swings in wholesale price, electric power prices are the most volatile of any commodity traded today.

In the face of this uncertainty, what's a power plant to do? A power plant does have some operational flexibility, and can use this in responding to prices. When it is profitable to produce electricity, the plant should produce. And when it is unprofitable, the plant should try to shut down temporarily. (If the power plant has some contractual obligation to provide electricity to some customers, it may be profitable – or more precisely, less unprofitable – to shut down temporarily, and fulfill its obligation by supplying less-costly power purchased in the market.) But market prices are uncertain, so it is not known in advance when the plant will be profitable or unprofitable; hence, it is not known in advance whether the plant should be operating or shut down.

However, the operating policy for the power plant can be specified in advance. As prices are revealed in the marketplace, the power plant's operators can adjust the operating level of the power plant in response to the market prices, and in accord with the operating policy for the power plant. Furthermore, the plant's operating policy can be changed as market conditions change, as regulatory requirements change, or as plant ownership, control, or governance changes.

There are two conditions leading to an option associated with operational flexibility. First, market prices for electricity output (and fuel input) are uncertain. Second, a power plant has some capability to adapt its operations when the uncertainty is revealed.

Surprisingly to some industry modelers, this option is poorly captured by the production cost models described earlier. In spite of all their engineering detail, these models include limited sources of uncertainty. The production cost models thereby miss almost all of the value in a power plant's ability to respond to fluctuating market prices. This ability to respond, often referred to as "dispatchability" in the electric power industry, may be a significant component of the total value of the power plant, but is absent from an NPV calculated using the discounted cash flow approach.

Recognizing this operating flexibility as an option is crucial for the accurate valuation of the power plant. But it is not sufficient.

An option-based approach to valuing a power plant is often used, typically by financially-oriented power traders who come from other commodity backgrounds, especially natural gas trading. These traders recognize that a power plant (at least, a "merchant" power plant not owned by a regulated utility) has a right, but not an obligation, to generate electricity in the marketplace. These traders model a power plant as a strip of European call options on the Btu (British thermal units) spread. That does not mean anything to power plant engineers, and may not mean anything to telecommunications people, but the Wall Street folks understand what that means. Let's dissect this beast.

The Btu spread is the differential between an electricity price and a fuel price. Because prices for electricity and fuel are expressed in different units, fuel prices are typically transformed to units of electricity price. The arithmetic calculation includes an adjustment for the thermal efficiency of the power plant (how much fuel input is required to produce one unit of electricity output). Thermal efficiency is commonly expressed as the Btu required as fuel input to yield one kilowatt-hour of electricity output. Hence, the Btu spread is a measure of the power plant's relative economic efficiency, given particular electricity and fuel prices.

A call option grants the holder the right, but not the obligation, to take delivery of the underlying instruments at the strike price. A call option pays off – is "in the money" – when the value of the underlying instrument is greater than the strike price. A call option on the Btu spread is the right to purchase fuel and sell electricity at the specified differential in electricity and fuel prices. In this light, a power plant has an opportunity to make money on the difference between electricity and fuel prices by burning fuel and producing electricity. In some sense, the plant is arbitraging the separate markets for electricity and fuel. A European option means that the option can be exercised only at maturity, not before. Because electricity is not readily storable, this is appropriate. A power plant has such an option for each hour of production. The strip is the collection of separate hourly options.

This option-based approach is inaccurate. It typically estimates the value of a power plant at an amount too high to be believed. The problem is that this pure financial approach ignores the operating characteristics of the power plant. It includes an assumption that the power plant can costlessly respond to market prices by turning up to maximum capacity when the Btu spread is positive and by turning off when the Btu spread is negative. Power plants have some freedom to respond to market prices, but this freedom is constrained by the operating characteristics of the power plant. Precisely because this assumption is not true, production cost models include engineering and regulatory detail on the power plant's operating characteristics.

So the approach we have taken at PHB Hagler Bailly is a real options approach. Figure 1 displays a schematic of this approach. Our proprietary market valuation process, MVP℠, starts with a characterization of market price volatility, as does the pure financial options approach described above. The model then values the ability of the power plant to respond to fluctuating market prices. Unlike the pure financial options approach, this model accounts for the decrease in value associated with the lost market opportunities caused by operating "frictions" such as physical and regulatory constraints on the power plant. These frictional losses are valued using standard optimization techniques such as dynamic programming and linear programming. The frictional losses are linked to the financial strip by constructing a new derivative (in the financial sense). This new derivative is a modification to the strip of call options on the Btu spread. The new derivative is then valued.

MVP℠ has been used to value power plants at auctions and in syndication of debt financing. Table 1 compares the values yielded by MVP℠ with those yielded by discounted cash flow methods based on production cost models, and with values from the pure financial approach. Values are stylized and have been scaled to make it easier to compare results across plants and valuation techniques.

As Table 1 shows, there is generally an option premium associated with operating flexibility. The magnitude of the option premium depends on the specific operating characteristics of the power plant. A nuclear power plant has little operational flexibility and does not readily respond to price signals, so the option premium is negligible. At the other end of the spectrum, oil plants used to meet peak conditions have high optionality. In most cases, the frictional losses due to operating constraints are substantial, so the pure financial option approach grossly overestimates the value of a power plant.

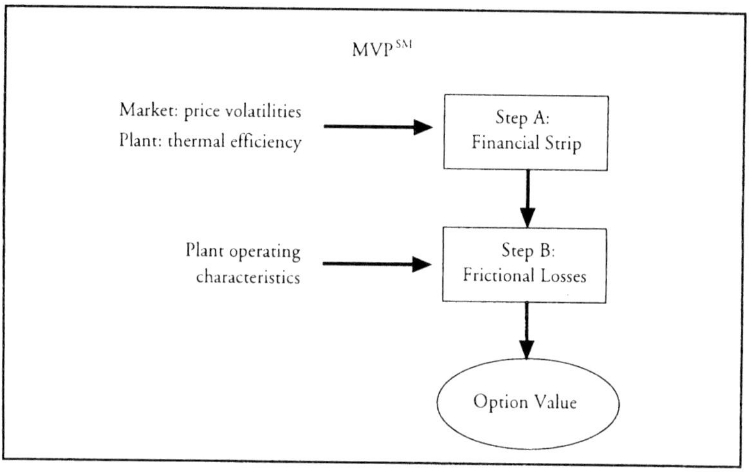

Figure 1: Real options approach to valuing a power plant

Table 1: Power Plant Values

Power Plant Type	DCF value	MVP℠ value	Financial Strip Value
nuclear plant A	100	100	110
coal plant B	100	134	> 300
natural gas plant C	100	200	250
coal plant D	100	229	> 500
oil plant E	7	100	300

2. LESSONS

Before gleaning some lessons for telecommunications from this electric power application, some salient features of electric power should be identified, with attendant comparisons for telecommunications. First, industry deregulation and restructuring are turning wholesale electric power into a commodity, with commodity markets. Second, there is no inventory because bulk electricity is difficult and costly to store. Third, electricity is transmitted over a network grid. The network is unswitched; electricity flows according to Kirchhoff's Law in physics. Fourth, electricity production has significant variable operating costs for most of the technologies in existence today. This is not true for solar power, but is true for fossil-fuel burning power plants.

Telecommunications has many similar features. The commodity seems to be bandwidth. There is no inventory: any bandwidth not used in one time period is forever unutilized. Telecommunications operates over a network grid. However, the network is switched, with much less network congestion. The greatest difference between telecommunications and electric power seems to be that telecommunications has negligible variable operating cost.

The electric power example above, of optionality in operating flexibility, hinges on variable operating cost. There appears to be no immediate analogous application of the model to telecommunications. This is fine. The most important lesson is to focus on the assets of interest, study the crucial characteristics associated with optionality, and build an appropriate model.

Focus on the assets of interest. In electric power, production cost models typically model wide swaths of regional electric power systems, in great detail. Much of this detail is extraneous. It does not materially affect the value of the assets of interest, and is not pertinent to the decisions of interest. Assembling the data inputs needed and debugging outputs for the wide swaths frequently divert time and money from the crucial modeling issues, such as validating important assumptions and assessing important sensitivities.

Study the characteristics of the assets of interest. This is accomplished by focusing on the crucial characteristics associated with optionality. PHB Hagler Bailly's first cut at an option valuation approach for power plants took us along the well-worn path of the pure financial option approach. But the operating characteristics of power plants yield constrained flexibility, and the standard option approach developed for pure financial options missed this. So we were confronted by the collision between the financial and engineering paradigms. The first step was to carefully identify the relevant details each paradigm framed best. The financial paradigm focused on price uncertainty – the strip of call options on the Btu spread. The engineering paradigm focused on operating constraints – the operating detail input to the production cost model.

Build an appropriate model. The MVP℠ model focuses on the key characteristic of market prices – volatility – to value operating flexibility. It distills from the host of power plant information input to production cost models the operating characteristics of the power plants of interest. For the power plants of interest, the model makes use of additional operating detail not typically part of the production cost model data set. The modular design of the MVP℠ process facilitates focusing on the assets of interest.

More generally, the way we integrate financial option models with engineering suggests a general modeling approach to value operating flexibility in network industries or services such as telecommunications and transportation. We link the engineering model with the financial model by creating a new financial derivative that synthesizes the operating characteristics of the power plant. This general idea appears promising for applications to other network industries.

Another important lesson is to customize generic analytical tools. I must admit, this is rather self-serving. I am a consultant, and do this for a living. But this lesson is based upon many hours of sweat equity. We started out using adaptations of the standard Black-Scholes formula. They did not work for a variety of reasons. We ended up with a solution tailored to our particular application. The real options methodology is a generic methodology. Make it your own. Focus on the particular business problem you face, and tailor the solution to the problem.

Principles

5 Cost Models: Comporting with Principles

Richard Emmerson, Ph.D.
INDETEC International, Inc.

Abstract - Recent public policy initiatives in telecommunications prescribe tying certain prices and subsidies to cost. The apparent motive behind these policies is a desire to mimic competitive outcomes when markets are too frail to be trusted with the task of achieving economic efficiency. Indeed, it is true that an outcome of "perfect competition" as portrayed in university textbooks has all prices equal to respective marginal costs. However, the conditions behind this relationship include an onerous requirement that all markets be present and operating. Missing in telecommunications are markets for the present and future use of the network capacity created by both incumbent and new firms. Just as "real options" in financial markets allow for the present trading of future options to purchase financial securities, options to presently trade future network capacity would greatly improve the incentives to build optimal network capacity. In addition, such options would provide a mechanism to realize present financial rewards for the expected future value of those networks. Yet economic efficiency requires that prices reflect the option costs in addition to the costs of productive resources. Because the "cost" of capacity options is not available today, any attempt to link regulated prices to resource costs could result in prices very different than market prices. Perhaps the wiser public policy is to encourage the development of present and future capacity markets, complete with associated real options.

Standard economics pedagogy tells of firms maximizing profits through the selection of market-priced inputs, prices, and output levels that bring marginal cost into perfect alignment with market prices. It is a familiar story: costless entry and exit into and out of industries; the self-serving expansion and contraction of output by these profit-maximizing firms moves society's resources according to the needs and whims of consumers.

Recent literature pertaining to "real options" suggests that firms cannot function so in the real world. Entry decisions entail irreversible resource commitments. Uncertainty about future demand makes it difficult to justify the employment of resources, thus putting wealth at risk. But this notion of "real options" is not new. This paper reflects on some early microeconomic literature to shed light on the conformance of the pertinent cost models (models designed to formulate public policy in telecommunications) with the principles of real options.

1. MARGINAL COST PRICING

The basic principles of marginal cost pricing were developed more than a century ago. Adam Smith's "invisible hand" (1776) would silently move resources to their highest and best use in response to the selfish actions of protfit seekers and informed buyers. More formal and mathematically complete analyses began in earnest with Walras (1877), who worked out the first formal statement of the conditions for general equilibrium. During this century, increasingly advanced mathematical techniques have revealed virtually all of the conditions that must hold for there to be a general equilibrium at which prices bear mathematical relationships to cost. The results are taught in every economics program today: economic efficiency as defined by economist Vilfredo Pareto (1909), is achieved when market prices equal long-run marginal cost. It is long-run marginal cost that is relevant because the presence of fixed costs (then presumed to be only a short-run phenomenon) may require deviations from marginal cost pricing.[1]

Further insight into this peculiar p = mc relationship was gained in the 1950s and 1960s when Kenneth Arrow, Gerard Debreu (1954), and others revealed that these efficiency relationships were not just due to the convenient conventions of calculus. Using the mathematics of topology, it was discovered that, with certain "continuity" and "convexity" assumptions, competitive prices would support an efficient allocation of resources, and that each such allocation could be supported by a set of competitive prices. In an obscure way, this meant that competition would bring about economic efficiency through forces that would set prices equal to marginal cost.[2] These results were soon taken to be a prescription for economic efficiency in addition to being a descriptive characteristic of that state of affairs. But, the issues raised by the "real options" literature call this practice into question.

2. REAL OPTIONS: THE PROBLEM

"Separating hyperplane theorems," or a variant of these theorems, were the primary tool used in deriving the relationship between prices and costs. In essence, the set of possible output combinations and the set of most desirable consumption options were separated by a hyperplane that touched each set at a point where they met. The fact that the two sets met indicated that supply equaled demand. The hyperplane had a "slope" that represented the marginal costs of outputs and prices of consumable goods. Two critical assumptions embedded in the mathematical derivations of these conditions for general equilibrium did not escape the notice of mathematical economists. The mathematical results could not be produced without assuming *complete markets* and that all resources were *perfectly divisible*[3] (tiny fractions of resources such as machines and people must be available to be employed). At first, little concern was raised since one could, in principle, "rent" arbitrarily small fractions of resources rather than buy them.[4]

Soon, however, when real options to employ resources were recognized, new mathematical techniques unambiguously revealed broken ties between marginal cost pricing and economic efficiency. In a world that offers up indivisible units of resources or requires that minimum thresholds of activities be attained to be efficient, competitive prices can bring about less than efficient resource allocations. Likewise, a fog bank of uncertainty about the future demands the introduction of infinitely more markets to place prices on contingencies that depend on unknown future states of nature and the economy. The culprits, of course, are the twin assumptions that made the early mathematical results so easy to derive: the perfect divisibility of resources and the completeness of markets.

2.1 Indivisibilities

Two papers published in the late 1960s and early 1970s showed that when firms do not have real options to buy resources in arbitrarily small amounts, or when efficient levels of resource use are available at only selected scales of employment, competitive prices might be associated with inefficient resource allocations.[5] That is, the traditional laws of supply and demand might bring about equilibrium market prices, but the resulting state of affairs could be inefficient. It is precisely these market failures that invite laws and regulations to overcome inefficient or abusive practices. For example, when an incumbent firm is viewed to have good reason to operate under less than competitive market conditions (a natural monopoly, for instance), regulators may attempt to impose a set of prices and subsidies equal to or formulated from long-run marginal (or incremental) cost.

A question of foremost concern in telecommunications is whether certain prices (or prices plus subsidies) should be set at long-run marginal cost to simulate efficient prices. Indivisibilities are relevant to answering this question; their presence in telecommunications may cause fixed and common costs to exist in the long run. For example, just as the presence of fixed costs in the short run may require prices to be set above or below marginal cost,[6] the presence of fixed costs in the long run may require efficiently regulated prices to deviate from long-run marginal costs. Thus, the "real options" of firms to acquire inputs having lumpy capacities disturbs the desirability of marginal cost pricing.

2.2 Complete Markets

Perhaps more disturbing than input and output indivisibility is the problem of incomplete markets. The mathematical models that justify setting prices equal to marginal cost require that all prices have this relationship. Setting aside the well-known problem of "second best" prices, some critical prices are missing from the real economy. An example will serve better than theory to explain. When a firm is required to invest irrevocably in resources (e.g., building a wire line telephone network), invariably, there are some components of the investment in resources that cannot be liquidated if the productive capacity of the resources is not fully used. This does not present a problem to the student of general equilibrium (the discipline that deals with advanced models of marginal cost pricing); it is assumed there is a market for such risk. In the real world, insurance markets and futures markets play this role. But there are not enough insurance or futures markets to set prices for every contingency faced by telephone companies, incumbent or newly forming. Thus, financial markets imperfectly reflect the *overall* risk of the company (e.g., through the beta component of the return on equity). But one price (the risk-adjusted cost of money) is not sufficient to meet the requirements of complete markets; more prices (in theory, one for each unique risk) would be needed for markets to be complete.

This issue is relevant to the present debate: prices set equal to long-run marginal costs are not sufficient to achieve efficiency if only the costs of the physical and financial resources were included in the calculations. Additional prices are needed for the various irreversible and risky resource commitments that accompany the business. Because the real options of the operating company are limited, costs and associated prices will be missing from the calculation.

3. HOW DO THE MODELS COMPORT WITH THEORY?

All of the cost models now under scrutiny by the FCC (the BCPM, HAI, and HCPM) attempt to adhere to a set of rules set out in the FCC's dictums, beginning with the First Report and Order and proceeding through the many subsequent meetings and processes. These rules require that only the most efficient means of serving inhabited (or perhaps habitable) areas be used in the cost calculations. Prices and subsidies are then calculated to equal an approximation of long-run incremental cost. This approximation calculates the incremental costs of the service(s) in question and adds a parsed component of common costs under the presumption that true long-run marginal costs would include these costs.[7]

The models have captured, at least in spirit, the problem with indivisible resources and related matters of fixed and common costs. But the models have not captured the remainder of the real options characteristics. Among the reasons why none of the models under consideration comports with the real options are two of particular importance. The first is practical: a model sufficiently complex to capture real options is simply beyond the state of the art and science of modeling today, or at least beyond the resources of the models' sponsors. The second is the present inability of models to simulate complete markets. Each point is taken in order.

The current cost study practices in telecommunications generally accept that there are fixed and/or common costs in long-run cost studies. By acknowledging that common costs may exist and that such costs would be reflected in competitive prices, the models do comport in practice with the pertinent principles. Although the accuracy and elegance of the solutions could be improved, at least the conceptual structure of the models allows for appropriate inclusion of the proper considerations.

On the other hand, the models are not sufficiently complex to capture certain other "real options." At the simplest level, none of the models builds a network that has been demonstrated to be functionally real. For example, the BCPM recognizes that network construction encounters concrete and asphalt only in proportion to their incidence in the overall terrain being served. The reality is that plant is built on rights of way having a very different mix of such terrain. The HAI and HCPM models collect customers into distribution areas that disregard physical barriers such as freeways and rivers. Any model will necessarily fall short of the real options due to the sheer magnitude of complexities that must be considered. Of course, this is the nature of modeling. A model is deliberately an abstraction from reality and therefore ignores details of reality that do not materially affect the uses of the model. Do the models abstract too much or too little? This is the subject of ongoing debate and adversarial proceedings, and one that cannot be resolved here. "Informational deficiencies" do not by themselves render a model impotent.

The second issue, incomplete markets, is the area where the models seriously fall short, in theory and practice, of "real options." Even if it were demonstrated that the models reflect a telephone network that can operate at a point in time, it is unlikely that any company would construct such a network, either in a cost minimizing monopoly or competitive environment.

The reason is simple: the rules of model construction require that an efficient network underlie the cost calculations. This network is constructed to an existing set of premises (just which premises differs by model) using the technology commercially available today. The "real options" open to any operating company are: a) to build the most efficient *increment* to an *existing* network that evolves (and minimizes cost) over time, not knowing just where and when new premises might appear; or b) to construct a *new* network to a set of existing premises anticipating what market shares or customers might demand service. Besides the uncertainty and irreversibility for which there may be no costs modeled in these scenarios (recall the incomplete markets problem), the rules require that each model build a network assumed to be the only network serving the area. Thus, another incomplete market surfaces: under the very competitive conditions that call for cost models, there will be underused network capacity in either scenario. Because there will be more than one competitive alternative, and because an efficient network operator will not engage in "just-in-time" network inventory practices, not every customer for which the network is built will opt to use that network.

This all points to the critical incompleteness of markets. The missing markets are most prominently capacity markets. There are not fully developed markets for selling the capacities (present and future) of telephone networks. While the clear impact (if not intention) of the FCC policies that have followed the Telecommunications Act of 1996 are to promote the sale and lease of network capacity (unbundled network elements and wholesale offerings), there are still limited opportunities to trade future network capacities in robust markets like those for financial securities.[8]

Can the missing capacity market problem be fixed in the context of the current models? In part yes, in part no. There are, in each of the models, parameters that can approximate many of the costs of real options. By selecting the proper fill factors (the size of the modeled network in excess of the current demand) and uncertainty in demand, a risky but possibly efficient anticipation of new premises can be accommodated. By selecting the proper depreciation rates and related cost of money, the "real options" associated with the general uncertainty and irreversibility (sunk costs) can be practicably incorporated. And so forth. However, these "fixes" can only be considered as rough and largely uninformed approximations to what real competitive markets would do.

4. THE COMPETITIVE MARKET STANDARD

Multiproduct firms in competitive markets price individual products and product lines more to meet the competition than to recover specific costs that may be allocated to those products. Common costs (using the FCC's definition)[9] are recovered from pricing above incremental costs (as they are defined today) according to the discipline exerted by competition. Similar firms, not entirely identical, are usually the source of this competition. Each firm examines its unique economies of scale and scope to determine what prices it can afford to charge. In order to remain profitable, or at least viable, firms choose to adjust combinations of prices and products. This results in a widely varying mix of markups over marginal or incremental costs that are easily formulated on paper. In other words, there is no cost-based formula that generates market prices; extensive information about demand must be taken into account.

In addition, entry into or exit from specific product markets or industries may entail costs associated with "real option" frictions as firms adjust their scope of services. The "real options" problem associated with the general issue of irreversible investments pales by comparison to the "real option" uncertainty that arises from the dynamics of market competition. It is inconceivable that adjusting cost-based formulas that reflect "real options" in a competitive environment could usefully proxy real-market prices. Only the evolution of markets for the capacities of the assets that are largely sunk upon entry will bring prices into alignment with "real options." A good central control mechanism that substitutes for well functioning markets does not exist.

5. POLICY IMPLICATIONS

The models proposed for use in developing public policy can certainly be improved by recognizing the "real options" phenomenon. Indeed, engineering assumptions, inputs (e.g., fill factors), and model parameters can partially incorporate such concerns in a crude but useful way.

However, the intention of the Telecommunications Act of 1996 appears to be one that supplants regulation with competition over time.[10] The "real options" problem is ultimately solved by competition itself. Competition presents "real options" to firms in complex and ever changing forms. Surviving in the real business landscape is both the challenge of successful companies and the beauty of the competitive process. The "real options" debate is really about how to best make the telecommunications industry competitive.

In the long run, the most important changes in public policy should not focus on revising models. The emphasis should be on creating policies that encourage the rapid development of capacity markets. Great strides in efficiency will come from facilitating the creation and evolution of spot and futures markets for the capacity of communications and information networks.

NOTES

1 An excellent discussion of the necessary deviations from marginal cost pricing in the presence of fixed costs is found in Baumol, W. 1988. *Superfairness*, Cambridge, Massachusetts: MIT Press, Ch. 7.

2 More accurately, the *ratios* of prices to one another would be equal to the respective ratios of marginal costs.

3 More generally, the topological properties of continuity and convexity used in the mathematical proofs were necessary to obtain the desired results. See Arrow, K. 1971. *General Competitive Analysis*. San Francisco: Holden Day.

4 Of course the fundamental problem remains: rental markets that would be capable of generating arbitrarily small amounts of each resource would themselves require resources that amount to an indivisibility.

5 Emmerson, R. 1973. *Journal of Economic Theory*, Starr, Ross. 1969. "Quasi-Equilibria in Markets with Nonconvex Preferences," *Econmetrica* 37.

6 For example, textbooks frequently depict situations where average variable cost equals marginal cost. In these circumstances, prices equal to marginal cost provide no contribution to fixed costs.

7 Among many parties to this argument, there is a presumption that "all costs are variable in the long run" and therefore common costs are an artifact of the short-run nature of the real world analysis. As discussed above, indivisibilities can result in long-run fixed costs. Thus, the need to address common costs in the long run cannot be so conveniently discarded. An equally important misconception is that common costs are fixed costs. In fact, common costs may exist even if all costs were variable in the long run. In any case, the FCC has chosen correctly to recognize that common costs are included in competitive prices.

8 There are a few evolving international markets for trading country-to-country traffic. If these markets flourish and extend to intracountry traffic, the missing markets problem may be largely solved.

9 In re Implementation of the Local Competition Provisions in the Telecommunications Act of 1996, CC Docket No. 96-98, at & 677. Defining "common costs" as "costs that are incurred in connection with the production of multiple products or services, and remains unchanged as the relative proportion of those products or services varies."

10 Telecommunications Act of 1996. See in particular: SEC. 257. (a), (b) (MARKET ENTRY BARRIERS PROCEEDING); and SEC. 401. (REGULATORY FORBEARANCE) as amended by the new section SEC. 10. (COMPETITION IN PROVISION OF TELECOMMUNICATIONS SERVICE).

6 The Design of Forward Looking Cost Models for Local Exchange Telecommunications Networks

William W. Sharkey[1]
Federal Communications Commission

Abstract – In the last few years great strides have been made in the development of algorithms that design telephone networks. As computational capabilities improve it is possible to produce better results, both from an engineering and an economic standpoint. This paper considers the design issues that cost model developers have addressed successfully. Many of these issues are illustrated by a detailed description of a model developed by FCC staff, known as the Hybrid Cost Proxy Model (HCPM). HCPM is capable of utilizing very precise customer location data. From these data, the model uses clustering algorithms to identify serving areas that satisfy appropriate engineering constraints. Within each serving area, the model uses a modified minimum-cost spanning tree algorithm to connect actual customer locations to a serving area interface. The same tree algorithm connects each interface point to a switch. Within each path, the model performs intensive integer searches to find the cost minimizing, yet engineering-feasible, choice of technology and electronics for that path. The result is a-low cost, feasible network plan that gives an appropriate estimate of the forward looking cost of providing wireline telephone service to a particular area. This estimate should prove particularly useful in the ongoing debate about the size and make-up of the Universal Service Fund, and for other regulatory purposes such as the pricing of interconnection and unbundled network elements.

Engineering process (cost proxy) models have been developed in recent years as an alternative to more traditional econometric and accounting approaches to cost measurement. Because econometric models rely on assumptions of (smooth) functional forms, engineering process models offer a more detailed view of cost structures than is possible using econometric data. In addition, engineering models are better suited for modeling forward looking (long-run) costs because they rely much less on historical data than econometric models.

In the telecommunications industry, cost proxy modeling can play a particularly significant role for three reasons. First, the very rapid technological change in the industry compounds the standard econometric difficulties in using historical data to estimate a forward looking cost function. Second, many applications of cost studies in telecommunications require highly disaggregated levels of detail, which can capture regional variations in cost and the costs of specific network components. Finally, a growing awareness of the benefits of deregulation in the public utility sector industries generally, has given rise to a demand for a new set of tools that can be used to promote competition and advance the pace of deregulation in the industry.

The deregulatory goals for telecommunications are explicitly set out in the Telecommunications Act of 1996,[2] in which Congress sought to establish "a pro-competitive, de-regulatory national policy framework" for the U.S. telecommunications industry. In the two full years following this act, the Federal Communications Commission has undertaken proceedings on universal service,[3] interstate access charge reform,[4] and local exchange competition[5] to overhaul its current regulations in light of the 1996 Act. In these proceedings, the Commission has examined, in varying degrees, the use of forward looking economic cost methodologies as a basis for determining universal service support levels, cost-based access charges, and pricing for interconnection and unbundled network elements. The 1996 Act has fundamentally changed telecommunications regulation by replacing the framework of government-recognized monopolies with one in which federal and state governments work in tandem to promote efficient competition and to remove entry barriers and regulations that protect monopolies. The 1996 Act, when fully implemented, should greatly reduce the legal, regulatory, economic, and operational barriers to entry in the local exchange and exchange access market, while preserving and advancing enhanced universal service goals.

The local competition provisions of the Act confer three fundamental rights on potential competitors to incumbent local exchange carriers (LECs): the right to interconnect with other carriers' networks at rates based on cost, the right to obtain unbundled network elements at cost-based rates, and the right to obtain an incumbent LEC's retail services at wholesale discounts in order to resell those services.[6] The Act also requires a fundamental restructuring of current regulatory mechanisms for funding universal service goals. For this purpose, the FCC must first define the services to be supported by federal universal service mechanisms, and then determine a mechanism to estimate the cost of such services in a manner that is "explicit and sufficient to preserve and advance universal service."[7] In its recently initiated access reform proceeding, the Commission also seeks to reform its system of interstate access charges to make it compatible with the competitive paradigm established by the 1996 Act and with state actions to open local networks to competition.[8]

Forward looking economic computer-based cost models could enable regulatory authorities to estimate the forward looking cost of network facilities and services without having to rely on detailed cost studies, prepared by incumbent LRCs, that would otherwise be necessary. In addition, a publicly available cost proxy model could be useful to regulators by providing an independent check on the accuracy of incumbent LEC cost studies. During the course of the model development process, several industry-sponsored models were submitted to the FCC for evaluation. These include the Benchmark Cost Proxy Model (BCPM) sponsored by US West, Sprint and Bell South and the HAI model sponsored by AT&T and MCI. Simultaneously, staff members of the FCC worked on an internal model known as the Hybrid Cost Proxy Model (HCPM), which incorporated elements of both of the industry models in addition to a set of new loop design and clustering algorithms developed internally. In October 1998 the Commission adopted a synthesis model consisting of the HCPM clustering and loop design modules in combination with HAI switching, transport and expense modules as a platform for the forward looking mechanism for determining high-cost support for non-rural LECs.[9] Subsequently, the FCC initiated an investigation of appropriate input values for use in the model. In May 1999, tentative input values were released for public comment. A final order recommending the use of the model and a set of input values for the purposes of determining high-cost support is expected in September 1999.

1. CRITERIA FOR EVALUATING THE UTILITY OF ECONOMIC COST MODELS

This section briefly discusses the criteria the FCC uses for evaluating forward looking economic cost models.

1.1 Use of Forward Looking Economic Cost as a Basis for Pricing

In dynamic, competitive markets, firms base their actions on the relationship between market-determined prices and forward looking economic costs. Forward looking economic costs are the costs that would be incurred if a new element or service were provided, or that could be avoided if an existing element or service were not provided, assuming that all input choices of the firm can be freely varied. This is often referred to as long-run economic cost. This "long-run" approach ensures that rates recover not only those operating costs that vary in the short run, but also fixed investment costs that, while not variable in the short term, are necessary inputs directly attributable to providing the element or service. If market prices exceed forward looking costs, new competitors will efficiently enter the market and bring pressure to bear on prices. If forward looking economic costs exceed market prices, new competitors will not enter and incumbent firms may decide to exit. These voluntary actions by firms produce efficient resource allocation by adjusting price and output until the value to consumers of additional output is just equal to the cost of the resources required to produce it. In contrast, basing prices on embedded costs would fail to establish the critical link between economic production costs and market prices, and would be inconsistent with the goal of efficient competition.[10] Pricing based on forward looking costs enables efficient providers to cover their costs and make new investments, while facilitating efficient market entry by potential competitors.

1.2 Use of Proxy Models for Multiple Objectives

For the purposes of determining universal service support levels, the FCC determined that a cost proxy model should, at a minimum, be able to estimate the full stand-alone cost of the minimum set of network elements capable of delivering traditional voice telecommunications service and narrowband data services, at currently acceptable quality levels, to customers of the public switched network and to private line users. Because incumbent local exchange carriers may choose to construct network facilities capable of providing services that require higher transmission speeds ("broadband" services), it is also necessary that a cost proxy model be able to model a network capable of providing these services if the model is to be used for the purpose of setting prices for unbundled network elements.

1.3 Consistency with Independent Evidence

It may be possible to obtain independent estimates of the costs of some network elements as a check on the validity of model estimates. For example, it may be feasible to compare estimates of loop costs with competitive bids for installing loops or the costs that cable networks incur in installing similar networks. Econometric studies might also provide a check on model results.

1.4 Potential for Independent Evaluation

The algorithms in a proxy model should be clearly identified and explained so they can be independently evaluated by state or federal regulators. It must be recognized, however, that this criterion may be in partial conflict with the overriding goal of obtaining accurate cost estimates. For example, a model that utilized only publicly available information would allow full independent evaluation, but might be less accurate than a model that used proprietary information (such as vendor pricing data).

1.5 Flexibility

Some jurisdictions may possess detailed information about important model inputs (such as discount prices offered by switch vendors) that model designers could only estimate. In addition, these jurisdictions may possess detailed information on local conditions, such as zoning restrictions and labor rates, that they may wish to add as inputs to a model. As a general rule, cost proxy models should permit parties to utilize such information where available.

2. UNDERLYING STRUCTURE OF COMPUTER-BASED COST PROXY MODELS

An economic cost proxy model for estimating the cost of network elements starts with an engineering model of the physical local exchange network, and then makes a detailed set of assumptions about input prices and other factors. Such models estimate the total monthly cost for each network element. This section examines both model design and the use of variable input factors for network investment, capital expenses, operating expenses, and common costs.

2.1 Preliminary Modeling Issues

2.1.1 Existing Wire Center Approach

Each of the models submitted to the FCC for evaluation was based on an assumption that wire centers will be placed at the incumbent LEC's current wire center locations. Subject to this constraint, all remaining network facilities are assumed to be provided using the most efficient technology currently in use. The constraint to use existing wire center locations is not fully consistent with a forward looking cost methodology, and it should be recognized that over time, an existing wire center model may become less representative of actual conditions faced by new entrants and incumbents. For example, after existing wire center locations were chosen by incumbent LECs, larger capacity switches and fiber/digital loop carrier technologies became available. Both of these factors have significantly altered the fundamental trade-off between switching and transmission in the design of an optimal communications network. Because of ongoing advances in technology, facilities-based new entrants and incumbent LECs may in the future choose a much different network topology that will result in different forward looking costs than today's network. A closely related issue is whether the placement of remote switching units should be restricted to existing wire center locations, and if the models should assume that every wire center includes a (host or remote) switch. Similarly, in the future, wireless technologies may be capable of providing narrowband telecommunication services at a lower cost than wireline technologies.

2.1.2 Specification of Demand

An accurate estimate of the cost of serving a wire center or a serving area within a wire center depends on a reliable forecast of customer demand patterns within the area, and the number of residential and business lines. Proxy models rely on census data to determine residential demand. However, because census data do not report the number of business lines,[11] model designers must use indirect methods to estimate business demand. The potential for error in estimating business and residential demand creates certain difficulties. First, as noted below, fill factors or utilization rates may be expected to vary between business and residential lines.[12] Second, loop lengths are typically shorter for business lines than for residential lines. Thus, unless the differences in costs associated with different fill factors for business and residential areas happen to offset exactly the differences in costs associated with differences in loop lengths, the cost of serving an area will depend on the ratio of business to residential lines. An understanding of the magnitude of these competing effects, however, requires an accurate estimate of the number of business and residential lines in a particular area.[13]

The HAI model and the FCC synthesis model incorporate access line demand data from the Operating Data Reports, ARMIS 43-08, submitted to the FCC annually by all Tier 1 LECs.[14] These models incorporate data on the number of: 1) residential access lines, both analog and digital; 2) business access lines, which include analog single lines and multi-line analog and digital lines, PBX trunks, Centrex trunks, hotel and motel long-distance trunks, and multi-line semi-public lines; and 3) special access lines. The number of residential lines in each Census block is computed by multiplying the number of households in a block by the ratio of total residential lines, as reported by ARMIS, to the total number of households in a study area. The number of business lines in a wire center is determined by multiplying the number of employees, as reported by Dun and Bradstreet, by the ratio of business lines to employees, as determined from ARMIS data. Some refinements to this process have been made that take account of the different demands for telephone use per employee. For example, service industry demand for telephone service is most likely greater than demand in the manufacturing sector.

2.2 Loop Plant

The largest portion of a network's investment consists of its investment in loop plant. It is therefore vitally important that models estimate accurately the cost of loop plant sufficient to satisfy demand. "Loop plant" consists of all network facilities, including wires, telephone poles or conduits, drops, etc., connecting the end office switch and customers' premises.

All cost proxy models include assumptions regarding feeder and distribution utilization rates (also called "fill factors"). In each model, lower utilization rates increase total loop investment because the increase in capacity associated with lower fill factors increases the amount of loop plant used to deliver telecommunication services. Thus, the choice of fill factor can have a significant effect on total cost. While all models allow user inputs for these quantities, it is not obvious what levels should be used as inputs. In a well-engineered network, it is necessary to include unused capacity when constructing loop plant to reduce the likelihood of outages in the case of breakages and to account for growth in demand. Furthermore, optimal fill factors should vary over the service life of the plant, increasing as demand grows until more plant is put into service.

Fill factors may also differ between business and residential markets. In residential markets, LECs traditionally place multiple wire pairs per home in order to be able to provide a second or third line to premises without incurring construction costs. Thus, fill factors that are less than 50 percent may be reasonable for residential markets. In business-dominated wire centers, the rate of utilization depends on the proportion of businesses using Centrex service rather than PBX terminal equipment, because PBXs serve to concentrate traffic between the customer and the central office. Customers using PBX equipment therefore require fewer lines than customers using Centrex service. Depending on the relative use of Centrex to PBX equipment, and LECs' plans for marketing Centrex services, business fill rates could be either lower or higher than residential fill rates.

The forward looking cost of installing loop plant includes both the cost of cable and the cost of building or obtaining access to structures that support the loop plant. With respect to cable investments, all three models use default input prices to estimate the cost of loop plant, but allow users to specify different input prices. Structures for cable plant consist of aerial, buried, and underground (i.e., cable in conduit) facilities, and the plant mix assumptions used by a proxy model can have a significant effect on estimated model costs. A crucial variable is the proportion of plant that is installed in new developments (where installation costs are relatively low) to plant installed for existing business and residential users. Different assumptions about the sharing of structure costs can also have a significant effect on estimated model costs.

One issue that has been raised with regard to forward looking cost studies generally is the treatment of existing sunk investments in structure facilities. While the use of existing structure investments in a forward looking cost model would superficially appear to be related to the fixed wire center assumption that most models have adopted, there are important reasons for rejecting the use of embedded costs for structure investments. For example, the deployment of feeder plant depends critically on the trade-offs in the costs of cable and electronics, which can be accurately described only in a fully forward looking context.

2.3 Switching Investment

After determining the number of lines assigned to a wire center, a proxy model must determine the number and size of the switches to be placed in these wire centers. The HAI model and the FCC synthesis model determine the investment in switches and interoffice transport based on the number of lines and DEMs, along with Bellcore assumptions on busy hour call attempts. These models use data from a McGraw-Hill study of the central office equipment market to derive average per-line prices for switching investment, including separate costs for the buildings, land, and other inputs to determine investment in switching. Since switch vendors typically grant carriers substantial discounts when selling switches, and require carriers to sign nondisclosure covenants that they will keep confidential the actual prices for which switches are sold, proxy models must rely on indirect evidence about the magnitude of such discounts, which can be expected to vary with the size of the purchasing carrier.

Another important issue in the modeling of switching costs is the ratio of traffic-sensitive to non-traffic sensitive cost in a switch. This ratio may be specific to the particular switches designed by different vendors. If the non-traffic sensitive costs are not constant across all switches, one would expect, since switches depreciate relatively quickly, that cost-minimizing carriers would install switches whose costs are largely traffic or non-traffic sensitive depending on the type of traffic that will be switched in an area. For example, in an area that switches a large amount of traffic with long holding times, it may be cost minimizing to install a switch whose costs are largely non-traffic sensitive.

2.4 Expenses

Cost proxy models are deisgned to produce an estimate of the annual or monthly cost of producing a set of services, including local exchange and access to intra- or inter-state toll services. Annualized cost consists of the sum of the return on equity, taxes, interest, depreciation, network operations and support expense, customer operations, and corporate overhead. The expense side of a model can have a significant effect on the final cost estimate.

2.4.1 Capital Expenses

Capital expenses are computed as the sum of a return on investment, taxes, and depreciation. In the HAI model, the return on investment is equal to the net investment base (gross investment minus accumulated depreciation) multiplied by a rate of return equal to a weighted average of the cost of equity and the cost of debt, with weights equal to the corresponding percentages of equity and debt in total investment. Taxes in the model are equal to the product of the net investment base, the percentage return on equity, the percentage share of equity, and a "tax gross up" factor determined by the following equation:

$$Taxes = \%Equity \times \%Return\ on\ Equity \times Investment\ Base \times \frac{Composite\ Tax\ Rate}{(1 - Composite\ Tax\ Rate)}.$$

For each category of plant, the capital cost is computed for each year of the economic life of the plant and the resulting stream of returns is "levelized" through a net present value calculation to give a constant annual cost of capital for that category of investment.[15] Aggregate capital costs are then computed as the sum of the capital costs for each category of plant.

The second component of a capital expense computation is a model's choice of depreciation rates. Since higher levels of depreciation lead to lower levels of investment base, and consequently lower annual expenses associated with return on investment and income taxes, changes in annual capital costs caused by changes in depreciation rates will automatically be mitigated to some extent by offsetting changes in return and taxes.

Depreciation schedules specified in a forward looking proxy model should be based on forward looking costing principles and should reflect projected economic lives of investments rather than physical plant lives. For the reasons described above in Section 2.2, the reported plant lives for loop-plant structures, such as conduit, manholes, and poles, are particularly important. Because of the relatively large investment needed to construct such facilities, inaccurate estimation of the expected economic lives of such facilities may result in a significant under- or overestimation of the forward looking costs of these facilities.

2.4.2 Operating Expenses

All proxy models use annual cost factors to calculate non-capital-related expenses. An annual cost factor is the ratio of expense booked to a specific account and the gross investment booked to the same account. Typically, the expense associated with investment is the product of the model-generated investment and the associated annual cost factor. Annual cost factors are used by models, as well as by companies in individual cost studies, because methods for developing forward looking expenses are complex and contentious.

2.4.3 Joint and Common Costs

If proxy models are used to estimate forward looking economic costs, the question of joint and common costs must be addressed. In the case of unbundled network element pricing, costs that are common to a set of network elements can be allocated among the individual elements in that set. For example, shared maintenance facilities could be allocated to the elements that benefit from those facilities. Common costs also include costs incurred by the firm's operations as a whole. Given these joint and common costs, setting prices for individual network elements based on forward looking incremental costs alone would not recover the full forward looking cost of the network. Consequently, in order to recover the full forward looking cost, a reasonable measure of joint and common costs should be included in the prices for interconnection and unbundled network elements.

3. OVERVIEW OF THE HYBRID COST PROXY MODEL[16]

The HCPM consists of two independent modules: a customer location module and a loop design module. The customer location module first groups individual geographic locations of telephone customers into clusters, based on engineering considerations. Next, the customer location module determines a grid and microgrid overlay for each cluster, and places each customer location into the correct microgrid cell. The loop design module determines the total investment required for an optimal distribution and feeder network by building loop plant to the designated customer locations represented by populated microgrid cells. The number of microgrids in a grid can vary from 4 to 2500. When used with a source of geocoded customer locations and a maximum copper reach of 18,000 feet, a uniform microgrid size of 360 feet can be maintained. All customer locations can therefore be determined with an error of not more than several hundred feet. All modules are written in high-level programming languages, and compiled versions can be supported on a number of computing environments. In the following sections, a more detailed description of each of the modules is presented.

3.1 The Customer Location Module

This section describes a method of modeling customer location based on cluster analysis. This approach is designed to accept as input a set of geocoded locations for every customer. It then performs a "rasterization" procedure that assigns customers to small microgrid cells.[17] A cluster algorithm then groups the set of raster cells into natural clusters. Finally, a square grid is constructed on top of every cluster, and all customer locations in the cluster are assigned to a microgrid cell for further processing by the loop design module. The cluster module can also accept Census block-level data as an input. In this case, every block that is larger than a raster cell is broken up into smaller blocks, each no larger than a raster cell, and the population of the original block is distributed uniformly among the new blocks.

One of the primary tasks faced by the HCPM is to identify clusters of customer locations. Each customer in a particular cluster, or serving area, will then be connected to the feeder system through a single interface, the serving area interface or SAI.

The clustering task is difficult because both engineering constraints and the general pattern of customer locations must be considered. There are two main engineering constraints. First, a serving area is limited to a certain number of lines by the capacity of a remote terminal. Second, a serving area is limited to certain geographic dimensions by current technology, because as distance increases beyond a critical value, service quality is degraded.

Given the engineering constraints, one could create feasible serving areas by simply placing a grid containing cells of an appropriate dimension over the entire wire center. For this to be a cost-effective approach, however, customers would have to be located in a relatively uniform pattern across the entire wire center. But, people do not tend to live that way. They tend to live clumped together in towns and communities. This tendency creates areas of varying population density throughout the wire center. Under these conditions, a gridding approach may divide a natural grouping of customers into different serving areas when a single serving area would be more cost-effective.

The objective of a clustering algorithm is to create the proper number of feasible serving areas. Unfortunately, this is not a well-defined objective, because of the existence of both fixed and variable costs associated with each additional serving area. A fixed cost gives a clear incentive to create a small number of large clusters, rather than a larger number of smaller clusters. On the other hand, with fewer clusters, the average distance of a customer from a central point of a cluster, and consequently the variable costs associated with cable and structures, will be larger. In moderate- to high-density areas, it is not clear, *a priori*, what number of clusters will embody an optimal trade-off between these fixed and variable costs. However, in low-density rural areas, it is likely that fixed costs will be the most significant cost driver. Consequently, a clustering algorithm that generates the smallest number of clusters should perform well in rural areas.

While statisticians have studied a wide variety of clustering algorithms,[18] there are two basic approaches to clustering: the agglomerative or bottom-up approach, and the divisive or top-down approach. Each approach starts with an initial state where each customer location belongs to a particular cluster. The initial state is then improved upon according to some rule until no more improvements can be made. The clustering module for the HCPM contains three alternative algorithms that represent implementations of both of the above approaches.

In the initial state for the default divisive approach, each location belongs to a single parent cluster. This initial state is improved upon by dividing the parent cluster into a new parent cluster and a child cluster. This step increases the total number of clusters by one. The improvement step is repeated until every cluster is feasible from an engineering standpoint.[19] A child cluster is created from the parent cluster by choosing the customer location furthest from the parent's line-weighted center as an initial child cluster member. Then, customer locations that are closer to the center of the child cluster than they are to the center of the parent cluster are reassigned in an iterative manner, recalculating the cluster centers at each step. Customer locations are added to the child cluster until it is full, i.e., until no more locations can be added without violating engineering constraints.

Alternatively, in the initial state for all agglomerative approaches, each location belongs to its own unique cluster. This initial state is improved upon by merging the two closest clusters together, reducing the total number of clusters by one. The improvement step is repeated until merging is no longer feasible from an engineering standpoint. The clustering module contains two agglomerative algorithms that differ only in the way in which they measure the distance between clusters. In the standard agglomerative algorithm, distance is measured from the line-weighted center of one cluster to the line-weighted center of another. In the nearest-neighbor algorithm, distance is measured from the two customer locations, one in each cluster, that are closest together.

Once one of the clustering algorithms has been run, it has been found that the initial result can generally be improved by reassigning certain customer locations to different clusters. The clustering module contains two optimization routines that perform these reassignments. As a final step, the cluster module computes potential locations for either one SAI or pair of SAIs. The location for a single SAI is simply the line-weighted center of the cluster. The locations for a pair of SAIs are determined by dividing each cluster into a parent and child. The module then reports the line-weighted centers of the parent and child as potential locations of a pair of SAIs. The actual number of SAIs used is determined within the loop design module.

Output from the cluster module is illustrated in Figure 1. Each cluster, which represents a single feasible serving area, is represented by a set of customer locations connected to the cluster center by a straight line.

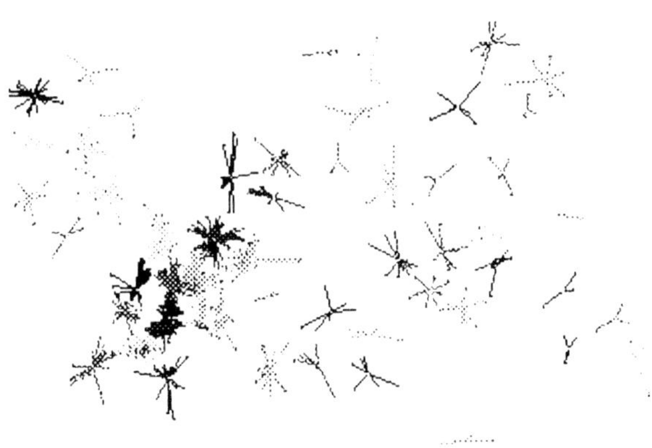

Figure 1: Clusters for the Wire Center GNSNCOMA

The final step in the customer location module is to convert the data from the cluster algorithm into a form that can be utilized by the loop design module. For wire centers that are sufficiently small, it would be possible to build plant to the exact customer locations determined by the geocoded data as processed by the cluster module. For larger wire centers, which may have 20,000 or more individual customer locations, it would be extremely time consuming to build distribution plant directly to each individual location. As in the clustering module, an acceptable compromise between absolute accuracy and reasonable computing time can be achieved by defining a grid on top of every cluster and assigning individual customer locations to microgrid cells within the grid. Customers within each microgrid cell are assumed to be uniformly distributed within the cell. If multiple customer locations fall in a single microgrid cell, the cell is divided into lots, as explained in the next section. Loop plant can therefore be designed specifically to reach only populated microgrid cells and the individual customer lots within each microgrid. For large wire centers, the number of populated microgrid cells will be much less than the number of customer locations, even when a relatively small microgrid size is specified. Therefore, with this approach it is possible to place an upper bound on computing time, while simultaneously placing a bound on the maximum possible error in locating any individual customer.

3.2 Loop Design Algorithms

The customer location module will report, for each cluster, the bottom-left and top-right coordinates of the overlay grid, the number of microgrid cells, the number of lines associated with each cell, and coordinates for the possible locations for the SAIs that could serve the cluster. Given the inputs from the customer location module, the logic of the loop design module is straightforward. Within every microgrid with non-zero population, customers are assumed to be distributed uniformly. Each populated microgrid is divided into a sufficient number of equal-sized lots and distribution cable is placed to connect every lot. These populated microgrids are then connected to the nearest concentration point (SAI) by further distribution plant. During this phase of the loop design algorithms, the heterogeneity of microgrid populations, and the locations of populated microgrids are explicitly accounted for. Finally, the SAIs are connected to the central office by feeder cable. On every link of the feeder and distribution network, the number of copper or fiber lines and the corresponding number of cables are explicitly computed. The total cost of the loop plant is the sum of the costs incurred on every link.

Distribution consists of all outside plant between a customer location and the nearest SAI. Distribution plant consists of backbone and branching cable, where branching cable is closer to the customer location. Feeder consists of all outside plant connecting the central office main distribution frame, or fiber distribution frame, to each of the SAIs. Feeder cable consists of main feeder, subfeeder and sub-subfeeder routes.

3.2.1 Distribution Plant Design

The distribution portion of the loop design module determines the cost of distribution plant for each cluster in isolation (ignoring information from all neighboring clusters). The algorithms described in the following sections compute the cost of all plant that is required to connect each customer within the cluster to the nearest SAI.

Each microgrid is divided into lots based on microgrid population. Distribution cable is built to touch every lot in the cell. Backbone cables, which connect cells to the SAI, are assumed to run horizontally and branching cables within a cell are assumed to run vertically along the grid lines of the cell. Branching cable is assumed to follow every other vertical lot boundary. Drop cable is designed to serve groups of four properties whenever possible.

Two algorithms are used to determine the correct amount of cable and structures that are necessary to connect each microgrid to the nearest SAI. In a fully optimizing mode, the model computes the cost of distribution plant for all clusters using both approaches, and selects the approach giving the lower cost.[20]

The first algorithm is most appropriate in densely populated clusters, in which the proportion of populated microgrids to total microgrids is relatively large. Backbone cables run along every other cell boundary and connect with the distribution plant within a cell at various points, as illustrated in Figure 2. The second algorithm generally gives a more efficient distribution network for clusters with a lower population density, where the number of populated microgrids is smaller. In this case, the construction of an optimal distribution network within a cluster is closely related to the problem of constructing an optimal feeder network for the entire wire center, and the same algorithm is used to provide a solution.

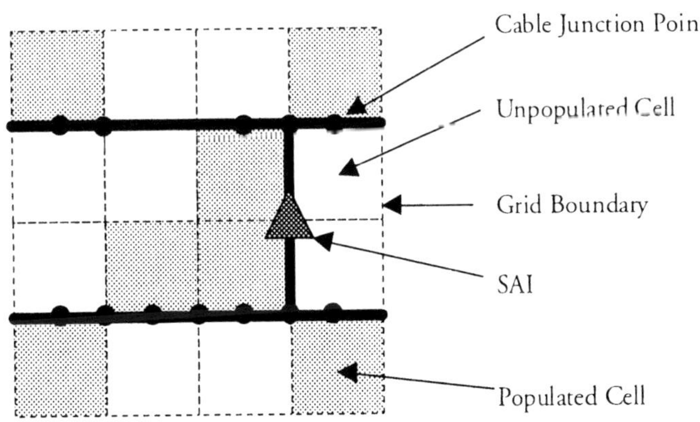

Figure 2: Connection of Cells to the Closest SAI

3.2.2 Feeder Plant Design

In previous versions of the HCPM and in other models of the local exchange, feeder plant was deployed in a "pine tree" network in which four main feeder routes emanate from the central office along east-west and north-south routes. Subfeeder routes perpendicular to the main feeder routes were then used to bring the feeder system closer to individual SAIs. This design proved to be highly efficient in terms of creating opportunities for the sharing of structure costs among feeder cables serving different SAIs. Lower structure costs made possible by increased sharing, however, came at the expense of longer feeder routes and correspondingly higher cable costs. In order to balance these two opposing tendencies, the HCPM examined a large number of possible feeder systems having different number of subfeeder routes, and chose the configuration giving the lowest cost.

The current version of HCPM uses a variant of an explicit optimization algorithm, discovered by Prim in 1957, to determine the trade-off between structures and cable costs. [21] This algorithm is based on some well known mathematical principles of network design based on techniques of discrete mathematics and graph theory. An abstract network consists of a single "supplier" node, a set of customer nodes, a cost function specifying the cost of connecting any two nodes, and a set of pair-wise traffic demands between any two nodes. In the application of the Prim algorithm to the feeder network, the supplier node is the central office for a given wire center, and the customer nodes are the remote terminals, or SAIs, that define the interface points between the feeder and distribution portions of the network. The algorithm can also be applied to determine cable routes for distribution networks within a cluster, as noted previously. In this case, the supplier node is an SAI within a cluster, and the customer nodes represent individual subscriber locations that are to be connected to that SAI.

In both the feeder and distribution portions of the network, the objective of the telecommunications engineer is to minimize the cost of connecting each customer node to the supplier node. While in general this is an extremely difficult problem to solve, there are several special cases in which efficient algorithms exist that define a fully optimal network solution. One special case of interest is the construction of a "minimum-distance spanning tree network" in which the sole objective is to minimize the aggregate length of communications links within the network. Such a network would be approximately optimal when traffic demands are sufficiently low that the actual cost of each link in the network is largely determined by the cost of structures (which depend only on distance).

A minimum-distance network can be constructed using the Prim algorithm in the following way. Beginning with a network consisting only of the supplier, find the nearest customer node that is not yet attached to the network and attach it. The network then consists of the supplier and one customer. The algorithm proceeds step-by-step in attaching customer nodes to the network on the basis of minimum distance. At any point in the algorithm, it chooses from the set of all nodes that have not yet been attached, a node that is closest to some node in the existing network. Prim demonstrated that this simple algorithm necessarily leads to a minimum-distance network.[22] In other words, when the algorithm is completed, there is no possible way to reconfigure the network so as to lower the aggregate distance of all links in the network.

As long as structure costs are significantly larger than cable costs, the original Prim algorithm provides a satisfactory solution. In the design of both feeder and distribution networks, however, a minimum-distance spanning tree network is not generally optimal.[23] While it minimizes the total distance of all links in the network, it does not minimize the distance between any particular node and the supplier. For example, if there is significant demand at a particular remote terminal for access lines to the central office, then the actual cost on the network between this node and the central office may need to be accounted for in the minimum-distance optimization problem. There are no simple algorithms that can be applied to give a completely optimal solution to the general problem. (A "star" network, which minimizes the cost of connecting each node to the central office, would not be optimal because it does not take advantage of potential sharing of structure costs in the network.) However, it is possible to modify the Prim algorithm to take account of the effects of traffic in the network on total cost, and generally to improve the performance of the algorithm computationally.

The HCPM makes two fundamental modifications to the Prim. First, the model creates a set of potential junction points that follow the location of the main east-west and north-south feeder routes in previous versions of the model. The algorithm permits, but does not require, these potential junction points to be used in creating the feeder network. Junction points create additional opportunities for the sharing of structure costs, and in some circumstances they can also reduce the distance between a terminal node and the central office.

The second modification of the Prim algorithm is in the rule used to attach new nodes to the network. Rather than minimizing the distance from an unattached node to the existing network, the algorithm minimizes the total cost of attaching an unattached node, and of constructing all of the lines required to carry traffic from that node back to the central office. A heuristic description of the algorithm is given below.[24]

Step 1: Begin with a network consisting of the central office alone.

Step 2: From the set of unattached nodes, find the node for which the average cost per line, including the cost of structures, cable and terminal electronics, is lowest for connecting that node to the existing network.

.

.

.

Step k: At any step in the algorithm, choose from the set of unattached nodes the node for which the average cost is lowest for connecting that node to the existing network. This cost will depend on the particular node in the existing network that is selected for connection, and will include the structure cost of connecting to that node as well as the incremental cable cost of carrying traffic from the new node to the central office along the currently existing network.

The algorithm terminates when all nodes have been attached. Unlike the Prim algorithm, it may be possible to lower total network cost by rearranging some of the links in the network after the algorithm terminates. However, the general optimization problem is computationally intractable, while the above algorithm is highly efficient. FCC staff have found that this modified Prim algorithm leads to lower feeder cost estimates than the unmodified Prim algorithm and the more traditional pine tree feeder route designs. Furthermore, the modified Prim algorithm provides a good approximation of the way in which real world engineers are likely to design the feeder network because the network grows naturally from the central office, by adding new nodes on the basis of minimum attachment cost as new communities are established.

In the construction of the feeder network, the HCPM allows the user to determine whether to use airline distances between nodes or rectilinear distances. The model also applies a road factor to all distance computations in the feeder network. This road factor is intended to convert distances determined by the distance function into actual route distances, which must account for the existing road network and other terrain factors. In principle, the road factor should be determined empirically for each region of the country by comparing actual feeder route distance to model distance computation. Clearly, a different factor should be applied to airline distance than to rectilinear distance computations. Some empirical evidence on the appropriate value for the road factor is given in Love et al. (1988).

Figure 3 illustrates the operation of the Prim algorithm and the HCPM modifications to it. A set of 15 locations representing one wire center (source) and 14 customer nodes were randomly generated. Each customer node was assigned a demand of one unit. A highly simplified cost function of the form *Cost per link* = $(P_S + T * P_C) * distance$, where P_S represents the price per foot of structures, P_C represents the price per foot of cable, and T represents the traffic carried on the link, was examined. In Figure 3a, we set $P_S = 1$ and $P_C = 0$. Since the only cost is the distance-related cost of structures, this example illustrates the outcome of the unmodified Prim algorithm. In Figure 3b, we set $P_S = 0$ and $P_C = 1$. In this case, the algorithm seeks to minimize the distance of every node from the central office, resulting in a "star" network. In Figure 3c, we set $P_S = 1$ and $P_C = 1$. This example illustrates a balanced network that would be constructed if cable costs and structure costs are both significant cost drivers. Figure 3d illustrates a balanced network assuming rectilinear distances rather than airline distance. Figures 3e and 3f represent the effect of creating possible junction points along the north-south and east-west axes emanating from the central office.

Figure 4 illustrates the feeder network constructed by FEEDDIST for a wire center in Montana. Solid circles represent SAIs, open circles represent junction nodes, and diamonds represent the center points of all populated microgrid cells.

Based on the feeder and distribution algorithms, the HCPM uses input data for the cost of structure, cable and electronics, as well as other engineering inputs, to determine a level of forward looking total investment in loop plant. Other model components of the synthesis model compute comparable investments in switching and transport plant. An expense module then converts these investment costs into annual and monthly cost estimates following the general procedures outlined in the previous section.

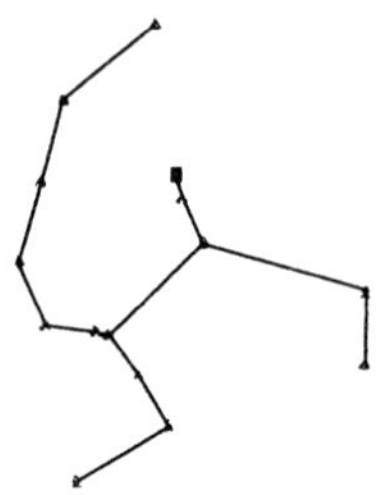

Figure 3a: Minimum Structure Distance Network

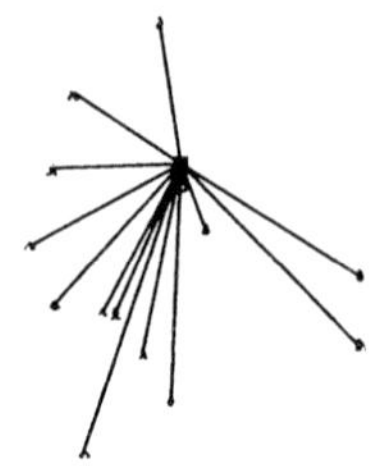

Figure 3b: Star Network

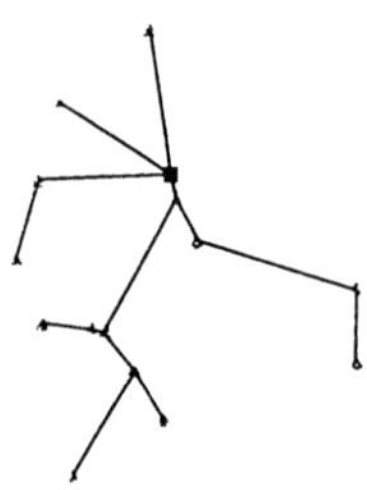

Figure 3c: Balanced Network

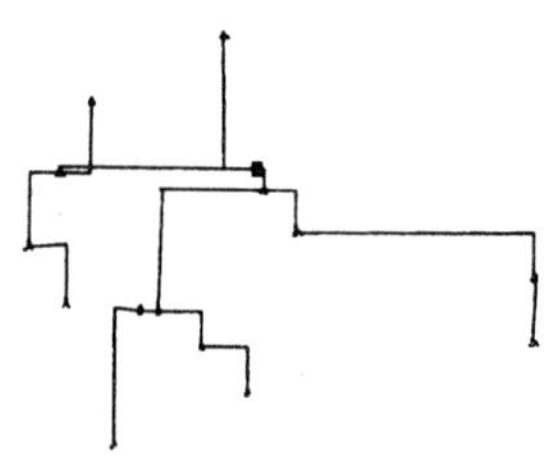

Figure 3d: Balanced Network with Rectilinear Distance

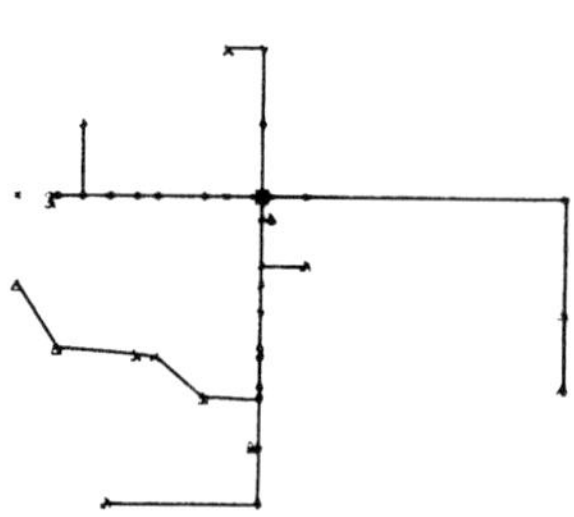

Figure 3e: Balanced Network with Junction Nodes and Airline Distance

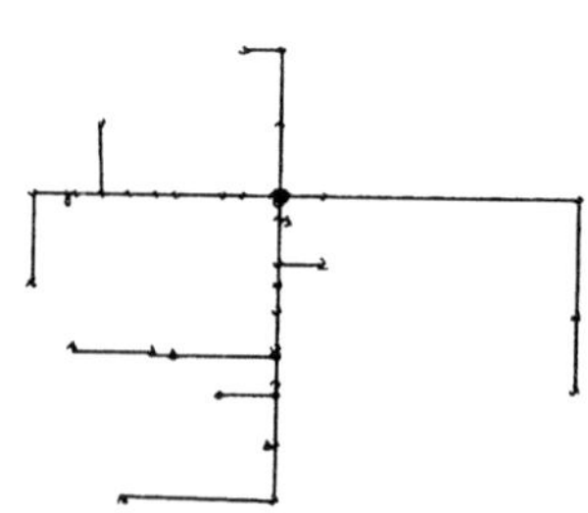

Figure 3f: Balanced Network with Junction Nodes and Rectilinear Distance

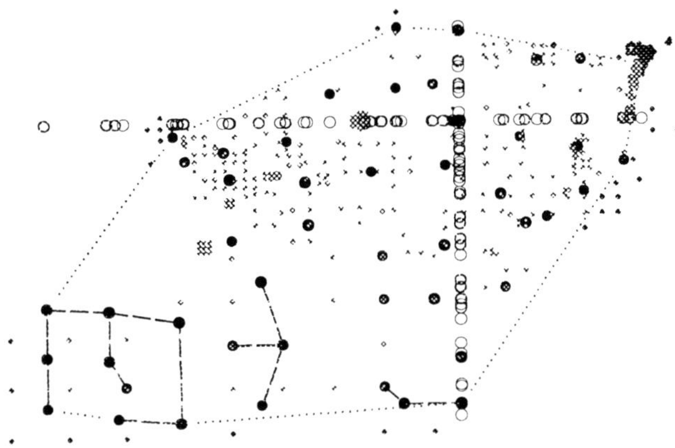

Figure 4: Feeder Network for the Wire Center ABSRMTXC

NOTES

1 The opinions expressed in this paper are those of the author and do not necessarily reflect the views of the Federal Communications Commission or any of its Commissioners or other staff.

2 47 U.S.C. §§ 151 *et seq.*

3 *In the Matter of Federal-State Joint Board on Universal Service*, CC Docket No. 96-45.

4 *In the Matter of Access Charge Reform*, Notice of Proposed Rulemaking, FCC No. 96-488, CC Docket No. 96-262 (rel. Dec. 24, 1996).

5 *Implementation of the Local Competition Provisions of the Telecommunications Act of 1996*, CC Docket No. 96-98, FCC 96-325 (released August 8, 1996), Order on Reconsideration *Implementation of the Local Competition Provisions of the Telecommunications Act of 1996*, CC Docket No. 96-98, 11 FCC Rcd 13042 (1996), *petition for review pending sub nom. and partial stay granted, Iowa Utilities Board v. FCC*, No. 96-3321 and consolidated cases (8th Cir., Oct. 15, 1996), *partial stay lifted in part, Iowa Utilities Board et al. v. FCC*, No. 96-3321 and consolidated cases (8th Cir., Nov.1, 1996).

6 47 U.S.C. §§ 251(c)(2)-(4), 252(d)(1).

7 47 U.S.C. § 254.

8 In providing interstate long-distance service, interexchange carriers use local telephone companies' facilities to originate and terminate calls. The use of local telephone company facilities to originate and terminate long-distance calls is referred to as access service. LECs receive access charges for providing interexchange carriers with access to the local exchange carrier's customers.

9 CC Docket 96-45 and CC Docket 97-160.

10 *Local Competition Order*, para. 706. The Commission adopted a forward looking incremental cost methodology known as total element long-run incremental cost (TELRIC) for use in setting interconnection and unbundled network element prices. *Id.* at para. 672. This provision was stayed by the Eighth Circuit Court of Appeals and later reversed by the United States Supreme Court.

11 Dun and Bradstreet report data on the number of daytime employees by CBG.

[12] Fill factors or utilization rates of loop plant are the percentage of a loop plant's capacity that is used in the network. Utilization rates are necessarily less than 100 percent so that capacity is available for growth or, in the event of breakage, to avoid outages. Lower utilization rates mean that carriers deploy more unused capacity, which increases the cost of loop plant.

[13] Alternatively, the differences in fill factors and loop lengths, and thus the cost of providing service to a particular area, may depend upon the density of customers, not the type of customers, in a particular area.

[14] Tier 1 local exchange carriers are companies having annual revenues from regulated telecommunications operations of $100 million or more. *Commission Requirements for Cost Support Material To Be Filed with 1990 Annual Access Tariffs, Order,* 5 FCC Rcd 1364 (Com. Car. Bur. 1990).

[15] Economic lives are specified for each of thirteen categories of plant.

[16] This section contains a condensed version of the HCPM model documentation, which is available on the internet at http://www.fcc.gov/ccb/apd/hcpm

[17] The size of a microgrid cell is specified by the user. The recommended size is a square with sides equal to 500 feet, but smaller cells can be chosen at the expense of increased computing time.

[18] For information about different clustering methods see: Everitt, Brian S. (1993).

[19] This and other stopping rules in the divisive algorithm can be adjusted to increase performance.

[20] In order to generate approximately optimal results using less computing time, the user has the option of computing distribution costs using both approaches only for the lowest-density grids.

[21] See Prim, R.C. (1957) for a description of an efficient algorithm for computing minimum distance networks. A computed coded version of the Prim algorithm, and some extensions, is contained in Gower, J.C. and G.J.S. Ross (1969).

[22] In fact, one can start with any initial node and be assured of reaching a minimum-distance network using the algorithm.

[23] The unmodified Prim algorithm is, however, used to connect multiple SAIs within a grid and for connecting drop terminal nodes to SAIs. In the mathematical literature on network design, networks that allow for the creation of junction points are known as "Steiner networks." [See Sharkey (1995)]. A Steiner network must always have a cost at least as low as a minimum-distance spanning tree network.

[24] This modification is due to Jeff Prisbrey.

REFERENCES

Atkinson, J. et al. 1997. *The Use of Computer Models for Estimating Forward-Looking Economic Costs: A Staff Analysis.* Federal Communications Commission, DA 97-56, released January 9, 1997.

Bush, C.A. et al. 1998. "The Hybrid Cost Proxy Model: Customer Location and Loop Design Modules," available from FCC internet site at http://www.fcc.gov/ccb/apd/hcpm/.

Everitt, Brian S. 1993. *Cluster Analysis,* Third Edition, London: Arnold.

Gower, J.C. and G.J.S. Ross. 1969. "Minimum Spanning Trees and Single Linkage Cluster Analysis." *Applied Statistics,* 18, 54-64.

Love, R.F., J.G. Morris and G.O. Wesolowsky. 1988. "Mathematical Models of Travel Distances." *Facilities Location: Models and Methods.* Amsterdam: North Holland.

Prim, R.C. 1957. "Shortest Connection Networks and Some Generalizations," *Bell System Technical Journal,* 36, 1389-1401.

Sharkey, W.W. 1995. "Network Models in Economics." Chapter 9 in M.O. Ball et al., eds., *Network Routing: Handbooks in OR and MS.* Vol. 8. Amsterdam: North Holland.

7 Forward Looking Telecommunications Cost Models

Timothy J. Tardiff
National Energy Regulatory Commission

William Sharkey's paper provides a useful overview of the mechanics, processes, and environment in which cost studies are being performed in support of prices for unbundled network elements and determining universal service support. His discussion explicitly or implicitly raises several issues that go to the heart of the telecommunications industry's regulation:

- The enormous task regulators face in determining costs and setting prices
- The importance of understanding the intent of regulatory actions and how outcomes can differ from the intended results
- Whether the stated objectives can be obtained by prescribing outcomes or through a process that allows competition to produce its results.

1. FORWARD-LOOKING COSTS

Models developed to produce the forward-looking costs of local exchange services are immensely complicated for a number of reasons. First, in their intent to capture the costs of a complex network in a single computer model, these models attempt to represent a large number of day-to-day engineering design decisions in a simplified form. These actions, in turn, forced regulators to make sense of, and render judgment on, a number of contentious design issues. These include 1) how long can copper phone lines serving customers be, and still produce adequate levels of quality, 2) what type of electronics is most efficient with fiber optic facilities, and 3) how should customers be grouped together when designing the local distribution areas that determine the design and cost of telephone lines? These questions and others had to be answered in the long debate over how to develop a model platform (i.e., a representation of the local network).

Once a platform is selected, regulators must wrestle with the inputs: how much should local telephone companies pay for equipment, should they be sharing support structures (such as telephone poles) with other utilities, and when should they use poles or place wires underground? Again, there is considerable controversy and uncertainty regarding these inputs.

Finally, because telephone equipment tends to have long economic lives, cost models essentially become a long-term forecast of a pattern of prices. The mathematical formulas that convert up-front investments to monthly charges (based on return on investment, economic lives, and taxes) ask and answer the following question: what single price can the firm charge over the life of its investment so that it just recovers its capital and earns a reasonable return on its investment?

The consideration of these complications clearly leads to an appreciation of the hard work that regulators have undertaken in posing these questions. In fact, the daunting task of developing forward looking costs raises the issue of whether these questions are even answerable. In this regard, the theme of this conference and Professor Trigeoris' discussion of real options become germane. Professor Trigeorgis pointed out that in the real world, businesses must make decisions constantly and be willing to change decisions they made earlier. In contrast, forward looking cost models are implicitly built on numerous up-front decisions that remain unchanged for many years.

2. INTENT VERSUS OUTCOME

How a policy is implemented has a crucial impact on whether its objectives are met. For example, the FCC and other regulators have professed the entirely proper belief that the prices established by regulation neither favor nor disadvantage particular firms (or types of competitors). Whether this objective is attained depends on the delicate balance among the incumbents' retail prices, prices for resold services, prices for unbundled network elements, and the underlying costs for facilities-based entry. These prices, in turn, are influenced by how vigorously certain firms participate in the regulatory proceedings in which these prices are established.

Not surprisingly, there is a "squeaky wheel" phenomenon at work here. To illustrate this, at the beginning of 1998, there was a widespread belief that local exchange entry was proceeding at a disappointing rate, in part fueled by the laments of firms such as AT&T and MCI. Later in the year, reports by investment analysts such as Salomon Smith Barney[1] and Merrill Lynch[2] demonstrated that new firms were entering at a healthy pace, attracting considerable amounts of investment, and may in fact be ahead of the pace that firms such as MCI and Sprint had attained at a comparable point in the development of long-distance competition. Indeed, both AT&T, by acquiring Teleport and planning to acquire TCI, and the completion of the MCI WorldCom merger quicken the pace of local exchange competition.

Another example of how results can deviate from intent relates to the objective that prices should promote efficient investment and entry. Again, imbalances among various prices can frustrate this objective. For example, unduly favorable prices for resale services can dampen the incentives for facilities-based entry, which economists generally agree brings the largest benefits to consumers. A revealing illustration of this phenomenon is the existence of certain competitive local exchange carriers that target information service providers (ISPs). Because ISPs for the most part receive calls (e.g., from their subscribers accessing the Internet), but make few calls, their local exchange carriers can earn large amounts of revenue from charges imposed on the carriers of the ISP's subscribers for terminating traffic. Thus, the business strategy of these carriers has responded to anomalies in interconnection prices, rather than efficient market prices. Further, carriers exploiting this advantage argue strenuously to perpetuate it in regulatory proceedings.

3. MARKET OUTCOMES VERSUS MARKET PROCESSES

The introduction of forward looking cost models can also be viewed as a profound shift in the regulatory paradigm. In the early 1990s, the regulation of local exchange carriers shifted from cost-based to price-based, under the prevailing beliefs that: 1) limiting prices provided better incentives than prescribing costs and 2) management discretion, rather than regulatory fiat, better promotes economic efficiency. The prices subject to regulation, in turn, were set at prevailing rates, with mechanisms to update them annually based on changes in inflation and productivity.

In contrast, forward looking cost models resemble the old-style cost-based regulation with a forward-looking twist (in effect, a review of prudent investment before the fact). And rather than starting with current prices and letting management decisions and competitive outcomes dictate the course of future prices, the use of these models is an attempt to produce prices that would putatively prevail under competition. In fact, some forward looking cost models imply that an efficient carrier could produce service at roughly half the price that incumbents are charging today. This perspective raises the fundamental question of whether we should rely on models to produce results that some claim competition would produce, or, as in the case of long-distance competition and price caps, should we start with prices that are consistent with current prices and let the competitive process itself determine the outcome?

NOTES

[1] Salomon Smith Barney. May 6, 1998. *CLECs Surpass Bell in Net Business Line Additions for the First Time.*

[2] Merrill Lynch, September 1998. *Telecom Services – Local.*

Implications of Neglecting Real Options

8 An Institutional Perspective on Assessing Real Options Values in Telecommunications Cost Models

Barbara A. Cherry
Michigan State University

Abstract - Under section 251(c) of the Telecommunications Act of 1996, Congress imposed a duty on incumbent local exchange companies (ILECs) to provide unbundled network elements (UNEs) on a nondiscriminatory basis at just and reasonable rates. This statutory obligation can be viewed as granting an option to competitive local exchange companies to "wait to invest" in their own facilities, but its quantification for inclusion in UNE prices would be controversial. This paper shows that, from an institutional perspective, there is a sound analytical basis for guiding public policy decisions on this issue. More specifically, given the U.S. constitutional framework, which constrains government regulation, the consequences of overestimation as opposed to underestimation of ILECs' costs are dramatically different. As shown, given the uncertainty of the "true" option value, a regulatory policy based on a cost methodology that tends to overestimate rather than underestimate the option value is more consistent with Congressional policy favoring regulatory intervention that encourages the deployment of an advanced telecommunications infrastructure. Therefore, for purposes of determining prices for UNEs, policymakers should err on the side of overestimating the option value.

In response to the desire – arising from both technological developments and political forces – to increase reliance on competitive forces, Congress passed the Telecommunications Act of 1996. The new Act provides a revised framework for regulating the telecommunications industry. An important feature of this framework is the imposition of certain statutory obligations on incumbent local exchange companies (ILECs) governing their relationship with other telecommunications carriers (referred to here as competitive local exchange providers, or CLECs) that want to utilize ILEC facilities. Among these obligations is the duty under section 251(c) to provide unbundled network elements (UNEs) on a nondiscriminatory basis at just and reasonable rates.

During the conference on The New Investment Theory of Real Options and Its Implications for the Cost Models in Telecommunications, held on October 2, 1998 at Columbia University, many of the presentations were devoted to the issue of whether the ILEC's obligation to provide UNEs constitutes the grant of an option to CLECs. For example, Jerry Hausman stressed that the nature of the option granted to CLECs consists of the option to invest in their own facilities or to wait by purchasing access to ILECs' facilities. Under such circumstances in a world of uncertainty, there is a "reward to waiting" given to CLECs. Therefore, according to the investment theory of real options, the sunk costs of the ILECs should include a markup factor to reflect the full costs of their investment. In turn, the costs upon which the regulator relies in approving prices to be charged by ILECs for access to UNEs should include such a markup factor. Hausman claimed that as it is currently calculated, the total element long-run incremental cost (TELRIC) model used by the Federal Communications Commission (FCC) does not include the relevant markup factor. The solution, he suggested, is either: 1) to have CLECs enter into long-term contracts with ILECs that cover the life of the UNE investment, in which case there is no option and thus no need for a markup; or 2) to have agreements between CLECs and ILECs with a duration shorter than the life of the UNE, in which case there is an option and the TELRIC cost standard should be modified to include an appropriate markup factor.

There were numerous responses to such claims of an option. Interestingly, virtually all presenters agreed that a CLEC's ability to wait to invest is an option whose value should be included in the cost model utilized for determining UNE prices. However, there was disagreement as to the size of that value and the extent to which current cost methodology already reflects the option value. For example, William Lehr disagreed with Hausman's assessment that current prices based on TELRIC do not include the necessary markup factor to reflect the option value, claiming that Hausman has overstated the degree to which prices need to be adjusted. Nicholas Economides questioned the degree of uncertainty faced by ILECs regarding local loop investment and therefore, the significance of the level of the option value. And, the eminent William Baumol agreed that, under those circumstances where the ILEC obligation to invest is operative, TELRIC costs need to be modified to reflect the value of the "waiting to invest" option provided to CLECs.

A review of the various positions and insights of these accomplished economists makes it is clear that agreement on the quantification of option values to CLECs will not be easy. Such difficulty will then, of course, pose consternation for policymakers. In light of the lack of agreement among industry players and experts, on what basis should regulators ultimately determine UNE prices? From an overall public policy perspective, is it preferable for regulators to overestimate or underestimate the option value to be included in UNE prices?

The purpose of this paper is to show that, from an institutional perspective, there is a sound analytical basis for guiding the public policy decisions of regulators on this issue. More specifically, given the constitutional framework within which government regulation in the United States operates, the consequences of overestimating and underestimating ILECs costs are dramatically different. As will be shown, given uncertainty over the "true" option value, the consequences of a regulatory policy that adopts a cost methodology tending to overestimate rather than underestimate the option value is more consistent with Congressional policy favoring regulatory intervention that encourages the deployment of an advanced telecommunications infrastructure. Therefore, policymakers should err on the side of overestimating the option value.

1. INVESTMENT DECISIONS IN THE UNITED STATES FROM AN INSTITUTIONAL PERSPECTIVE

An industry's economic performance and private investment decisions are influenced by the institutional endowment of a nation (North, 1990). This endowment comprises five elements: 1) the nation's legislative and executive institutions, 2) its judicial institutions, 3) the customs and informal, but broadly accepted, norms that constrain the actions of individuals or institutions, 4) the character of contending social interests within a society and the balance among them, including ideology, and 5) the administrative capabilities of the nation (Levy & Spiller, 1996).

The special characteristics of telecommunications investments – economies of scale and scope, high asset specificity and non-redeployability, and a broad range of domestic users – make them highly vulnerable to expropriation by government. For this reason, a regulatory regime must provide sufficient constraints on arbitrary government power in order to be compatible with sustained private investment in telecommunications infrastructure. Levy and Spiller (1996) show that a wide range of regulatory regimes are suitable, as long as three complementary mechanisms restraining arbitrary administrative action are in place: 1) substantive restraints on the discretion of the regulator, 2) informal or formal constraints on changing the regulatory system, and 3) institutions that enforce the above formal, substantive or procedural constraints. In particular, they note that utility regulation is likely to be more credible and regulatory problems less severe when a nation's political system restrains executive and legislative discretion, and provides a strong judiciary to limit administrative discretion. The constraints on executive and legislative discretion include separation of powers among the branches of government, a written constitution limiting legislative and executive power, a legislative branch with multiple chambers, and checks and balances between legislative and executive powers. A strong judiciary frequently includes a body of administrative law, a tradition of upholding contracts and property rights, and an historical ability to act independently from other government branches.

The U.S. Constitution is an important element of the institutional endowment of the United States. It defines the structure of the federal government, enumerates the powers of the federal and state governments, and provides express limitations on government action. As Cherry and Wildman (1998) describe, the U.S. Constitution was designed to constrain the potential abuse of government power and creates a structure of government that provides the critical mechanisms identified by Levy and Spiller for achieving sustainable investment from the private telecommunications sector. Constitutional constraints are of two types: 1) indirect limitations on government power through structural design, and 2) direct limitations on government power, such as the Bill of Rights, which are judicially enforceable guarantees.

There are several aspects of structural design under the Constitution that constitute indirect limitations on government power. For example, the Constitution separates the power of the federal government into three branches - legislative, executive and judicial - with checks and balances among them. It also expressly enumerates certain powers to the federal government, while placing residual powers in state governments. Finally, the judiciary is established as an independent branch of government with authority to enforce constitutional constraints, through judicial review, on the actions of other branches of the federal government as well as state governments.

As for direct limitations on government power, the one most relevant here is the Takings Clause found in the Fifth Amendment of the Constitution. It applies directly to the federal government, providing in relevant part: "nor shall private property be taken for public use, without just compensation." It has also been held applicable to state governments by virtue of the Due Process Clause of the Fourteenth Amendment (Missouri Pacific Ry. v. Nebraska, 1896), which provides that "no person shall be . . . deprived of life, liberty or property, without due process of law . . . ."

Initially illegal takings were found only in the context of physical invasion of property, such as the exercise of eminent domain power. However, since Pennsylvania

Coal Co. v. Mahon (1922), unconstitutional regulatory takings have also been found with regard to government's exercise of its police power. This is because the purpose of the Takings Clause is "to bar Government from forcing some people alone to bear public burdens which, in all fairness and justice, should be borne by the public as a whole" (Armstrong v. United States, 1960, p. 49). Therefore, even if government exercises its power for the purpose of improving social welfare or efficiency, however defined, the Takings Clause limits the exercise of that power due to its effect on individuals. Depending upon the circumstances, an individual's remedy for an illegal taking is either compensation or invalidation of the government action.

In the public utility context, regulatory takings have been found when government regulation, such as rules related to utility ratemaking, constitutes a confiscation of a private utility's assets (Pierce, 1989; Madden 1989). This is because government regulation must provide the private utility and its investors with a reasonable opportunity to recover the costs of the business, including returns on investments comparable to those of enterprises with comparable risks (FPC v. Hope Natural Gas Co., 1944, p. 603).

Cherry and Wildman (1998) explain that both direct and indirect limitations on government power serve purposes other than efficiency goals in two respects. First, the indirect limitations on structural design create multiple governmental bodies that are required to interact in a manner which, from a transaction cost perspective, is inefficient. Thus, indirect limitations create organizational (or structural) inefficiency by purposefully fragmenting government power in order to protect individuals from the effects of majoritarianism. Second, the judicially enforceable direct limitations on power prohibit the exercise of government power when it has certain effects on private parties - notwithstanding otherwise laudable goals of efficiency or efficacy - because the Constitution recognizes the "higher value" of protecting the rights of the citizenry. The following is a clear expression by the U.S. Supreme Court as to these limitations on the pursuit of efficiency goals:

> The establishment of prompt efficacious procedures to achieve legitimate state ends is a proper state interest worthy of cognizance in constitutional adjudication. But the Constitution recognizes higher values than speed and efficiency. Indeed, one might fairly say of the Bill of Rights in general, and the Due Process Clause in particular, that they were designed to protect the fragile values of a vulnerable citizenry from the overbearing concern for efficiency and efficacy that may characterize praiseworthy government officials no less, and perhaps more, than mediocre ones. (Stanley v. Illinois (1972), p. 656; footnote omitted, emphasis added)

In this regard, it bears emphasizing that the Bill of Rights includes the Takings Clause. Thus, under the U.S. Constitution, government is constrained in its pursuit of efficiency goals, whether the goal is to make government operate more efficiently or to improve societal efficiency.

These limitations on the government pursuit of efficiency goals, however, do not mean that the enforcement of constitutional rights is devoid of any efficiency properties. The economic theory of the regulatory contract emphasizes the need for government to make credible commitments so that private parties will continue to contract with it in the future (Goldberg, 1976 & 1980; Sidak & Spulber, 1996). In order to procure investment in the public utility context, such credible commitments may include the need to maintain entry barriers or to compensate incumbents for unrecovered past (yet prudent) investments, thereby forgoing some of the gains from subsequent entry or competition. This means that some inefficiencies, particularly those in the short run, may need to be tolerated in order to promote desirable long-term investment. Without appropriate incentives for such long-term investment, society will likely lose the benefits of dynamic efficiency. It is precisely this role that the institutional endowment of a nation plays in providing an environment conducive to credible commitments by government which, from the institutional perspective, reveals that regulatory decisions designed to achieve short-run efficiency outcomes may actually undermine beneficial long-term investment in utility infrastructures (Cherry & Wildman, 1998).

Given this background as to the constitutional limitations on government pursuit of efficiency goals and the possibility that credible commitments may require society to bear some inefficiencies in order to achieve long-term investment, we now have the context within which to evaluate the respective consequences of a regulatory decision that overestimates, as opposed to underestimates, the option value associated with the CLECs' opportunity to purchase UNEs under section 251(c). The analysis below shows that, under the Constitution, the difference in the consequences among these regulatory decisions arises from the juxtaposition of the constitutional rights of the ILECs to the statutory rights of the CLECs and consumers.

2. THE CONSEQUENCES OF OVERESTIMATION VERSUS UNDERESTIMATION OF THE OPTION VALUE TO CLECS

As previously discussed, the CLECs have a statutory right under section 251(c) of the Telecommunications Act of 1996 to purchase UNEs from ILECs on a nondiscriminatory basis at just and reasonable rates. Consumers also have the statutory right under the Act to purchase telecommunications services from telecommunications carriers upon reasonable request at just and reasonable rates and without unjust discrimination (sections 201, 202). [1]

Meanwhile, ILECs' private property is protected from confiscation under the Takings Clause. In this regard, it is not so much the methodology upon which government regulation is based that matters, but what the end result of implementing the regulation is on the carrier (FPC v. Hope Natural Gas Co., 1944). Thus, if the end result of government regulation is that the ILEC is not given a reasonable opportunity to recover the costs of its business, then there is an illegal regulatory taking.

The significance of ILECs' constitutional rights under the Takings Clause is that they override the statutory rights of other parties, whether CLECs or consumers. This is because statutory rights, by definition, arise only from the legislative actions of government, which, in turn, are constrained by constitutional limitations. Such limitations include the direct limitations under the Bill of Rights, such as the Takings Clause. Therefore, if government actions to implement or enforce the statutory rights of the CLECs or consumers violate the ILEC's constitutional rights, then such actions are invalid.

Thus, in evaluating the consequences of regulators' decisions related to the option value of CLECs regarding UNE prices, it will be essential to determine when such decisions may constitute illegal takings of ILEC property. In this regard, it should be noted that takings can be classified into two groups, only one of which encompasses the real options problem.

One type of taking may occur when past investment becomes stranded due to changes in regulatory policy. This is a confiscation problem created by the transition from one set of regulatory rules to another. The second type of taking may occur when compliance with regulatory rules (whether in isolation or in combination) on a prospective basis makes costs unrecoverable. For example, if regulation requires a firm to invest and does not provide a reasonable opportunity for the firm to recover such investment, then the end result may constitute confiscation. It is the latter form of taking that applies to the real options scenario discussed here. In particular, ILECs are required to provide adequate facilities to consumers and to sell UNEs to CLECs under the Act. Yet ILECs may not be given a reasonable opportunity to recover those costs because regulators constrain the prices that can be charged to consumers, and restrict the level of UNE prices charged to CLECs by utilizing a costing methodology that may underestimate the option value granted to the CLECs.[2] The following analysis of the consequences of overestimating or underestimating the option value associated with ILEC provision of UNEs considers the possibility of an unconstitutional taking of property under this second type of taking.

3. OVERESTIMATION OF THE OPTION VALUE

Assume that the regulator utilizes a costing methodology for setting or approving UNE prices which, due to the means by which it quantifies the value of the CLEC's option to wait to invest, tends to overestimate the costs of providing UNEs by ILECs. There are several consequences that are likely to ensue from such an approach.

First, given that the ILEC's costs will tend to be overestimated, there is unlikely to be an underrecovery of costs by ILECs associated with providing UNEs. For this reason, there should be no ILEC claim of confiscation under the Takings Clause.[3] Furthermore, this tendency to overestimate the ILEC's costs would provide assurance to the ILECs that, at least with regard to government intervention on UNE prices, they will be given the opportunity to recover their costs. Such assurance provides a credible commitment by government to enable the ILECs to recover their costs, thereby creating an environment conducive to continuing long-term investment by ILECs in telecommunications infrastructure.

Second, the tendency to overestimate ILEC costs will also affect CLEC behavior. With respect to allocative efficiency, the overestimation of ILEC costs would lead to inefficiently high prices for UNEs. In the short run, this will deter CLECs from purchasing UNEs and slow their entry into the local exchange market on this basis. But, CLECs would then have the incentive to invest in their own facilities. This would likely lead to an increase in facilities-based competition; although, to the extent that CLEC facilities are more costly than the ILEC's "true" costs, such competition would be inefficient. To the degree that such inefficiencies do occur, there would be some loss in social welfare to consumers.

4. UNDERESTIMATION OF THE OPTION VALUE

Now assume that the regulator utilizes a costing methodology for setting or approving UNE prices that, due to the means by which it quantifies the value of the CLEC's option to wait to invest, tends to underestimate the costs of providing UNEs by ILECs. A number of important consequences are likely to arise from this situation.

First, given that the ILECs' costs will tend to be underestimated, there is likely to be an underrecovery of costs by ILECs associated with the provision of UNEs. For this reason, the greater the underestimation of the costs, the greater the likelihood that the ILECs will file claims of confiscation under the Takings Clause.[4] These takings claims will create significant litigation costs, not only for ILECs but also for regulators to defend their decisions and for other parties with an interest in the litigation, as well as increased uncertainty for investors in telecommunications companies pending the outcome of the litigation. Furthermore, this tendency to underestimate the ILECs' costs would undermine the assurance by government that, over time, ILECs will be given the opportunity to recover their costs. Such lack of assurance seriously impairs government's ability to make credible commitments, thereby creating an environment that is not conducive to continuing long-term investment by ILECs in telecommunications infrastructure.

Second, the tendency to underestimate ILEC costs will also affect CLEC behavior. Unlike the overestimation scenario, the underestimation of ILEC costs would lead to inefficiently low prices for UNEs. As a result, CLECs will be deterred from investing in their own facilities. To the extent that the costs of CLEC facilities are less than the ILEC's "true" costs, such failure to invest would be inefficient, with a corresponding loss in social welfare to consumers.

5. COMPARING OVERESTIMATION AND UNDERESTIMATION OF THE OPTION VALUE

The alternatives available to regulators can now be understood by comparing the consequences of overestimation and underestimation of the option value to CLECs. With overestimation, the benefits are a reduced likelihood of takings claims as well as more credible commitments by government to support long-term ILEC investment. The costs include possible overinvestment by CLECs in facilities-based competition with its corresponding loss in social welfare. On the other hand, underestimation of the option value increases the likelihood of takings claims and their associated costs, undermines credible commitments by government that are needed to support long-term ILEC investment, and encourages underinvestment in facilities-based local exchange competition.

Thus, regulators essentially have the choice of creating an institutional environment that 1) is conducive to supporting long-term investment by ILECs at the cost of some overinvestment in facilities-based competition by CLECs, or 2) discourages both long-term investment by ILECs and investment in local exchange facilities by CLECs, while encouraging takings claim litigation. The former arises from the regulator's use of a cost methodology that tends to overestimate the value of the CLEC's option to wait, whereas the latter arises from use of a cost methodology that tends to underestimate the option value.

Therefore, the greater the value that a nation places on the availability of and investment in telecommunications infrastructure, the more preferable is the institutional environment (of the first type) created by the overestimation scenario. Congress demonstrated its desire to encourage the deployment of advanced telecommunications infrastructure in numerous provisions of the Telecommunications Act of 1996. For example, section 706 requires the FCC and each state commission to encourage the deployment of advanced telecommunications capability to all Americans "by utilizing, in a manner consistent with the public interest, convenience, and necessity, price cap regulation, regulatory forbearance, measures that promote competition in the local telecommunications market, or other regulating methods that remove barriers to infrastructure investment." In addition, section 254 requires the FCC and state commissions to implement universal service policy consistent with the principle, among others, to provide access to advanced telecommunications and information services in all regions of the nation, including all public and non-profit elementary and secondary school classrooms, health care providers serving rural areas, and libraries.

With regard to the implementation of cost methodology, the institutional environment created by a tendency to overestimate rather than underestimate ILEC costs is more consistent with these Congressional statutory mandates. Thus, if regulators are uncertain as to the value of the option granted to CLECs under section 251, as a matter of public policy they should err on the side of overestimating rather than underestimating the option value. The inefficiencies from CLEC overinvestment in local exchange facilities that are likely to arise under such a regulatory policy are the cost that society may need to bear to promote desirable long-term investment.

6. CONCLUSION

The Telecommunications Act of 1996 provides a revised framework for regulating the telecommunications industry. This framework is based on increased reliance on competition to promote the deployment of an advanced telecommunications infrastructure to all Americans. As part of this framework, Congress has provided CLECs with a statutory right under section 251(c) to purchase UNEs from ILECs on a nondiscriminatory basis at just and reasonable rates.

By employing the new investment theory of real options, economists have identified this statutory right as an option "to wait" with regard to investment decisions. The prices of UNEs that ILECs charge to CLECs should reflect the value of this option; however, there is disagreement as to how to quantify this value and whether current costing methodology already sufficiently accounts for this value. Given that industry participants are unlikely to agree on the appropriate level of the option value, regulators will be required to decide how to reflect the option value in the costing methodology for UNEs.

In making this decision, regulators must be mindful of the fact that the institutional endowment of a nation greatly affects the incentives of private parties to invest in telecommunications infrastructure. In this regard, it is essential that the institutional (political, social, and legal) environment provide sufficient constraints on arbitrary government action so as to create credible commitments by government consistent with long-term private investment decisions.

In the United States, an important element of the institutional endowment is the federal Constitution. The Constitution consists of both direct and indirect limitations on government power. Indirect limitations place constraints on government power through structural design, such as separation of powers and various checks and balances among the branches of government, which purposefully introduce organizational inefficiencies. Direct limitations are express, judicially enforceable prohibitions on government action, such as the Takings Clause. Both forms of limitations constrain government power in order to protect the interests of individuals, notwithstanding the underlying goals, such as efficiency, of government policies.

Given the institutional endowment based on the U.S. Constitution, a regulatory policy that adopts a costing methodology which tends to overestimate, as opposed to underestimate, the option value conveyed under section 251(c) has very different consequences. The differences arise, in large part, from the fact that an ILEC's constitutional right to seek protection from the confiscation of its property under the Takings Clause supersedes the statutory right of CLECs to purchase UNEs as well as the statutory right of consumers to purchase telecommunications services upon reasonable request at just and reasonable rates without unjust discrimination.

Because Congress has clearly articulated a policy in favor of encouraging the deployment of advanced telecommunications infrastructure throughout the nation, a regulatory policy based on adopting a cost methodology that errs on the side of overestimating, rather than underestimating, the value of the CLEC option "to wait" is preferable. This is because a regulatory policy based on a tendency to overestimate is more likely to create an institutional environment conducive to infrastructure investment by both ILECs and CLECs as well as avoid the costs of litigation incurred by ILECs' pursuit of takings claims. The inefficiencies associated with potential overinvestment by CLECs in their own local exchange facilities under such a policy is the cost society may need - and, given Congress' statement of policy, should - bear in order to promote the deployment of advanced telecommunications capabilities in the nation's telecommunications infrastructure.

NOTES

1 There is also a requirement that the rates be affordable under section 254(b)(1) on universal service.

2 It is under this second type of taking that William Baumol agreed that the price of UNEs should increase to reflect the option value to CLECs.

3 This is true assuming that the combination of all the federal and state regulatory rules – such as for UNE pricing, consumer prices, and universal service obligations – provide the ILEC with a reasonable opportunity to recover its total costs. At least for the purposes of the discussion here, a confiscation claim would not arise solely due to inadequate recognition of the CLEC's option value.

4 Of course, the likelihood of a takings claim will increase if the combination of other federal and state regulatory rules, such as those restricting end-user prices or estimating universal service costs or contributions of carriers, do not provide the ILEC with a reasonable opportunity to recover its total costs.

REFERENCES

Armstrong v. United States, 364 U.S. 40 (1960).

Cherry, Barbara and Steven Wildman. June 1998. "An Institutional Perspective on Regulatory Regimes and Investment Decisions by Telecommunications Providers." Paper Presented at the International Telecommunications Society Conference, Stockholm, Sweden.

FPC v. Hope Natural Gas Co., 320 U.S. 591 (1944).

Goldberg, Victor. 1976. "Regulation and Administered Contracts." *Bell Journal of Economics*, 7, pp. 426-448.

Goldberg, Victor. 1980. "Relational Exchange." *American Behavioral Scientist*, 23, pp. 337-352.

Levy, Brian, and Pablo Spiller (eds.). 1996. *Regulations, Institutions, and Commitment: Comparative Studies of Telecommunications*. New York, New York: Cambridge University Press.

Madden, Sean. 1989. "Note: Takings Clause Analysis of Utility Ratemaking Decisions: Measuring Hope's Investor Interest Factor." *Fordham Law Review*, 58, pp. 427-446.

Missouri Pacific Ry. v. Nebraska, 164 U.S. 403 (1896).

North, Douglass. 1990. *Institutions, Institutional Change, and Economic Performance*. Cambridge, Massachusetts: Cambridge University Press.

Pennsylvania Coal Co. v. Mahon, 260 U.S. 393 (1922).

Pierce, Richard. 1989. "Public Utility Regulatory Takings: Should the Judiciary Attempt to Police the Political Institutions?" *Georgetown Law Journal*, 77, pp. 2031-2077.

Sidak, Gregory and Spulber, Daniel. 1996. "Deregulatory Takings and the Regulatory Contract." *New York University Law Review*, 71, pp. 851-999.

Stanley v. Illinois, 405 U.S. 645 (1972).

9 Real Options Applications for Telecommunications Deregulation

Greg Hallman and Chris McClain
PHB Hagler Bailly, Inc. and Vouchsafe, Inc.

Abstract - Competition in local phone markets has not developed as envisioned in the Telecommunications Act of 1996. One reason for the lack of competition is that the prices for unbundled network elements (UNEs) are likely set too low. A major reason for UNE underpricing is that the FCC's TELRIC-based pricing methodology ignores the option component of the CLEC's decision to purchase UNEs from ILECs. A real options framework for pricing UNEs is illustrated that demonstrates how TELRIC-based prices result in underpricing. Additionally, the real options framework suggests policy changes that could mitigate this underpricing problem and enhance local market competition.

... I want to state for the record that I am not patient enough to wait ten years to see true competition in this market. Ten years is far too long for small businesses and consumers to wait for the benefits of competition. We want to see competition developing in the short term, and if it doesn't we will need to seriously consider new legislation.

U.S. Senator Mike DeWine (R-OH), Opening Statement,
Antitrust Subcommittee Hearing, September 15, 1998

Since the Telecommunications Act of 1996 (Act) was passed, regulators, policy makers, and some telecommunications industry participants have been disappointed with the seemingly low levels of competition in the U.S. local telecommunications markets. The evidence is not necessarily slanted in favor of those who would call the Act a failure because competition is vigorous for profitable services in business markets. Most incumbent local exchange carriers have already lost about half of their intraLATA toll and switched access market share in business markets. However, it is undeniably true that competition in the industry's most visible markets - those for residential customers and for alternatives to the incumbent's local line services -have been less intense than expected. Indeed, the Federal Communications Commission's (FCC) second survey on the state of local competition indicates that Regional Bell Operating Companies (RBOCs) still provide local line service to 95 to 99 percent of residential customers in the United States.[1] Three alternative networks to the copper local loop - modified cable TV, wireless local loop, and satellite-based wireless - are emerging, but at slower rates than had been promised by the networks' owners and developers.[2]

When the Act was passed, Congress and the FCC envisioned local competition unfolding faster than long distance competition. Much of the blame for today's local competition predicament may lie with Judge Green's Modified Final Judgement (MFJ), which set up an awkward system of subsidies between artificially high-margin wholesale network access prices and below-cost basic retail line service prices. Low-priced basic line service is at the foundation of the policy of "universal service," which courts and regulators are determined to preserve. The creation of high-margin switched access prices to subsidize below-cost lines may be the most significant reason why the focus of local competition has been on avoiding switched access fees rather than on winning unprofitable local line services. The MFJ did successfully stimulate competition for long distance minutes. AT&T's share of minutes has steadily dropped since 1984, and many alternative long distance networks have been constructed.[3] The pace of build, in fact, continues to increase in long-haul networks, and innovation in network design and protocol, especially those having to do with Internet technologies, continues at a rapid clip.

Why is competition for local line services proceeding more slowly than had been expected? As is typical with any policy-related question, the answer depends on which side of the table you sit. New market entrants blame the incumbents. Alleged slow order processing, slow movement in negotiating interconnection agreements (through which new competitors buy access to incumbents' networks and the "last mile" to homes and businesses), and the slow implementation of necessary systems interfaces on the part of the large incumbent local exchange carriers (ILECs) deny new competitors access to local market dollars. Indeed, it is true that ILEC order processing systems have been complex to build and that interconnection agreements often end up being finalized in the courtroom. New entrants argue that even the slightest delay in providing service to customers who are willing to switch away from the incumbent is enough to spoil a significant percentage of sales. Policy makers at the FCC also appear ready to blame the ILECs for delays. And, the ILECs' successful challenge to the Act's constitutionality in the Eighth Circuit Court of Appeals last year was not received well by Reed Hundt, then chairman of the FCC. Last, potential entrants believe that even with federally mandated resale discounts and cost-based pricing formulas, wholesale prices for local services are too high.

As one might expect, the incumbents blame their accusers for the delay. ILEC managers suspect that there is gaming by long distance companies. RBOC entry into long distance markets is contingent on the vague predication that the capability for competition in local markets must be in place. The local market entrants that are most capable of making a significant impact on local share distribution are long distance carriers like AT&T, Sprint, and MCI/Worldcom. However, these companies would like to steer ILEC competition away from their core long distance markets for as long as possible. It is obvious, say the ILECs, that long distance carriers are waiting to enter local markets in the hope that local competition rules will be changed in their favor, making it easier to compete in local markets and further delaying RBOC entry into long distance. In the meantime, other competitive local exchange carriers (CLECs) continue to pick off the ILECs' best local customers, further weakening the incumbents' financial position. In addition, the FCC continues to attempt to drastically reduce the ILECs' surest sources of margin, switched access and intraLATA toll, primarily in response to interexchange carrier pressure. This is paramount to eliminating the franchise upon which ILECs have been built and upon which shareholders have invested their money, leaving ILECs no choice but to fight FCC mandates in the courts.[4]

In addition, the ILECs are under tremendous pressure to continue to innovate in their networks to accommodate demands to transport larger and larger quantities of traffic, primarily data traffic. The Act, however, requires that ILECs lease any new services to competitors at a discount, virtually eliminating any incentive for ILECs to innovate. After all, why innovate when your competitors are given access to your innovation at a discount the instant it hits the market? This point was made effectively by an unlikely spokesperson, C. Michael Armstrong, AT&T chairman and CEO. In response to suggestions that AT&T-TCI should follow the same local competition rules AT&T has advocated for ILECs, he stated that other telecommunications companies should not be given a "free ride" on AT&T's investment in the TCI network. "No company will invest billions of dollars to become a facilities-based broadband services provider if competitors who have not invested a penny of capital, nor taken an ounce of risk, can come along and get a free ride on the investments and risks of others."[5]

Another reason why the pace of local competition is slower than expected could be that the FCC's rules for pricing unbundled network elements (UNEs) are fundamentally flawed. Those rules mandate that UNEs be priced at incremental, forward looking cost, which, ILEC management argues, is equivalent to "giving away the store" to CLECs. To be sure, mispriced UNEs would result in inefficiencies in the market. UNEs priced too low leave ILECs with the unattractive prospect of losing high-revenue customers but still carrying the burden of federally mandated universal service obligations under which incumbents must provide service to high-cost customers at below-cost prices. Under-priced UNEs reduce incentives for competitors to build alternative networks because local services can be provided without the risks of building a network. Excessively low UNE prices deter investment in competitive networks and thwart FCC goals of opening local markets in a non-discriminatory and economically efficient manner. The competitive stimulus that regulators hoped for when setting UNE prices low has not occurred because of the complex options competitors have available to them when entering local services markets.

This paper explores further the claim that UNEs are mispriced. Although the broad concepts upon which the FCC's UNE pricing methodology are based may be sound, the implementation of those concepts has proven to be a much greater challenge than anyone expected. There has been a movement afoot lately to propose that a modification to the FCC's method is appropriate. The proposed modification would apply real options theory to the calculus of forward looking incremental costs and subsequently, UNE prices. The rationale for this is that the traditional discounted cash flow method of valuing investments like those made in telecommunications networks does not capture the entire present value of those investments. The value of the option that management has to delay, contract, expand or otherwise modify making those investments must be included in decision making.

The research of Dixit and Pindyck demonstrates conclusively that investments that are irreversible and in which a firm can invest in the future as an alternative to investing today can potentially benefit, on a net present value basis, from a premium inherent in management's option to wait to invest.[6] The application of real options techniques to the forward looking cost analysis used to derive UNE prices will enhance the efficiency of local market competition. And proper valuation of the options that competitors consider in entering local markets can enable regulators and public policy makers to establish local competition rules that achieve public policy goals.

1. FCC PRICING METHODOLOGY

There are basically two sets of wholesale prices that are important to competitive local exchange carriers: local resale prices and unbundled network element prices. Setting resale prices is less complex than setting UNE prices. State commissions discount retail prices to the extent that costs are avoided in the provision of a service as wholesale rather than retail. If an ILEC charged $15 per month for a retail flat rate local access line, and it avoided $2 of marketing, advertising or product management costs, and $1 of other strictly retail-related costs, the price of a resale flat rate local access line would be $12 per month. Although the disputes about what costs are actually avoided in resale versus retail products have been heated, the rules are generally understood and are less subject to dispute than unbundled network element prices. Real options techniques can be applied to the proper setting of the resale discount. But since the resale discount is less controversial, this paper's focus is on UNE pricing.

It is now generally agreed that the most effective method of entering local markets is to lease lines connecting customers to switches and to purchase and install switches. This is being called the "smart-build" model. The lines may be unbundled network loops from an ILEC or lines from another competitor. FirstWorld Communications, Inc. started to install fiber in local markets, but then adopted the "smart-build" model and "the economics look a whole lot better," according to Sheldon Oringer, FirstWorld's president and CEO. "It doesn't take a whole lot of capital," he goes on to say, "to move forward with a switch-based plan."[7] A great deal of analysis has been done by competitive local exchange carriers (CLECs), ILECs, and Wall Street analysts that demonstrates that combining an incumbent's unbundled local loop with a CLEC switch provides CLECs with an attractive vehicle through which to avoid paying switched access charges to ILECs and offer high-margin value added services – call waiting and caller ID, for example – at low operating costs. The unbundled loop is the only portion of ILEC networks that is a critical ingredient in the "smart-build" model, and its pricing is a key determinant of the model's profitability.

In order for competitive markets to evolve, prices for unbundled loops must be set at levels that market participants would pay in a competitive market. The FCC determined that in order for UNE prices to be economically efficient, they would have to be set at forward looking economic cost, calculated using a total element long-run incremental cost (TELRIC) method. TELRIC attempts to capture the costs for all inputs to supply an unbundled network element on a long run, forward looking, least cost, incremental basis. Firms buying UNEs priced at TELRIC (correctly calculated) can, in theory, rest assured that they are paying prices that are economically efficient and that imitate prices that a new market entrant might endure if entering a competitive market.

Unsurprisingly, ILECs claim that UNE prices are too low. They note, for instance, that the sale of UNEs at incremental cost by definition leaves ILECs with no margin to cover the overhead costs associated with running the business. CLECs, on the other hand, claim that UNE prices are too high, citing especially high nonrecurring charges that ILECs demand to cover costs generated by new processes and procedures required to provision a UNE. At first blush it may be unclear which party is correct. If prices are too high and do not imitate competitive prices (ostensibly giving ILECs an advantage), local markets should observe quite a bit of competitive network build to capture local profits. If prices are too low (which would give CLECs a short-term advantage), CLECs should be winning large numbers of local customers using UNEs. However, as noted earlier, there has been little competition in residential local markets, and there has been little competitive network build.

2. UNE PRICES APPEAR TO BE TOO LOW

The only viable competitive local network technologies now appear to be cable TV, wireless local loop, and some adaptation of global satellite. Low investment levels in alternative local networks is a sure indication that UNE prices are too low. Although the FCC's rules were meant to jump start competition by allowing competitors to use discounted resale lines or unbundled network elements priced at incremental cost to enter the market quickly, the concept of the Act was not to price UNEs in a way that deterred competitive build. TELRIC pricing rules, unfortunately, have had that effect. If it were less expensive for a CLEC to build its own facilities in local markets than to buy UNEs, CLECs would inarguably build networks. However, there has been little network build. Probably the primary reason TELRIC-based prices did not accomplish Congress' and the FCC's goals is that they do not accurately reflect the investment decisions that telecommunications firms face when evaluating network build opportunities. In short, TELRIC-based prices are inaccurate because they are set without consideration for the value of the options new entrants have for entering local markets.

Because TELRIC methods are forward looking, cost analysts using the method are required to make estimates of many future parameters. For example, projections of future network factor prices must be made. Levels of demand and type of demand must be taken into account so that the network's capabilities reflect market expectations. Engineering design and the expenses associated with provisioning and running a network must be predicted. One characteristic that is common to all of these parameters is that they are dynamic. Factor prices, demand levels, engineering design specifications, and operating expenses, to name only a few relevant parameters, all change over time. Any firm making an investment decision of the sort that CLECs and ILECs face would need to estimate the degree of change in all of them. In fact, this is common practice in finance departments in all telecommunications companies when three- to five-year business plans are developed. TELRIC, however, calls for these variables to be static. It is fairly simple, in fact, to compile a laundry list of TELRIC's shortcomings. Some of the items that would be included in that list are:

- TELRIC assumes that prices, output levels, and expenses remain static over time.
- Depreciation is based on accounting methods that allocate costs arbitrarily over time, do not calculate economic depreciation, and include depreciation improperly in pricing formulas.
- Quantities do not rely at all upon demand elasticities or market shares, and are constant throughout time.
- There are no economies of scale or scope, no technological substitution, and no factor price considerations in TELRIC's engineering design and relationships.
- Rate base calculations are without dynamics, including input and output price, and discount and interest rate dynamics.
- Investments are assumed to be one-time with static factor prices, constant capacity, no differentiated risk, and no real options.
- There are no competitive impacts or market share losses due to changes in price.[8]

Clearly these are major weakness in TELRIC methodology. Perhaps with the best of intentions, it has oversimplified the investment decision-making process.

Another defining feature of TELRIC that appears to fall short of ideal is that it relies on discounted cash flow (DCF) methods. In short, TELRIC-based prices reflect the discounted net present value of an investment in the local network made sometime in the future. Although DCF methods are frequently used by business decision-makers, they alone are not appropriate for the purpose of pricing UNEs.

Making the simplifying assumption that the TELRIC method is a satisfactory way to estimate the incremental costs of constructing telecommunications networks (although the authors do not feel it to be appropriate), TELRIC-based prices should exactly equal the discounted net present value of an investment made in building a network (see Relationship A below). In other words, a new entrant into the local market would be indifferent between building its own network or leasing it from an ILEC. If investors are indifferent, one would expect to see an equal mix between customers served by CLEC facilities and those served using ILEC UNEs. The evidence shows that there is not an equal mix between the two types of service provision.

TELRIC price = Cost to build (Relationship A)

Still, using this simplifying assumption, there is a way to account for this disparity. CLECs purchasing UNEs incur costs in addition to UNE lease prices because there are transaction costs when buying UNEs from ILECs. CLECs must negotiate contracts, participate in arbitration proceedings, set up departments to interface with ILEC wholesale operations, and invest in computer systems to ensure compatibility with ILEC operations support systems. In addition, having to rely on a competitor as a supplier brings with it some costs. These are real costs, and many CLECs would agree that they are significantly higher than expected when CLECs drafted their business plans. Now that CLECs have had two years to estimate these costs accurately, which the authors will assume are now known to be fairly high, and if TELRIC-based prices exactly equal the discounted net present value of investing in a network, one should again expect to see more build (see Relationship B).

TELRIC Price + ILEC Transaction Costs > Cost to Build (Relationship B)

Once again, prices based on TELRIC seem to result in irrational investment decisions on the part of CLECs. Assuming CLEC managers are not irrational, the only way one can account for this is that there must be another cost on the right side of Relationship B that is unaccounted for in this simple analysis.

There is, in fact, a cost that has not yet been unaccounted for in this analysis. When a telecommunications firm is making a decision on whether or not to build a network, it faces various degrees of uncertainty. Many sources of uncertainty are obvious. Will there be sufficient demand to justify capital outlays? What customer segments will be targeted? Where are they located? What demand is there to satisfy? Will that demand change over time? What technology should be deployed (CDMA vs. TDMA and IP vs. circuit switched, for example)? What competitive response can be expected? Any financial analyst evaluating this investment would need to address these sorts of questions.

Typically, strategic planners and financial analysts would account for uncertainty by changing the discount rate in their NPV calculations. Indeed, the discount rate is the primary variable through which uncertainty or risk is measured and applied to the analysis using discounted cash flow methods. Discount rates can be estimated in a variety of fashions, each of which has proponents and each of which employs a large amount of time in corporate finance departments. That so much energy is expended in calculating discount rates is an indication of how complex a variable it is. Indeed, cash flows in DCF analyses are projected with certainty, and DCF relies almost exclusively on the discount rate to factor uncertainty into analyses of future projects.

How is this relevant to the discussion about TELRIC-based prices? TELRIC methods rely on estimating, as closely as possible, the net present value of constructing a network in the future based on DCF methods. However, of late, there has been quite a bit of research in finance that challenges the validity of the DCF and NPV approach to evaluating projects.[9] If DCF opponents are correct, DCF does not accurately measure the true present value of many future projects because it does not accurately reflect the effects of uncertainty on a project's value. DCF, by necessity, assumes that uncertainty or risk decreases the value of a project. Larger payoffs are required (i.e., a risk premium) to reward an investor for increased risk. In general, this phenomenon can be reflected in the following way:

$$\uparrow \text{Uncertainty} \rightarrow \uparrow \text{Discount Rate} \rightarrow \uparrow \text{NPV}$$

(Relationship C)

3. OPTIONS THEORY APPLICATIONS TO DCF/NPV AND UNE PRICES

It is not difficult to illustrate that DCF methods fall short of accurately reflecting the complete value of a project when uncertainty exists. Dixit and Pindyck offer the following simple example to illustrate how DCF methods are inadequate for evaluating many investments under uncertainty, as well as the need to include the value of the option to wait to invest in a project.[10]

Dixit and Pindyck propose to evaluate a firm's decision to invest in a factory that produces widgets. They assume that the factory cannot produce anything but widgets once it is built. In other words, factory costs are sunk after the factory is built. Factory output is limited to exactly one widget per year. The cost of building the factory is $1,600, and the factory produces widgets with $0 operating costs. Today's price for a widget is $200, but the price will permanently change to either $300 or $100 with probabilities q and (1-q), respectively, next year. Dixit and Pindyck assume as well for simplification purposes that the firm does not have any firm-specific risk and that it should discount cash flows at the risk-free interest rate, which is assumed to be 10%. Under these circumstances, Dixit and Pindyck ask if this is a good investment.

Calculating net present value is straightforward. The expected price for widgets is $200 (a 50 percent probability that future price will be $300 and a 50 percent probability that future price will be $100). NPV, then, is

$$NPV = -\$1{,}600 + \sum_{t=0}^{\infty} \frac{200}{(1.1)^t} = -\$1{,}600 + \$2{,}200 = \$600 \qquad (\text{"Static NPV"})$$

Since this project's NPV is greater than $0, it appears that the project should be pursued.

However, Dixit and Pindyck then go on to analyze the value of this investment under slightly different behavior. Indeed, if this firm waits one more period and invests in the factory only if the price of widgets rises, the NPV calculation looks a little different. First, there is no money spent in year 0. Second, $1,600 is invested only if widget prices rise in year 1. Assuming that the probability of prices rising is once again 50 percent, the investment analysis looks like:

$$NPV = (0.5)\left[\frac{-\$1{,}600}{1.1} + \sum_{t=1}^{\infty} \frac{\$300}{(1.1)^t}\right] = \frac{\$850}{1.1} = \$773 \qquad (\text{"Expanded NPV"})$$

So, net present value today is significantly higher if the factory investment is made next year instead of today. The firm maximizes its net present value, then, by waiting until next year to invest. Dixit and Pindyck's point in introducing the second NPV calculation is to show that the first NPV calculation did not account for the opportunity cost of investing now instead of waiting to invest next period when it will be clear if widget prices rise or fall. In fact, the firm derives value from having the option to wait that is equal to $173, the difference in the two NPVs. This analysis can be expanded beyond the simple binomial example presented here, but the point remains - uncertainty can be valued and is a critical consideration in the correct valuation of any investment.

Proponents of options applications to project valuation under uncertainty often refer to the first NPV calculation as "static NPV" and the second NPV calculation as "expanded NPV." Expanded NPV is a more thorough measure of the value inherent to a project that is irreversible and in which a firm can invest in the future as an alternative to investing today. Looking back at Relationship A, one sees that uncertainty in a project does not necessarily decrease that project's value and that Relationship A, if it were to properly measure a project's present value, would have to include an option premium to reflect the value of having the option to wait:

↑ Uncertainty ➔ ↑Discount Rate ➔ ↓ NPV +↑option premium ➔ ↑ or ↓ NPV depending on the nature of the option

(Relationship D)

Investments in telecommunications networks naturally tend towards the expanded NPV evaluation method because they are for the most part irreversible, and firms can invest in the future as an alternative to investing today. If having the option to wait changes today's present value of a project, then clearly option premia need to be included in net present value calculations involving unbundled network elements.

4. REAL OPTIONS VALUATION SHOULD BE INCLUDED IN UNE PRICES

The Dixit and Pindyck example clearly illustrates that a project has an option component when a firm has the ability to postpone the project. Its value derives from uncertainty in either the cash inflows that will be realized in the future or cash outflows necessary to undertake the project. In the Dixit and Pindyck example, cash inflows are uncertain because the firm does not know the future selling price of widgets. Because the firm has the ability to postpone investment and there is uncertainty regarding the value of the investment, however, the project has a valuable option component.

Under the current structure of the local market, CLECs have the ability to postpone investments in real network assets without sacrificing the ability to invest later. Additionally, there is a great deal of uncertainty about the costs to construct network assets and about future cash flows that will be generated by those assets. Just like the firm in Dixit and Pindyck's example, CLECs own a valuable option.

Given that the CLECs own a valuable option, it is easy to show that TELRIC-based prices are too low. If the goal of FCC pricing rules is to exactly reflect the costs a firm would incur when investing in a network, then the option value of waiting to build must be included in the pricing formula. TELRIC prices are designed to capture the costs of construction and operation only, and the value of the option to postpone is not included. By definition, therefore, TELRIC prices are too low. Any telecommunications firm determining whether or not to build a network would have a higher investment threshold than TELRIC would predict because a firm would have to forego the option to wait to build.

Another way to illustrate that TELRIC prices are too low is to show what a CLEC both pays and receives from building a network and from buying UNEs. If a

CLEC chooses to build a network, then it pays the construction and operation costs of the network, and it receives cash inflows from selling services "produced" by the network. On the other hand, if a CLEC chooses to buy UNEs, it pays a price that is designed to be equivalent to the costs of the network's construction and operation, and it receives cash inflows from selling services "produced" by the network plus the option to build its own network at a later date. Given that the option to build at a later date is always valuable, a CLEC is always better off buying UNEs at current TELRIC prices because it simply gets more for its money.

In terms of the earlier pricing relationships, the value of the CLEC's option to wait needs to be added to the right-hand side of Relationship B. Reflecting the value of the option, Relationship B becomes:

TELRIC Price + RBOC Transaction Costs =
Cost to Build + Value of Option to Wait (Relationship E)

A firm facing this investment decision would be indifferent to the build-versus-buy decision, which would go a long way towards achieving the FCC's goals of stimulating competition in local markets.

It is clear that options theory is relevant to the CLEC's build-versus-buy decision. Under the FCC's pricing rules, CLECs have been given the option to delay investing in networks today in favor of waiting to invest in networks in the future. Indeed, both the build and buy decisions have the characteristics of options. Both have a strike price and a finite time horizon. The value of financial options increases as their time horizon increases, and the same holds for the real options available to CLECs. There is no compelling reason for CLECs to exercise their option to build before the option expires. Furthermore, the option is costless to the CLEC because it did not have to purchase the option. The most rational decision for CLECs to make under this pricing structure is to test local markets using UNEs, gather more information, and invest in networks later when sure payoffs are available.

5. OPTION VALUATION

It is clear that CLECs own a valuable option. What remains is to assess the value of that option. Although it can be complicated to derive the exact value of a real option, and it is not calculated here, it is still useful to discuss some general rules and relationships that can be employed.

Option valuation rules have been derived through extensive research on financial options.[11] The simplest financial option is a call option on a stock. A call option gives the owner of the option the right, but not the obligation, to purchase a stock at a prespecified price over some prespecified time period. The prespecified price at which the stock can be purchased is called the strike price or exercise price, and the prespecified time period is defined by the option's expiration date. Valuation research has shown that the value of a call option is a positive function of the profitability of exercise (which is the difference between the current value of the stock (S) and the exercise price(X)), the time to maturity, and the volatility of the stock price. This research has also shown that an option always has a positive value, because an option is a right, but not an obligation, to purchase a stock.

When studying the effects of the three variables that determine the value of an option (profitability of exercise, time to maturity, and volatility), the effects of profitability of exercise and time to maturity are the easiest to understand. The effect of profitability of exercise, for example, simply predicts that the option to purchase the stock for $X becomes more valuable as the positive difference between the current price of the stock, $S, and the exercise price, $X (i.e., S-X) becomes larger. The effect of time to maturity of the option simply predicts that, all else being equal, an option is more valuable if it has a longer life.

The valuation effect of volatility, on the other hand, is less intuitive. Options research shows that the value of an option increases as the volatility of the underlying asset increases. In other words, all else being equal, an option on a more volatile stock such as Yahoo! is more valuable than an option on a less volatile stock like AT&T. The reason for this is that an increase in volatility increases the chance that the stock price will experience a large upward move which, in turn, increases the profitability of exercising the option in the future. Of course, an increase in volatility also increases the chance that the stock will experience a large downward move in price, but this is of little consequence to the owner of a call option because the downside of a call option position is simply the cost of the option. Remember, a call option gives the owner the right, but not the obligation, to purchase the stock. In the event of a large downward movement to the point where the value of the stock ($S) is less than the exercise price ($X), the owner of the call option does not exercise the option and loses only the amount paid for the option. It is important to note that the positive effect of volatility on the value of an option comes from the fact that the owner of the option is not obligated to purchase the stock, and the option will only be exercised (i.e., the call option's owner will use the option to buy the stock for the exercise price $X) if it is profitable to do so.

These valuation effects can be applied to the real option component of CLECs' build-versus-buy decisions, although not all of these effects are directly relevant. One of the effects that is not directly relevant is profitability of exercise. Because a CLEC can realize profits from local markets by either buying UNEs or building networks, the profitability of exercise does not affect the value of the option component in the CLECs' build-versus-buy decision. Time to maturity, on the other hand, is more relevant. Because CLECs appear to face no imminent expiration date on their option to build, their option has a long life and is therefore more valuable than if it had a defined expiration date.

Probably the most important insight into the value of the CLECs' option to build comes from the idea that volatility, or uncertainty, increases the value of this option. Various sources of uncertainty in the local market are discussed in the next section, but suffice it to say that given the high degree of uncertainty in the local market, the CLECs' option to postpone investment in building network assets is very valuable. And because a CLEC's option ceases to exist the moment it commits to building, the most rational decision for a CLEC is to test local markets using UNEs purchased at low TELRIC-based prices and keep its valuable option alive. As was pointed out in Relationship E in the previous section, the only way for the FCC to alter this decision is to capture the value of the option in UNE prices.

6. UNCERTAINTIES

As discussed above, one of the most powerful insights that real options analysis has on business decision-making is that uncertainty does not necessarily decrease the value of a project. Indeed, if firms have the option to wait, increased uncertainty, as in Dixit and Pindyck's simple example, can generate greater value as measured in net present value terms. If real options are to be applied to TELRIC-based pricing (and other) decisions in telecommunications, it is worth spending a little time discussing the uncertainties that currently characterize the industry and that would lend themselves to increasing the value of the option to wait.

Uncertainties in the telecommunications industry are vast, which explains to a large extent why there has been little change in the distribution of market share in local markets. The decisions that make the largest net impact on local market participants are regulatory. The Act has been thrown into question, and it is unclear if and how it will be modified after sustained and repeated legal challenges to its constitutionality. Certain FCC mandates could be suspended indefinitely, for instance, completely reversing the course of local market entry and rendering CLEC investments in local markets useless until subsequent legislation is written and passed by Congress and ultimately upheld in the courts. RBOCs continue to press for within-region InterLATA market entry. So far, success has eluded them, but recently Joel I. Klein, assistant attorney general-antitrust, prognosticated "that within a year to 18 months, Bell companies will begin winning approval to offer in-region interLATA services."[12] RBOC entry into long distance within 18 months would change the business landscape for interexchange carriers, ushering highly capitalized, well-branded competitors into the long distance market and, presumably, forcing interexchange carriers to be more aggressive in local competition to offer full service "one-stop-shop" packages.

Competition in local markets generates a great deal of uncertainty. Through June 1998, CLECs had raised about $20 billion in investment since the Act was passed.[13] Investors and market participants are placing their bets on many different types of firms, all of which are looking for growth opportunities in both traditional and new segments of the local market. With CLECs of all sizes and telecommunications equipment firms angling at different segments of the market, even large CLECs must continually reevaluate local market opportunities. If one type of competitor emerges with a distinct advantage, many other CLECs may follow. Until then, some firms seem willing to wait to see who can offer the most compelling package.

Rapid technological changes are enabling new forms of CLECs and are rendering other CLECs obsolete just as rapidly. One of the most dramatic changes has been in the movement of data (and soon voice) traffic away from circuit-switched networks and towards packet-switched networks. Wireless local loops still appear to be cost-prohibitive for the replacement of all local lines, but each year wireless costs decline, making wireless local loops a more viable alternative. PCS and cellular services are offering inexpensive, flat-rate pricing plans that are leading customers to use wireless phones for many calls that would have previously been made on a wireline phone. Wireless services involving toll calls are now competing with wireline services. Meanwhile, consumers are also demanding that the copper network be able to handle significantly larger volumes of traffic, and equipment companies are developing inexpensive technologies that can do just that. It is difficult to tell which technologies will prove to be winners in this environment.

As in any market, it is difficult to predict what services the market will demand in the future. As consumer preferences, regulation, competitive landscape, and technology change, market demands continue to reshape. No one predicted ten years ago that the mass market would be demanding third and fourth access lines into the home for multiple modem connections to ISPs. Nor could anyone have predicted that in two years seven RBOCs would consolidate into four, that Worldcom would become the nation's second-largest long distance carrier, or that AT&T would spend tens of billions of dollars to acquire cable TV assets. All of this activity generates uncertainty. And all of that uncertainty enhances the value of the option to wait or the option to take alternative actions. Public policy decisions must consider the impact of these options, and real options analysis must be included in pricing methodologies for the deregulation of the telecommunications industry.

7. PENETRATION OF RESIDENTIAL LOCAL MARKETS

The introduction of this paper notes that there has been little competition in residential local markets. Although the focus here has been on the effects that UNE prices have had on CLEC build-versus-buy decisions, there are clearly other reasons for limited competition in residential markets. Perhaps the most important of these has to do with the "low hanging fruit" strategy many CLECs have employed. Average business customers make more calls and overall pay higher rates than average residential customers. So, CLECs entering local markets have by and large targeted business customers first. Indeed, even before the Act, competition for large and medium-sized businesses was fierce, and competitive access providers had laid thousands of miles of competitive fiber in all large metropolitan areas in the country. Today, any business owner located in a metropolitan area with average or higher toll calling volumes, even a small business, is frequently approached by CLEC salesforces offering them discounts from ILEC rates. With most of their energy concentrated on high-margin business customers, CLECs may not have had the resources for broad residential market entry.

Another explanation for low residential penetration levels is that the vast majority of residential customers are unprofitable. Estimates are that ILECs make profits on only 30 percent of residential customers, who cover much of the losses associated with the other 70 percent of customers. If a CLEC were to try to win a portion of residential local revenues away from an ILEC, it would have to be able to find a way to target the 30 percent of the residential market that is profitable. However, unlike business customers, which are typically clustered in business parks or in downtown metropolitan business districts, high-usage residential customers are not typically clustered together. CLECs might be able to target residential areas, like California's Silicon Valley, where there might be high usage on local lines, but CLECs run the real risk that these customers are not using their lines for attractively priced toll calls, but instead are paying a low flat monthly charge and dialing into their Internet service providers for hours at a time. Profitable residential customers are those who make a large volume of intraLATA toll calls and long distance calls. It is not likely that these customers are clustered together, which raises marketing and selling costs, and also renders the use of unbundled loops less attractive. On an aggregate basis, residential margins may not be high enough to justify CLECs deploying switches in residential areas where the CLEC succeeds in winning only a few high toll usage customers.

8. CONCLUSION

Senator Mike DeWine, who is quoted in this paper's preamble, articulates nicely the frustrations that policy makers, industry participants, and the public have voiced over what they see as failure to achieve the goals of the 1996 Telecommunications Act. Many factors account for the current levels of competition in local markets. One of the most compelling is the uncertainty surrounding the direction and extent of ongoing regulatory rule making. Because the value of many local market investments hangs in the balance with each local market regulatory decision, competitors are reluctant to make major investments.

At the most fundamental level, however, it appears that the pricing of unbundled network elements may be a cause of some of the delay in network investment by CLECs. The FCC's TELRIC-based pricing methodology has many shortcomings, not the least of which is that it does not measure all of the costs attributable to a forward looking investment in telecommunications. Real options frameworks supply a new and more exact way to view telecommunications investment and UNE pricing.

The proper valuation of unbundled network elements is critical to the efficient operation of competitive local exchange markets. If UNE prices are too high, competitors are left without a good short-term method for entering the market. If they are too low, competitors have a low-cost method for entering local markets quickly, but are left without an incentive to build competitive networks. And, incumbents are left without the ability to earn on added investments. Neither result is ideal from a public policy standpoint, and every effort should be made to ensure that UNE prices are efficient. Using current methodologies, they certainly are not.

The more uncertainty that exists surrounding the local markets, the more valuable the option to wait to enter or to wait to build local networks becomes. Regulatory decisions, with billions of dollars hanging in the balance, continue to be unpredictable. Competitors are raising money and staking claims to the portions of the local market that are attractive now, but they are forced to delay entry into some larger segments of the market until the regulatory and competitive landscapes are more clear. Technological advances have served both as a shield and a threat to ILECs as the types of technologies that make it possible for ILECs to offer new services over old networks allow competitors to exploit their advantages in organizational speed and time to market. But they have also made it much less clear which technology is most appealing to customers, providing yet another reason to delay until the local market is more well defined.

Real options techniques can help to explain the current state of competition in local markets and to understand CLECs' choices of market segments and investment plans. Real options techniques can also be used to identify the conditions necessary to stimulate greater investment in local networks and to promote CLEC penetration of the residential market. Understanding why CLECs have made their current decisions and what changes could stimulate different investment decisions would be valuable in the development of improved public policies and regulations. The pricing of ILEC wholesale services, like unbundled loops, is just one of the important factors. Many other factors are important to achieving public policy goals as well. Under the current circumstances, with a great deal of uncertainty and variety of local strategies to choose from, options valuation is clearly the most appropriate foundation for decision-making in the telecommunications industry, for both business decision makers and public policy makers.

NOTES

1 FCC, "Responses to the First Common Carrier Bureau Survey on the State of Local Competition," March 27, 1998. See http://www.fcc.gov/ccb/local_competition/survey/responses/.

2 Hume, Barbara. 1988. *Local Loop Competition.* Masters thesis, University of Colorado.

3 The FCC estimates that AT&T's share of long distance minutes has dropped from 85% in 1984 to about 55% today. See Zolnierek, James and Katie Rangos. January 1998. *Long Distance Market Shares – Third Quarter 1997*, FCC, p. 29.

4 Pacific Telesis offered the following summary of the problems associated with FCC Access Charge Reform proposals in its Comments on the Commission's Notice of Proposed Rulemaking, FCC Docket No. 96-262. *See http://www.fcc.gov/Bureaus/Common_Carrier/Comments/access_reform/samples/0155376.htm*

"The current access charge system is designed to recover all costs allocated to interstate access service, including all current costs. These current costs are allocated between the intrastate and interstate jurisdictions by arbitrary formulae that have one over-riding objective: to keep basic exchange rates low. Interstate costs are recovered by access charges. Access charges also recover some costs of the current Universal Service Fund, which is used to subsidize high cost carriers in rural areas. Likewise, interstate access charges also recover current and embedded LEC costs including investment being depreciated more slowly than economically justified to keep current rates low, as well as the cost of plant that may be stranded due to competition. Plainly, LEC shareowners will be subject to a new, fundamentally different and greatly increased risk if access reform creates a 'regulatory squeeze' by moving prices to economic costs without providing for the recovery of all current costs outside of the access charge regime.

The Notice proposes to reform access charges by several possible means: changing the rate structure; reducing or eliminating regulation to allow market forces to work; and/or continuing to regulate prices but with a changed basis. The ideal thrust of each of these proposals would be, in the Commission's view, to 'make [the] system of interstate access charges more economically rational and compatible with competitive local markets.' [As discussed in detail below, the likely reality of certain proposals would be quite the opposite.] To the extent that the Commission's access charge reform reflects a single-minded principle that prices must be lowered to recover no more than forward looking costs, the real current costs now included in access charges will be unrecovered and land solely on the shoulders of LEC shareowners. Under some of the options proposed, LECs would be precluded from recovering any costs other than forward looking costs in their access charges. Under other options, certain access charge elements might theoretically include a portion of these costs, but given competition, cost recovery would be impossible, leaving LEC shareholders 'holding the bag.'"

5 *Telecommunications Report*, Nov. 2, 1998.

6 Dixit, Avinash K. and Robert S. Pindyck. 1994. *Investment Under Uncertainty.* Princeton, NJ: Princeton University Press.

7 *Telecommunications Reports*, Nov. 9, 1998.

8 See Alleman, James, "The Application of Real Options to Cost Models," this volume. This list is largely based upon Alleman's presentation at CITI's October 2, 1998 real options conference.

9 For a good example of this, see Ross, S. Autumn 1995. "Uses, Abuses, and Alternatives to the Net-Present-Value Rule." *Financial Management*, Vol. 24, No. 3, pp. 96-102.

10 Dixit and Pindyck, op. cit., pp. 26- 29.

11 The seminal work in this area is: Black, F. and M. Scholes. May-June 1983. "The Pricing of Options and Corporate Liabilities." *Journal of Political Economy*, and Merton, R. Spring 1973. "Theory of Rational Option Pricing," *The Bell Journal of Economics and Management Science*, Vol. 4, No. 1.

12 *TR DAILY*, Nov. 20, 1998.

13 Madden, Andrew P. October 1998. "What Happened to the Telecom Act?" *The Red Herring*. See http://www.redherring.com/mag/issue59/telecom.html.

10 The Poverty of Cost Models, the Wealth of Real Options[1]

James Alleman
University of Colorado at Boulder
and PHB Hagler Bailly

Abstract - The attempts to estimate forward looking costs worldwide are based on cost models whose foundation is traditionally applied discounted cash flow analysis - exactly the method that the real options methodology has shown can give terribly wrong results. However, these cost models are ideal vehicles to adapt to the real options methodology. This paper develops a stylized cost model to quantify several deficits associated with the cost models in use today. Even without the application of real options methodology, the stylized results show a significant difference between the revenue requirements model and a traditional discounted present value model. With the application of real options techniques, the differences become much greater.

The implications are significant. Policymakers who attempt to use proxy cost models to emulate the market behavior of firms in competition without considering real options are acting unwisely. Policies that deal with costs cannot be effective without a fundamental understanding of the implications of real options theory.

1. OVERVIEW OF COST MODELS

This paper reviews and critiques the proxy cost models that have recently been developed for the telecommunications industry. While these cost models go into great detail on the engineering aspects of the telephone network, they lack a fundamental understanding of economics and finance by failing to apply the appropriate traditional techniques of engineering economics. Some do not use discounted cash flow (DCF) techniques to evaluate capital investments.[2] Instead, they simply use a revenue requirement method, based on arbitrary cost allocations. These cost models have ignored DCF's major contribution to asset valuation.[3]

More recently, valuation analysis has been enhanced with "real options theory," which accounts for the investment uncertainties, subject to probability distribution, that are fundamental in the DCF analyses. Applying the real options methodology to DCF analysis can produce a significant change in the valuation – by as much as a factor of two or more.[4] However, all of the cost models ignore the real options effect. The results of the stylized model presented in this paper indicate the underestimation is on the order of 40 to 60 percent.

Given this enormous disparity and major methodological problem, it would be irresponsible to use these cost models for determining access/interconnection prices, unbundled network elements (UNEs), or universal service obligations.[5]

2. SCOPE OF CRITIQUE

While there are several generic problems with the existing telecommunications cost models, this paper cannot hope to go into detail or even enumerate all of them. It attempts to show, however, that the models can be modified to correct the more egregious faults and offers suggestions on how to include the real options effects. The reader should be warned that while the framework of the current models may be salvageable, this does not mean that a simple "adder" can be appended to the results to determine "the number." The corrections introduced by real options considerations are nonlinear. The nonlinearity precludes "additive solutions," but requires the explicit incorporation of a different approach into the models.

The cost models are based on engineering relationships using traditional telecommunications plant design with the best available technology. The network is laid out to meet the quantity demanded, and is designed in extensive detail.[6] It is granular in terms of equipment and geography. For example, version 5.0a of the HAI model has nearly 200 input parameters and would include, *inter alia*, the hardness of the ground for laying transmission facilities (HAI Consulting, Inc., 1998b).

This class of models is generally known as engineering process models.[7] They design the network "on paper," and estimate the physical investment required to serve demand as well as other factors needed to develop the costs associated with the level of investment. This paper is only concerned with the step after the estimation of the physical investment required to serve the demand: the economics/financial methodology of the cost calculation.

Stripped to their simplest form, the engineering process models begin with an estimate of the demand to be served and then design the system to serve this demand based on standard engineering practices and relationships using the latest technology available. This determines the investment required in physical units. The results are then used as a basis for virtually all other calculations:

- The physical units are multiplied by the unit cost of the investments to obtain the total investment cost.

- The expenses are determined as a proportion of investment costs; thus, the level of investment is critical for the determination of the expense elements of costs.
- The annualization of the investment is based on the depreciation schedule and the cost of capital.
- The revenue requirement is the value of the annualized investment, expenses and overheads.
- Dividing the revenue requirements by the quantity defines a "price" (see Figure 1).

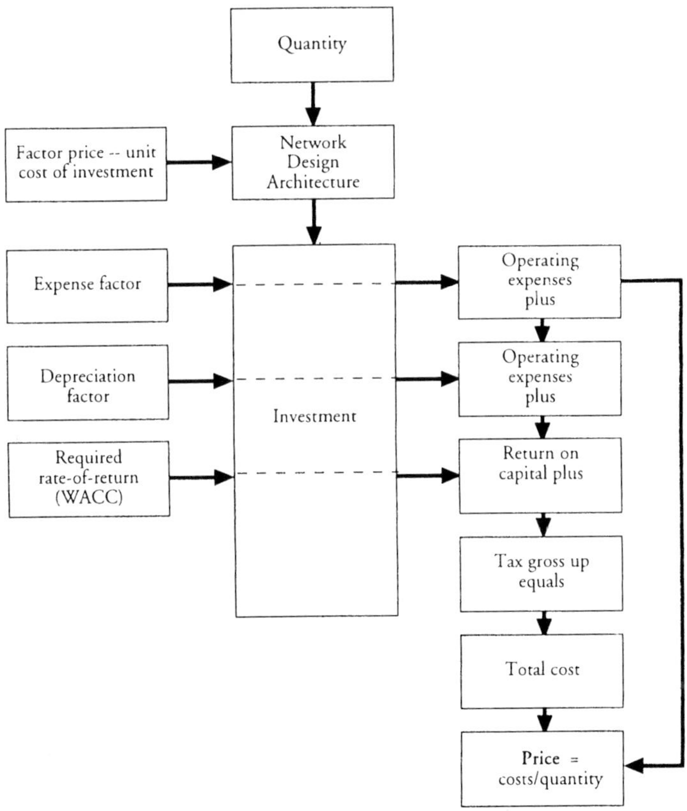

Figure 1. Engineering Process Model
Rate-Base, Rate-of-Return Cost Model Calculation

3. STYLIZED COST MODEL

3.1 A One-Period Model

Virtually all of the models describe in extensive detail how their model networks were designed and built, but the financial and economics descriptions are limited to a few paragraphs (HAI, 1998; NERA, 1999). As a result, the models' economics/financial structure is ambiguous. Explicit interpretations of the calculations are presented below along with discussions of the problems with this approach. A distinction is made between traditional DCF analysis and the revenue requirements (RR) method; various forms of the latter are used in the current cost models. The difference between an RR model and the traditional approach is over 10 percent. This paper shows where real options can be useful in enhancing the accuracy of cost estimates and increasing the exchange access price by up to 60 percent.

Initially, for expository purposes, assume only one period, no depreciation, no taxes and no operating expenses. Then, in their simplest form, RR models compute the price/cost in the following manner. First the required output is determined, followed by the equipment needed to provide this output based on telecommunications engineering principles. That is, with these quantities, the network is sized based on standard engineering design relationships – the size of the central office required for the number of loops to serve this demand, etc. Next, the price of the equipment is determined. The prices of the input times the quantities required determines the total investment. A cost of capital factor is used to compute the revenue requirement, which is then divided by the output to determine the price. To illustrate these points, assume only one type of capital is needed and is used up in this period.

$$Q = F(K) = \updownarrow K \tag{1}$$

If Q is the output, K is the capital required, and w is the price of the capital equipment. Using the subscript $_0$ to indicate the value of the variables and assuming that $\updownarrow = 1$, then:

$$Q_0 = K_0 \text{ and} \tag{2}$$

$$P = w_0 K_0 / Q_0 \tag{3}$$

This is the revenue requirement model in its most basic form. Obviously, this is too simple. However, it illustrates several points about the models that are examined below: 1) the price is driven by the estimate of capital requirement, 2) demand is assumed to be invariant, no mater what the price, and 3) investments and revenue are assumed to occur instantaneously. All these deviations from reality are maintained in all the models under discussion.

3.2 Quantity Determination

As indicated, the quantities necessary to meet demand are first determined via telecommunications engineering relationships. However, no consideration is made for price effects on the quantity demanded. But not having this demand parameter implies a perfectly inelastic demand. That is, no matter what the price, there will be no change in quantity demanded. This, of course, belies all the demand studies made in the telecommunications industry since the late 1960s (Taylor, 1980).

In this module no accounting is made for the decline in either market share due to market competition or, conversely, the increase in demand due to market growth for the services. The local exchange carrier's (LEC) demand, as opposed to the industry demand, will certainly diminish as competition enters the market. This is ignored in the engineering process models.

Moreover, the models do not allow for demand growth (or shrinkage) over time, but are designed to meet the maximum demand. This implies that investments are not added incrementally, but at once. A related assumption of these models, which ignores reality, is that the investment and the revenues derived therefrom occur instantly.

These problems can be summarized as follows:

- The demand is assumed to be perfectly inelastic
- Output is constant
- There is no decrement in market share.

3.3 Multi-Period Models

Expanding the model to multiple periods is the next complication. This introduces several issues. How is the capital treated over the time periods? When does the capital become productive? How does it deteriorate? Must it be augmented? Must it all be in place initially? Does it have any salvage value at the end of its life? How should the time-value of money be handled? And when are revenues received? The method of treating these issues will determine how well the models reflect the realities of the marketplace. The following sections contrast the traditional method of project evaluation with the RR method.

3.4 Traditional Valuation

Traditional project evaluation treats the time periods explicitly using what is known as discounted cash flow (DCF) techniques. The cash flow over time generated by a project or service is estimated; and then the cash flow is "discounted" or reduced over time by the factor $1/(1+r)^t$, where t is the period in which the cash flow occurred.[8] The discount factor, r, represents the opportunity cost of capital for the firm, or what the firm could earn in the marketplace in its next-best alternative.[9]

If the sum of these discounted cash flows, known as the present value (including the initial and any intermediate investments), is greater than zero, the project is "profitable." In a properly constructed cost model, this present value would be set to zero; that is, the discounted revenues just cover the discounted costs and the "revenue requirements" are met. If there are no taxes (yes, an heroic assumption in today's world, but it is dropped later), then accounting depreciation is of no concern. Indeed, economic depreciation is of no concern except in the last period, when the economic depreciation represents the salvage or market value of the investment – what the investment will sell for in the marketplace (or what will be the cost to remove it). The investors are only interested in earning their money back on the investment after accounting for the time value of money (the fact that the cash earned tomorrow is not as valuable as the same amount of cash earned today) plus a return on the investment.

The cash flow is composed of the revenue earned and the cash outlays during the period. While it may seem trivial to note that the revenue is composed of the price of the service times the quantity, this appears to have escaped the cost modelers' notice. The price is endogenous. But what the modelers are attempting to determine is the price. It is axiomatic for economists to consider that price and quantities interact. The downward sloping demand curve is in every economist's tool kit. One cannot determine the quantities without the prices and vice versa. However, this is what the cost modelers have done. Quantities are estimated without regard to prices, and then prices are determined as an output of the model.[10]

3.4.1 Taxes and Depreciation

Before considering how depreciation is handled in the DCF models, it is worthwhile noting how it is handled in the revenue requirement (RR) models. In the RR models, it is added as an expense and reduces the magnitude of the capital upon which the rate of return is calculated.

$$P = [w_0(K_0 - \Sigma D_t) + D + \alpha (K_0 - \Sigma D_t)]/Q_0 \quad (4)$$

Thus, the choice of depreciation can make a significant difference in the price. In the revenue requirement models, the modelers offer it as a parameter to be used to adjust the pricing.[11] This is incorrect. The only factor that should be used is the one the government requires for tax purposes. Any other will not reflect the reality of the tax system and will be inappropriate.

Taxes. In the traditional DCF models, the depreciation required by the tax code is used. It is included because it enters as an accounting expense, which reduces the tax liability. Otherwise, it is an accounting artifact. Taxes are thus calculated based on the depreciation actually used (and required by the tax code).

Depreciation. In the cost models, depreciation schedules are used to determine the number of years over which to annualize the investment. The discount factor used to annualize the investment is the weighted-average cost of capital.

The depreciation schedule is also used to determine the life of equipment. This is needed to annualize the equipment life in the discounting formula. For example, in the HAI model, the depreciation schedule comes from the Joint Board's determination of what the life of the asset should be for regulatory accounting purposes.[12] It is most definitely not the economic life, which can only be determined with knowledge of the output prices. Moreover, it is commonly known in the industry that this schedule is biased toward long-lived depreciation rates, since a very long-lived asset has the effect of keeping exchange rates low.[13]

The DCF model can be rewritten with these changes:

$$DCF = \Sigma\{[(P_tQ_t - CFO_t) - tx_t\,(P_tQ_t - Exp_t - D_t\,)]/(1+r)^t\}, \quad (5)$$
$$\text{summed over } t = 0, T$$

Where P_tQ_t is price times the quantity sold (revenue) or cash inflow, CFO represents the cash outflow (that is, any capital outlays along with expenses (Exp_t) or non-capital cash outlays), and tx is the tax rate on net income. The tax burden is represented by the second term in the summation. It is the operating income before taxes. Note that taxes are reduced, *inter alia*, by the accounting depreciation, but this is not a cash outlay and only represents an allocation of an earlier capital outlay.

The more familiar form of the cash flow model is the earnings after taxes plus depreciation, which is equivalent to the above expression (assuming no intermediate capital investments).

$$DCF = \Sigma[(1 - tx_t)(P_tQt - Exp_t - D_t) + D_t]/(1+r)^t \quad (6)$$

In other words, the firm's only concern with the accounting depreciation is its impact on its tax liability and hence, its cash flow. When the project terminates, depreciation (both accounting and economic) becomes a concern. The difference between the salvage value (or the market value) of the asset, and the asset's book value gives rise to a positive or negative (accounting) capital gain.[14] This capital gain or loss is subject to a tax liability or credit. This book value is determined by the accumulated accounting depreciation less the initial cost of the asset.

The difference between the original market price of the assets and its current market value represents the accumulated *economic* depreciation. This suggests that the only depreciation that should be considered for any of the cost models is the depreciation required for tax purposes and an estimation of the salvage value less the book value at the termination of the project. In the United States and most other countries, these schedules are quite precise and codified in the tax law.

While depreciation is important, it is not treated appropriately by modelers. The manner of handling depreciation in these models is suggested when the model treats it as an input or a variable, which can be changed under different scenarios.[15] The arguments as to the use of accounting or economic depreciation are misdirected. In these discussions, the modelers are considering the rate-base, rate-of-return models, where they wish to capture the "using up of capital" in that period. Here, the economic depreciation would be the correct solution, but only if this calculation were made year-by-year. Moreover, the market value of the asset is determined primarily by the price of the output the assets support, which was noted is endogenous. Even then, the tax liability would have to be considered, which is based on the accounting depreciation.[16] What the modelers are attempting to do is the impossible. They are trying to find the output price for a service in a particular year, but then assume that this will be adequate for the remaining life of the service. This makes an additional, inappropriate, assumption: In addition to the previous problems, the following are added:

- Certainty is assumed
- Accounting depreciation is treated as a real cost
- An incorrect discount rate is employed

- Tax treatment is inappropriate
- No growth in demand is assumed

3.4.2 Other Issues

At the risk of being pedantic, the above points can be demonstrated by developing a stylized example of traditional project evaluation, which can be contrasted with the current cost models. It will consist of an eleven period (from 0 to 10) model, which will include, ultimately, all the features an *ab ovo* project should consider.[17] To evaluate the project, the investment and other costs are judged against the income. But, as noted earlier, income is determined by the demand relationship and is endogenous. Assuming this problem away for the moment by assuming a perfectly inelastic demand for the service, the cost side can be examined. Second, just as Rome was not built in a day, the telecommunications network cannot be built instantaneously, although the cost models not only assume this is the case but also that the associated revenue is obtained instantaneously. Thus, this paper's model has the investment occurring in the zero period (that is, in the first year of operation) and the revenue and associated expenses occurring in the later periods. This has at least two impacts that the cost modelers ignore: the delay before income accrues – a return on the investment is required during this gap. It also demonstrates the lack of dynamics in the cost models.

Turning to the traditional evaluation method once more, it can be seen that demand does not remain constant over the periods. This implies that the initial investment can be augmented over time and that both revenue and, perhaps, expenses will increase during this time period. At least two of the cost models handled this dynamic by assuming that the service is provided for the maximum demand anticipated. Thus, until demand grows to this level, capacity is underutilized, even if, as is likely the case, the capacity could have been added incrementally. Neither demand, investment, nor expenses grow. This gives an obvious bias to the results.

This is the first instance where real options methodology can be applied. Demand and its growth are uncertain. If the initial demand does not manifest itself, the firm has the option not to invest and expend additional operating funds; indeed, it has the option to contract its investment. This active management flexibility is not captured by the traditional models, but can be incorporated with real options methods. While analysts may disagree on the characterization of the probability density function, the methodology does make the assumptions explicit and, not as the author was informed recently by a regulator, that they would account for these considerations based on "judgment."

The traditional method evaluates the project in a crude dynamic – estimates of the prices, quantities, expenses, investments and other costs are forecasted for input into the cash flow analysis. Interest rates, economic conditions and other market factors are considered in a sophisticated analysis. Risk or uncertainties are handled in a variety of ways: capital asset pricing methods (CAPM), sensitivity, decision tree, and/or simulation analyses. Real options methodology creates a sophisticated dynamics that none of the models has captured, as is demonstrated below.

Investment Costs. The cost of the investment is determined by multiplying the input price (the unit cost) of the investments by the quantity of the physical investments. The investment input prices are at the "list" price, which could be subject to quantity discounts, but this is not considered.

Expenses. Expenses are determined as a factor of the specific investments. Where available, these factors are based on historical relationships and vary by the specific investment.

Once again, the expense factor shows a lack of economic considerations. The expense factors enter the model as a proportion of the particular investment. And while they may be based on historical relationships, they do not comport with the realities of today's marketplace. There is no ability to tradeoff the expense factors with the magnitude of the investment. The expense factors contain a large amount of labor in their components. Every beginning economist is confronted with the necessity of learning about the tradeoff between labor and capital. As the price of labor goes up, capital is substituted for labor and vice versa. Within the context of these models, this is not possible.

Table 1 summaries these faults in the cost models. But even if the modelers corrected these deficiencies, one glaring defect remains. The new investment theory, known as real options, has not been considered.

Total Cost. The annualized investment, expenses and overhead costs are added together to determine the total cost. This is then divided by the quantity, which started the process, to determine a price.

Additional Problems. Before turning to real options considerations, other points should be noted regarding this modeling.

The prevailing models are static models – what the real options, in part, correct – and are known in economist jargon as light bulb or "one-hoss shay" models (that is, the investment functions as if it were new and needs no maintenance until it

Table 1: Engineering Process Model Modules and Problems

Module	Problem
Quantity	Constant output
Engineering design and relationships	No technological substitution No economies of scope No factor price consideration
Investments determined	One-time investment Static factor costs/prices Light bulb model No economies of scale/scope Static discount/interest rate Constant capacity factor No differentiated risk profile No real options consideration
Expenses	Annualized (constant) as proportion of investments No labor/capital substitution
Depreciation from schedule	Not economic, but accounting Not tax, but regulatory Schedule from Joint Board Certainty of life Non-economic calculation
Rate-base, rate-of-return revenue requirement	No dynamics One price No change in input or output prices Static discount rate
Revenue requirement/quantity **determines price!**	No price (demand) effects Revenue requirement level No competitive impacts No market share loss

suddenly "blows out" or dies). Everything is calculated at the beginning of the period and built instantaneously. There is no allowance for growth in demand or changing factor prices over time. Finally, differential risk profiles, irreversibility and the sunkenness of various investments are ignored. This is critical when considering real options, as shown in the next section.

3.5 Real Options: A Brief Sketch[18]

Real options is based on the fact that one can evaluate real (i.e., physical) assets with the same tools as financial options. Since the Black Scholes method of pricing options was developed over a quarter of a century ago, the methodology has been refined and extended. The essence of the method ensures that the option is evaluated in a risk-neutral way.

3.5.1 What are Real Options?

As outlined above, the traditional approach to project evaluation and investments uses discounted cash flow (DCF) methods. These methods explicitly assume the project will meet the expected cash flow with no intervention by management in the process. All the uncertainty is handled in the (risk-adjusted) discount rate. It is static. At most, the expected value of the cash flow is incorporated into the analysis. Management's flexibility to make decisions as states of nature are revealed is assumed away. However, management discretion has value, which is not incorporated into the DPV. The real options methodology goes beyond this naïve view of valuation and more closely matches the manner in which firms operate. It allows for the flexibility the firm has to abandon, contract, expand or otherwise modify its actions after nature has revealed itself. This is another lesson for the policymakers – if they wish to emulate the competitive process, they cannot rely on applications of traditional DCF methods in cost models.

Decision-tree analysis (DTA) moves the analysis one step forward by allowing that decisions can be made after information has been received. But, as in the case of DCF, the appropriate risk-adjusted discount rate is virtually indeterminate.[19] Using the firm's opportunity cost of capital is inappropriate if the project does not correlate with the company's cost of capital – another lesson for the telecommunications industry. Unbundled network elements have different levels of risk. For example, the operator services element's risk/return is much different from that of the local loop element. Calculating the cost/price of these elements using the same discount rate would be incorrect.

However, none of the traditional approaches to dealing with uncertainty such as decision-tree analysis, simulations, and sensitivity analysis has the capacity to deal with uncertainty as meaningfully as real options.

The second insight of the theory is the recognition that a well-developed financial/portfolio theory applies to asset/project evaluation. This allows for the integration of capital budgeting issues with physical (i.e., "real"), assets on the one hand, and the incorporation of decision-tree analysis on the other. A portfolio of securities is created which is (perfectly) correlated with the investment. The portfolio's price and return are known. Rather than considering the expected value of outcomes, it incorporates the probability density function within the analysis. It is not necessary to determine a risk-adjusted discount rate. Uncertainty is not eliminated, but it is accounted for in the density function and the twin portfolio. The construction of an equivalent portfolio to the asset in question can be evaluated with the techniques that have been developed for financial options, for example, the Black Scholes (1973) methods of option valuation.[20, 21]

3.5.2 Concepts and Applications

Real options is a means of capturing the flexibility of management to address uncertainties as they are revealed. Present value methods fail to account for this flexibility. While much of the debate in telecommunications focuses on the irreversibility of investments, the flexibility that management has goes beyond deferring sunk costs, and includes: abandon, shut down and restart, expand, contract, and switch use.

The key valuation concept is that an option can be priced based on the construction of a portfolio of a specific number of shares of an underlying asset, and that one can borrow against the shares at a riskless rate to replicate the return of the option in a risk-neutral world.

The options theory is able to overcome the deficiencies of the traditional present value technique through an understanding of the interactions, interdependencies, and competitive interactions among projects.

The framework for the application of real options to investment opportunities is concerned with discrete (binomial) events or with continuous distributions.

The intuition of real options, by accounting for this asymmetry in outcomes, is simple, but profound – management's decisions skew the distribution of possible outcomes toward the upside. Real options methodologies can take the best features of DCF and DTA without their failings.

Real options can be applied to a variety of cases including competitive interactions. However, a simple linear addition to the valuation of a traditional discounted cash flow analysis cannot correct for the real options impact. This method can make a significant difference in the valuation, as shown below. It expands the notion of manager's flexibility and strategic interaction in skewing the results of the traditional DPV analysis which, as with financial options, allows for gains on the upside, and minimizes the downside potential, thus increasing the valuation. Viewed in light of traditional economic theory, real options suggests that the traditional theory needs re-evaluation.

> No ad hoc, exogenously provided, single risk-adjusted discount rate properly captures the interdependencies between current and future decisions in the presence of managerial flexibility, since risk changes endogenously in time, with the underlying uncertain variable, and with managerial response. Since the value of a flexible project and the optimal operating (exercise) schedule must generally be determined concurrently, the dis-

count rate must, in effect, be imputed *endogenously* within a forward-looking dynamic programming process.

An option-based (expanded-NPV) analysis bypasses the discount-rate problem by relying on the notion of a comparable security to properly price risk while still being able to capture the dynamic interdependencies between cash flows and future optional decisions (Trigeorgis 1996, p. 200).

Assume that a project requires an investment of $104 and has a value of $100 in the first period.[22] It has a return in the second period of either $180 or $60, with an equally likely probability of occurrence. The comparable security is $20 initially and $36 or $12 in the next period. This implies that the cost of capital is 20 percent. If one calculated the DCF of the expected value of the project, the DCF is $ - 4 < 0. Thus, it would not be undertaken. But with management flexibility, the firm could wait one period to see what the state of nature would be. Evaluating this using real options tools, one would solve for the value of the twin security such that it would be risk-neutral (that is, the purchase of the security and borrowing of an amount at the risk-free interest rate that replicated the return). In the example, this implies purchasing 2.82 shares and borrowing $31.33. Solving this for the initial conditions, the value is $25.07. Thus, the option valuation is $29.07 = (($25.07 – ($ - 4)).

This is different from the value calculated with the opportunity cost of capital, which overestimates the value of using the-risk free rate, which underestimates the value. In other words, alternative discount rates cannot correct the deficiencies that real options reveals.[23]

While the example used here is the deferral of the investment, the methodology applies to other areas of management discretion: expand, contract, abandon, and start up or shut down.[24]

While there is a debate about the extent of irreversibility in the local loop, a contraction of the market is also possible with the introduction of competition in the exchange market.

Changes in valuations due to competitive interaction can be dealt with – both exogenous entry and endogenous reactions. Although real options theory is increasingly used in industry,[25] it has not been applied in the telecommunications industry.[26] But, as will be argued below, telecommunications is ripe for this methodology.

3.5.3 Model Discussion

To crudely estimate some of the deficiencies described above, the author built a stylized model based on the traditional cash flow (CF) approach to project evaluation. The major parameters from the HAI model were used. In addition, the price of the revenue requirements (RR) models was forced to $20 a month as a reference point. Twenty dollars is approximately the current national average of the price of exchange access estimated by the hybrid FCC model. The RR model underestimates the CF model by approximately 10 percent. But the main purpose of this construction was to apply the real options methodology to this cash flow. Depending on the volatility factor assumed, the underestimation from the RR model can be as much as 60 percent.

Before discussing these results in detail, the model, including its strengths and weakness, is described. The purpose is not to estimate "the price," but to show the poverty of the RR models in determining "the price" of access and to indicate how inaccurate the estimations are with the correction of only a few of their deficiencies.

The model follows the RR models by assuming that the level of investment, which in turn is determined by the demand, drives the model. However, it was assumed here that the demand grows over time. Arbitrarily, it was also assumed that the demand is 100 units in the initial period. The base case is one percent (1%) per year over the ten-year life of the project. Second, it was assumed that it takes a year to build to the incremental demand. The demand is multiplied by the investment factor and the input price (the cost per unit of investment). This determines the required investment and cost in each period. For simplicity, a straight-line depreciation over ten years was then assumed. It would be preferable to use actual tax depreciation, as noted above, but to compare with the RR this simplifying assumption was made. Had tax depreciation been used, the schedule would have had more depreciation in the early periods, thus providing a larger tax shield in the earlier periods, reducing taxes in these periods and improving the cash flow (lessening the outflow).

Next the expense factor, interest, debt to equity ratio, and tax assumptions of the HAI model were employed. These provide sufficient information to develop the cash flow. First, the costs for tax purposes were calculated (expenses plus interest charges plus depreciation) and then the taxes. (Because only costs are dealt with here, this represents a tax credit to the firm.) To develop the cash flow, investment for the period was added to the expenses, interest and tax charges. (Note, as previously indicated, depreciation is only used for the tax calculation.)

The traditional DCF analysis then applies the discount rate to the cash flow. The proper method to handle this is to use the risk free-interest rate to discount the investments and a risk-adjusted rate to the balance.[27] In the traditional approach, the risk-adjusted rate to use is one that is appropriate to the risk of the project. Thus, a project such as operator services would have a different discount rate from exchange loops. More sophisticated analysis uses the capital asset pricing model (CAPM) to determine the proper discount rate. The CAPM determines the risk-adjusted rate based on the systematic risk associated with the project. The cost models ignore this refinement and simply use the weighted average cost of capital (WACC) for the discount rate.[28] For comparative purposes, this analysis used the WACC rate as a discount rate for the balance of the cash flow.

Using these parameters, the RR model was then set up. Even with these modest corrections to the RR approach, the difference is over 10 percent.

In order to develop the real options methodology, the RR model was solved for a price of $20 by varying the input price of the required investment. With this price of the inputs, the traditional model was solved for the price that would generate sufficient discounted revenues to cover the cost using the traditional method.

The above procedure corrects for the deficiencies of the RR models by ensuring accurate discounting of the investment stream, the appropriate handling of depreciation in calculating taxes, and the growth of demand.

What it does not correct for is the appropriate depreciation rate, the inflexibility of the expense function, the correct risk-adjusted discount rate, price/demand effects, and other problems listed in Table 1. Moreover, the subject of this volume, real options, was not corrected for. Many uncertainties exist in the telecommunications industry, which suggest that real options methodology is appropriate. The most obvious of these impacts is the speed and magnitude of competitive entry in the exchange market, and the uncertainty of judicial and regulatory actions. This refinement is discussed next.

The method selected here to incorporate real options was to use the Black Scholes algorithm to calculate the option value of the service. It was assumed that the risk-free discount present value of the investment is the strike price of the option, and the risk-adjusted discounted stream of non-investment cash flows is the stock price. The risk-free interest rate, the eleven periods of the cash flows, and various volatility rates in the algorithm were employed. This shows that the price may be underestimated by as much as 60 percent.

Because not all of the criticisms of the cost models were incorporated in these calculations, a precise estimate of the misspecification was not possible. However, the objective was not to determine the size of the underestimate, but to show that ignoring real options can make a significant difference in the estimation of costs, which has been done.

4. SUMMARY AND CONCLUSIONS

Attempts to estimate forward-looking costs in both the United States and abroad are based on cost models whose foundation is traditionally applied discounted cash flow analysis – exactly the method that real options methodology has shown can give terribly wrong results. These cost models are ideal vehicles to adapt to the real options methodology. All the data are in a form to which real options considerations can be applied without a measured change in their structure. However, it should be cautioned that the results are nonlinear, that is, the modelers cannot simply add an "'additive'" factor to the results of their models to "correct" for the real options impact.

This paper has shown that the cost models have fundamental methodological flaws, even when considering a traditional approach to valuation. Moreover, the models neglect the latest application of valuation theory – real options – and it has been demonstrated that this can make a significant difference in costs. This is consistent with others' results (Dixit and Pyndick, 1994; Hausman, 1998).

Policymakers are ill advised to use these cost models to determine universal service funding, unbundled network elements, or interconnection charges. The magnitude of the error can result in hundreds of millions, if not billions, of dollars of misallocated resources. Incorrect price signals will retard investment, research and development. The mis-estimations can equally cost consumers hundreds of millions, if not billions, in lost welfare. It would be highly irresponsible for policymakers to make decisions without considering the real options impacts. Policies dealing with costs cannot be effective unless they are made with a fundamental understanding of the real options theory's implications.

NOTES

1 The author would like to thank Larry Cole, Wynne Cougill, Barbara R. Miller, and Eli Noam for their useful comments and suggestions. The partial support of Curtin University of Technology, Perth, Australia, is also gratefully acknowledged. The usual disclaimer applies.

2 Also referred to as (net) (discounted) present value techniques. These terms are used interchangeably here.

[3] For example, see National Economic Research Associates. 1999. *Estimating the Long Run Incremental Cost of PSTN Access*. Appendix C, pp. 80 ff.

[4] Dixit, Avinash K. and Robert S. Pindyck. 1994. *Investment under Uncertainty*, Princeton, NJ: Princeton University Press, p. 153.

[5] These models serve a variety of purposes: the calculation of universal service obligations, access charges, reciprocal compensation, or UNE prices. These are referred to as "prices" in the remainder of this paper.

[6] While these cost models go into great detail on the engineering aspects of the telephone network, many lack a fundamental understanding of economics and finance, i.e., they fail to apply the appropriate, traditional techniques of engineering economics. Some do not use present discounted value or discounted cash flow (DCF) techniques to evaluate the capital investments. They simply use a revenue requirement method, based on arbitrary cost allocations. Many of the cost models have ignored DCF's major contribution to asset valuation (e.g., NERA, 1999, pp. 80ff.)

[7] Unless otherwise specified, this paper's references to cost models are the HAI (1997); INDETEC International, Inc., et al. (1999), FCC (1999) (see http://www.fcc.gov/ccb/apd/hcpm/), and National Economic Research Associates (1999).

[8] Engineering economics texts best illustrate this approach. See, for example, deGamo et al. (1993) or Steiner (1996). These texts delve into the mechanics of DCF analysis and cost estimation methods, but have little, if any, discussion of the capital budgeting or financial considerations of project evaluation, or the determination of the proper discount rate.

[9] The more sophisticated analyses use the risk-adjusted rate of return, which is based on the capital asset pricing method (CAPM), one of the methods used to account for uncertainly in the marketplace. This, however, is not the same as the weighted average cost of capital (WACC) that the cost modelers use in their calculations. Indeed, the real options methodology suggests that the discount rate used in DCF calculations changes each period. See Trigeorgis (1996, pp. 38-52) and the references cited therein. For a brief general exposition of capital budgeting, see Trigeorgis (1996, Chapter 2, pp. 23-68); for an in-depth approach see Hull (1997).

[10] The modelers may argue that the demand is perfectly inelastic, or nearly so. If this is the case, then the universal service obligation cannot be met, no matter what the price of exchange access. No price will be low enough to bring on additional subscribers!

[11] See for example, NERA model, op. cit., HAI model (1999a) and Pelcovits (1999).

[12] The Joint Board is a legacy of regulation. If is composed of the FCC and state regulatory staff. It was designed to determine depreciation for ratemaking purposes, not tax purposes.

[13] See Salinger (1998) for an excellent analysis of the inappropriateness of depreciation handling within the engineering process models. He shows, *inter alia*, that economic depreciation cannot be determined from the engineering process models, since economic depreciation is dependent on the price of the outputs.

[14] In the case of removal costs, the capital gain is unequivocally negative. In other cases, the sign of the gain is indeterminate. The better the accounting depreciation matches the economic depreciation, the smaller will be the gain or loss.

[15] This is clearly the case in the NERA model, op. cit., and appears to be the case in HAI Model Release 5.0a (1998a), which uses the regulatory review process to determine depreciation inputs, not the tax code. Also see Pelcovits (1999) in this volume. See HAI Consulting, Inc. *Inputs Portfolio*, January 27, 1998, page 118 at http://www.hainc.com/hminputs.pdf. The URL for the HAI model descriptions can be found at http://www.hainc.com/ documentation.html.

[16] Salinger (1998) correctly critiques the method by which depreciation is handled in the cost models. Many of his points concern the attempt to capture the depreciation effects in the rate-of return type models.

[17] By convention the period labeled 1 is the end of the first period and the beginning of the second. For expository purposes, this period is assumed to be one year.

[18] This section is adapted from the author's forthcoming review of Lenos Trigeorgis. 1996. *Real Options: Management Flexibility and Strategy in Resource Allocation.*

[19] While it is possible to determine the risk-adjusted discount rate, it involves certainty-equivalent or risk-neutral probabilities, which are not easy to calculate. Moreover, real options methodology remedies this problem. See Trigeorgis (1996), pp. 58 - 68.

[20] See Hull (1997) for a complete description of options methods.

[21] A financial option is the right to buy (a call) or sell (a put) a stock, but not the obligation, at a given price within a certain period of time. If the option is not exercised, the only loss is the price of the option, but the upside potential is large. The asymmetry of the option – the protection from the downside risk with the possibility of a large upside gain – is what gives the option value. (A European option can only be exercised on a specific date, while an American option can be exercised any time before the expiration date.)

[22] This example is from Trigeorgis (1996). Also see Copeland et al. (1991).

[23] See Trigeorgis (1996) or Copeland et al. (1991) for the details of this type of calculation.

[24] Many of the commentators in this volume (e.g., Alleman, Noam) leave the impression that the irreversibility of investment is the only driver of the real options methodology. This is the impression left if one only looked at the economic literature and ignored the financial literature on the topic. For example, see footnote 3 in Clarke, this volume, which has no financial citations. Also, the commentators note that real options is only considered in a monopoly environment, but this is not true; for example, see Trigeorgis (1999) and the reference cited therein.

[25] See *The Economist* (1999) for the current state of play of real options in other industries.

[26] Hausman's (1997, 1998) application of options (not real options) theory to value unbundled network elements and Small's (1998) application to network pricing is as close as the industry has come to the author's knowledge.

[27] Many analysts discount the total cash flow by some risk-adjusted discount rate. This is inappropriate because uncommitted investment funds need not make the same return as the balance of the cash flow See Luehrman (1998a) and Alleman (1999).

[28] The WACC is the average of the equity return and the cost of debt weighted by the proportion of each.

REFERENCES

Alleman, James and Eli Noam (eds.). 1999. *Real Options: The New Investment Theory and its Implications for Telecommunications Economics.* Boston: Kluwer Academic Publishers.

Alleman, James. forthcoming. "Real Options by Lenos Trigeorgis" (a book review). in *Information Economics and Policy.*

Black, F. and M. Scholes. 1973. "The Pricing of Options and Corporate Liabilities," *Journal of Political Economy,* 81, 637-654.

Clarke, Richard N. 1999. "Rethinking the Implications of 'Real Options' Theory for the U.S. Local Telephone Industry." *Real Options: The New Investment Theory and its Implications for Telecommunications Economics.* Boston: Kluwer Academic Publishers.

Copeland, Tom and Jack Murrin Koller. 1991. "Using Options Pricing Methods to Value Flexibility." *Valuation: Measuring and Managing the Value for Companies*, New York: John Wiley & Sons.

DeGarmo, Paul E., William G. Sullivan, and James A. Bontadelli. 1993. *Engineering Economics*, 9th. ed. New York: MacMillan.

Dixit, Avinash K. and Robert S. Pindyck. 1994. *Investment under Uncertainty.* Princeton, NJ: Princeton University Press.

Dixit, A.K. and R.S. Pindyck. 1995. "The Options Approach to Capital Investments," *Harvard Business Review*, 73, 105-115.

"Economic Focus: Keeping All Options Open," *The Economist*, August 14 -20, 1999, p. 62.

HAI Consulting, Inc.1998a. *Inputs Portfolio*, January 27. At http://www.hainc.com/hminputs.pdf. The URL for the HAI model descriptions can be found at http://www.hainc.com/ documentation.html

HAI Consulting, Inc. 1998b. HAI Model Release 5.0a, "Model Description," Revised: February 16.

Hausman, J. 1997. Testimony before the California Public Service Commission, April 7.

Hausman, J. 1998. "Valuation and the Effect of Regulation on New Services in Telecommunications. Washington, DC: *Brookings Papers on Economic Activity: Microeconomics.*

Hull, J.C. 1997. *Options, Futures and other Derivatives*, 3rd ed. Upper Saddle River NJ: Prentice-Hall.

INDETEC International, Inc., BellSouth, Sprint and USWest. 1999. Benchmark Cost Proxy Model, Release 3.0, 1999.

Luehrman, T.A. 1998a. "Investment Opportunities as Real Options: Getting Started on the Numbers," *Harvard Business Review*, 76, 51-67.

Luehrman, T.A. 1998b. "Strategy as a Portfolio of Real Options," *Harvard Business Review*, 76, 89-99.

NERA. 1999. *Estimating the Long run Incremental Cost of PSTN Access, Final Report for ACCC (Australian Competition & Consumer Commission).* London.

Pelcovits, Michael D. 1999. "Application of Real Options Theory to TELRIC Models: Real Trouble or Red Herring," in Alleman, James and Eli Noam (eds.). *Real Options: The New Investment Theory and its Implications for Telecommunications Economics.* Boston: Kluwer Academic Publishers.

Salinger, Michael. October 1998. "Regulating Prices to Equal Forward Looking Costs: Cost-Based Prices or Price-Based Costs?" Paper presented at the Telecommunications Policy Research Conference 1998, Arlington, VA.

Small, John P. 1998. Real Options and the Pricing of Network Access. Working paper, Centre for Research in Network Economics and Communications.

School of Business and Economics, University of Auckland. June 1998.Auckland, New Zealand. See http://www.crnec.auckland.ac.nz/papers/wp16.pdf

Steiner, Henry Malcolm. 1996. *Engineering Economic Principles*, 2nd. ed. New York: McGraw Hill.

Taylor, L.D. 1980. *Telecommunications Demand: A Survey and Critique.* Cambridge, MA: Ballinger Publishing Co.

Trigeorgis, Lenos. 1999. "Real Options: A Primer". Chapter 1 in *Real Options: The New Investment Theory and its Implications for Telecommunications*, James Alleman and Eli Noam, eds. Boston: Kluwer Academic Press.

Trigeorgis, Lenos. 1996. *Real Options: Management Flexibility and Strategy in Resource Allocation.* Cambridge, Mass.: MIT Press.

11

The Forecasting Implications of Telecommunications Cost Models[1]

Timothy J. Tardiff
National Economic Research Associates

Abstract - The Federal Communications Commission and state regulators have relied on models of long-run forward looking costs when establishing prices for the services and facilities provided by incumbent local exchange carriers. These models produce results that are fundamentally complicated long-run forecasts: what constant price(s) can the incumbent charge for the output it produces that will just recover its expenses and allow it to earn a reasonable return on and of its capital investments. This paper discusses the underlying assumptions of these forecasts and identifies methods for properly representing their inherent uncertainty in the estimates produced by cost models.

The Federal Communications Commission and numerous state regulators have required the use of forward looking economic cost models to establish prices for network components that must be sold to the competitors of incumbent local exchange carriers (ILECs) and to establish the subsidy levels required for universal service.[2] While forecasting is typically associated with the demand, rather than the cost, side of a company's business operations, there are a number of implicit forecasting issues involved in proper cost calculations that are often either not recognized or ignored in practical applications.

When one looks at economic costs, in general, and those associated with assets with long lives, in particular, the essential role of forecasting becomes apparent. The economic definition of cost deals with the question of the expenditure of resources that will be incurred as the result of a decision to offer a product or service. Clearly, the answer to this question depends on how resources will be used in the future, i.e., a forecast is necessary. In the case of investments with short economic lives, such forecasts can be straightforward – what you recently paid for a quickly used-up resource is likely to apply in the near future. For assets with long lives, the forecasting becomes more complicated.

Consider the case of a telecommunications investment, such as a central office switch. Determining the economic cost of that asset is equivalent to a how a business determines whether it is economic to invest at all. In addition to the purchase price of the switch, the business must consider: 1) how long the switch will last (economic life), 2) the volume of products produced by the switch that will be sold (demand forecast), 3) the price at which switches will be sold, 4) how the purchase price of new switches will change in the future (economic depreciation), and 5) uncertainty in the "forecasts" just enumerated. A sound investment decision considers all of these factors, and so should a properly conducted cost study.

This paper elaborates on how forecasting impinges on the development of correct economic costs. Section 1 describes the typical approach to cost models and compares it to the conceptually equivalent approach to investment decisions. Section 2 identifies how the consideration of specific items subject to forecasting affects the development of correct costs. The last section concludes the paper.

1. TYPICAL COST MODELS AND INVESTMENT DECISION MODELS

Turning first to cost models, the analysis in models that have been recently adopted or are being considered by regulators consists of the following steps: 1) estimate the *investment* in new equipment necessary to serve a predetermined level of demand, 2) estimate the operating expenses required to operate the new equipment, and 3) convert these costs, which are forecasted to occur over the life of the investment, into annual (or monthly) costs.

A simplified view of this process can be represented by the following equation:[3]

PV asset = Value of Investment + PV (operating costs, life, discount rate)

In the equation above, PV denotes present value and the value of the investment accounts for tax considerations, i.e., depreciation is tax-deductible and equity earnings are taxed. Operating expenses are typically assumed to be constant over the life of the asset, so that their present value is determined by applying a present value formula found in spreadsheet software for a constant annuity over a period equal to the life of the project, discounted at a rate approved by the regulator.

The present value calculated above is then annualized, again applying standard financial formulas.[4] Note that the step of annualizing the present value of the investment creates a peculiar depreciation pattern that is quite different from any used in regulation, let alone the actual economic depreciation of telecommunications assets. Just like a personal financial transaction (e.g., a home loan), a constant annual amount implies that the investment is depreciating slowly at first (in the early years of a home loan, the payment is predominantly interest) and accelerates as the life of the investment unfolds (at the end of the home loan, the same payment represents mainly principal).

In contrast, the "text book" investment equations is:[5]

$$PV = -I_0 + \sum_{i=1}^{T} \frac{-I_i + (Rev_i - Op\ Cost_i)}{(1 + r)^i}$$

In the above equation, I denotes investment and r represents the (after-tax) discount rate. Comparing the cost model equation to the investment decision equation identifies a number of simplifying assumptions, which in turn impose powerful forecasting *assumptions* on the former. First, in general, investments can occur throughout the life of the project, while cost models typically assume that investment occurs up-front and that any subsequent investment occurs in replacing the asset after its life is over. Second, whether the investment is economic (PV > 0) depends on the revenue realized by the investment, and this revenue can vary over the life of the project. In contrast, the cost model implicitly produces a constant revenue over the life of the investment that makes the present value equal to zero. Third, the investment decision model allows operating costs to vary over time, while the cost model assumes that they are constant.

The revenue forecast implied by the cost model is especially stringent. Such models typically provide for facilities sufficient to accommodate a known level of demand. Therefore, the constant revenue outcome is fundamentally a forecast: the ILEC will be able to charge a single price over the life of the asset that will just allow it to recover its expenses, depreciate its plant, and earn a fair return on its investment. And this "forecast" is implicitly made independent of whatever is happening to the demand for the services produced by the investment — in particular, no consideration is given to factors such as how competition will affect demand, how changes in the prices of equipment will affect the market price for services produced by that equipment, and how the first two items might vary by geography, customer type, and service mix over the operations of the ILEC, and uncertainty in all three.

2. ACCOMMODATING ALTERNATIVE FORECASTS IN COST MODELS

The implicit forecasts of constant prices for both telecommunications equipment and the services produced by these investments defy expectations. In particular, at least for some types of equipment (mainly those based on electronics and computers, such as switches and fiber optic electronics), the expectation is for *decreasing*, not constant, prices. Similarly, there is a general expectation that the competition, which is the main backdrop in the development of the models in the first place, will drive the prices of services down.

Of course, it is important to recognize that the simple implicit forecasts have been adopted with good intentions: namely, to produce workable cost models that will provide prices that will start competition rolling. These models are already very complicated. In effect, the forward looking philosophy underlying these models calls for prices and quantities of numerous items that comprise a telecommunications network, based not on what can be observed outside, but instead on a hypothetical new company that serves demand by starting over with new equipment. Whether this task is doable in a reasonable time period is still an open question. In a sense, overlaying complicated price and demand forecasts on top of what is already there could make the whole enterprise impossible.

Fortunately, recent research as well as casual observation of other industries can produce results that 1) qualitatively explain the consequences of the implicit forecasts when they depart too much from reality and 2) suggest possible adjustments to the results produced by a typical cost study. Interestingly, while these emerging approaches tend to produce a series of prices that vary over the life of the project, they tend to focus on the prices for the first year. This focus makes sense in that the most immediate need is for prices that allow competition to get started. As that competition develops, alternatives to the products and services produced by the ILECs will emerge and the market, rather than regulators, will increasingly determine the relevant prices.[6]

2.1 Accommodating Non-constant Equipment and Output Prices

Hausman[7] and Krouse[8] have analyzed the impact of declining equipment prices on the costs and prices produced from a cost study. Turning first to declining prices for equipment, both Hausman and Krouse analyze the case of prices declining at a constant rate.[9] Mathematically, the effect of such a price pattern on the initial price is equivalent to increasing the discount rate by the rate of the price decrease.

Hausman provides the following equation that captures the effect of price changes.

$$PV = \int_0^\infty e^{-rt} \, (Pe^{-\alpha t}) \, \frac{1 - e^{-\delta t}}{\delta} \, dt = \frac{P}{r + \alpha + \delta} \qquad (1)$$

The integral contains three terms: the first converts future cash flows to present value, at the discount rate, r; the second depicts the decline in the output price at a rate of α from the initial level, P; and the third represents economic depreciation of input prices, at a rate of δ.

The right-hand side expresses the relationship between the value of the investment and the output price for the initial period. For a given level of investment, this relation implies that the higher the rate of decline in output and asset prices (α and δ), the higher the initial price has to be to make the investment economic.

Thus, according to the formula, when input and/or output prices are declining, the constant demand and price assumptions lead to an understatement of the initial period price by a factor of[10]

$$\frac{r}{r + \alpha + \delta}$$

For example, if the discount rate is 10 percent and the combined rate of decline in output and input prices is 5 percent annually, the correct price for the first period would be 50 percent higher than that produced by the typical cost model; alternatively, the cost model result is only two-thirds of the correct result.

Krouse discusses the relationship between prices in the initial and subsequent periods when the input price declines at a constant rate. The basic result is that the rate of change in the output price from one year to the next is the same as the rate of change in the input price.[11] The intuition behind this result is straightforward. Under competitive conditions, the decline in input price will be reflected in a decline in the output price. A firm expecting such a price decline would have to charge a higher price early on in anticipation of the decline in revenue that is expected to occur later. Although the present value of revenues recovers investments and operating costs in both the constant output price and declining price cases, a firm facing competition does not have the luxury of charging prices that are inconsistent with competitive conditions. At a constant price, it will recover too little in the early years because competition will drive prices down so that it cannot fully recover its cost from the declining revenues in the later years.

2.2 Accommodating Uncertainty

Both the standard cost model and the alternative case of declining prices assume certain forecasts. Of course, the transitions being experienced by the industry – towards more competition, industries converging, and technology advancing –

have made any long-term forecast of demand and/or cost characteristics problematic. One need look no further than how local competition is developing to see how hazardous such forecasting can be. When the Telecommunications Act was passed a little over three years ago, the then chairman of AT&T announced his expectation that his company would capture a significant share of the local market through a combination of its own facilities plus resale of ILEC services and network components. The current chairman is also predicting a large share, but through a different means – the upgraded facilities of the cable television firms it has already acquired or is in the process of adding. Clearly, to the extent that AT&T succeeds in its current strategy, it will likely result in a very different pattern of demand levels and prices for ILEC services and facilities than AT&T's initial strategy would have produced.

Recently, there has been increasing interest in "real options," which is essentially the conceptual basis for derivative investments in the stock markets. Two aspects of this approach have been suggested for telecommunications applications.[12] First, real options theory recognizes the inherent uncertainty facing many investment decisions and considers the value of alternative courses of action, such as delaying the initial investment, pulling out in the future if demand conditions do not materialize, and so forth. Such a view is the polar opposite of that assumed by recent cost models: the firm for which costs are needed is assumed to make all of the investments needed to serve a certain predetermined demand level up-front, with facilities available at certain input prices in return for a constant price that is supposed to recover these investments over a long period. Because options theory teaches that costs can be lower when uncertainty is accommodated, the very long-run perspective assumed in cost models may, in fact, increase costs, rather than provide the basis for efficient prices.

Therefore, the converse of the cost-reducing effect of keeping one's options open is the possibility that the cost estimates produced by a model that assumes certain demand and prices can understate the correct economic costs by a substantial amount. Hausman has identified four sources of uncertainty that produce higher costs: 1) uncertainty in demand, 2) output price uncertainty, 3) input price uncertainty, and 4) discount rate uncertainty.[13] Using an approach similar to the Black-Scholes option pricing model, Hausman concludes that the price determined in equation 1 above must be increased by a multiple, which in turn is determined by the amount of economic uncertainty in question.[14]

Hausman offers some indication of the amount by which economic uncertainty increases costs. He reports that previous calculations by MacDonald and Seigel[15] and Dixit and Pindyck,[16] where neither output nor input prices are expected to decline, has resulted in a markup factor of approximately two. Focusing on telecommunications, where such price decreases are anticipated, he estimates that the markup is larger – on the order of three.

2.3 Use of Long-Term Contracts

There appears to be widespread agreement that economic uncertainty increases costs, although there is considerable controversy over how large the impact is and what adjustments to the prices produced by cost models, if any, are needed. For example, the FCC has acknowledged the existence of risk and its cost-increasing effects, but has suggested that ILECs can employ long-term contracts to mitigate such risks.[17] When a buyer agrees to purchase output for the duration of the economic life of an asset, the seller's uncertainty is eliminated. In this case, the prices and costs produced by a typical cost model allow the seller to recover its economic costs, i.e., the mark-up factor discussed in the previous section would be 1.0.[18]

The solutions discussed in this and the preceding sections – a markup with no contract versus no markup with a full-term contract – define the extremes of a range defined by the length of the contract on the one hand, and the size of the markup on the other. Intermediate points on this range can be defined by assigning smaller markups to successively longer contract durations. For example, Hausman[19] has proposed a linear sliding scale over the range from the maximum markup (no contractual commitment) to no markup (contract duration equal to economic life).

The notion that contract commitments are accompanied by lower prices when assets are expected to decrease in the future is illustrated by the difference between lease rates and outright purchase prices for items such as computers. The monthly payments for a loan covering the purchase price of a computer are substantially lower than the monthly rate for a short-term lease.

2.4 Adjusting Standard Parameters in Cost Models

The preceding sections indicate that with the exception of long-term contracts for the life of the asset in question, current cost models will tend to understate economic costs in the presence of economic uncertainty. This finding suggests directional qualitative adjustments to standard parameters in cost models, particularly rates of return, depreciation lives and levels of spare capacity.[20] For example, the amount of spare capacity can be set to provide for efficient response to growth and spatial changes in demand, depreciation lives can be adjusted to reflect the impact of declining input prices on the required initial output price, and rates of return can be adjusted to reflect increased business risks.

Apart from these qualitative and probably ad hoc adjustments to model parameters, there is also the issue that any analysis in support of a particular quantitative adjustment is likely to be of a complexity similar to an analysis to quantify the factors in the more rigorous approached described above.

3. CONCLUSION

The long-run cost models that have gained prominence since the Telecommunications Act was passed have implicit long-run forecasts built into them. Both input and output prices are assumed to remain constant over the study period encompassed by the model and the ILEC is assumed to serve a pre-determined level of certain demand. Given the changes wrought by advancing technology and increasing competition, these implicit assumptions are at best heroic and most likely unrealistic.

Modifying these assumptions to more realistically match market conditions tends to increase the costs and prices produced by these models, especially in the early years. Declining prices for inputs and outputs impose a similar declining pattern on the economic costs of the ILEC. Even without uncertainty, declining costs imply that the ILEC must charged higher prices in early years in anticipation of prices and revenues being forced down by competition and technological progress in later years. Uncertainty in economic conditions causes an additional increase in economic costs, with estimates two to three times as high as the costs produced by typical cost models.

Perhaps more fundamentally, the long-run focus of the cost models and the need for firms to respond with flexibility to the technological change and growing competition that characterizes the telecommunications industry are mismatched. The long-run forecast is an attempt to *emulate* competition by anticipating the outcome of competitive processes. In contrast, in competitive markets, it is the often unpredictable actions of firms meeting the demands of consumers, and not attempts to predict the outcomes of this process, that determine what services will be offered and at what price. Establishing regulated prices that have a reasonable prospect of getting the *competitive process* moving would seem to be a better use of regulatory resources than attempts to forecast precisely the outcome of that process.

NOTES

[1] This paper was presented at the 1999 International Communications Forecasting Conference, Denver, Colorado, June 17, 1999.

[2] One interpretation of universal service is ensuring that any household that wants service is able to afford it. Historically and continuing under the terms of the 1996 Telecommunications Act, affordability has been ensured by limiting the price charged for basic telephone service. The universal service programs that are currently being designed and implemented pursuant to the 1996 Act will establish funding levels based on a comparison of a benchmark rate with the forward looking cost of basic service.

[3] Some models create a "revenue requirement" (a time series of annual depreciation and return on investment) corresponding to the initial investment, and then take the present value of that "cash flow." It turns out that this calculation is equivalent to the purchase price of the investment, reduced by the tax benefit of depreciation deductions. See Tardiff, Timothy J. and Miles O. Bidwell, Jr.. May 10, 1990. "Evaluating a Public Utility's Investments: Cash Flow vs. Revenue Requirement," *Public Utilities Fortnightly*.

[4] Some cost studies utilize an equivalent approach where annual capital factors, which account for depreciation, return, and taxes over the life of the investment, convert the investment to an annual equivalent and then add the annual operating costs to this amount.

[5] The cash flows in the equation are after-tax, i.e., annual revenues and expenses are reduced by the income tax rate and the tax-deductibility of depreciation is included as a positive cash flow. For simplicity, these effects are not explicitly depicted.

[6] One of the ironies of the debates that accompany the development of cost models is that some parties view the ILEC's facilities as having at least in part natural monopoly characteristics, and as a result, call upon the regulator to produce models that emulate the results of competition. As the previous discussion indicates, such a task could be virtually impossible because of the sheer complexity of the forecasts needed to model the workings of competition. Consequently, a process that produces reasonable starting prices and lets competition do the rest has considerable appeal.

[7] Hausman, Jerry A. 1997. "Valuing the Effect of Regulation on New Services in Telecommunications." *Brookings Papers on Economic Activity Microeconomics*, M.R. Baily, P.C. Reiss, and C. Winston, eds., pp. 1-38.

[8] Krouse, Clement G. 1999. "LRIC Pricing, Dynamically Competitive Markets and Incentives to Invest." Department of Economics, University of California, unpublished manuscript.

[9] Hausman also considers the impact of constantly declining prices for the output produced by the investment. The result is symmetrical and additive. That is, if output prices are decreasing in addition to the amount indicated by the decline in equipment price, the effect of first period price is equivalent to an additional increase in the discount rate.

[10] Hausman's formulation assumes an indefinite life for the investment. Krouse produces an equivalent result when investment lives are finite.

[11] Krouse also considers the case in which investment and operating costs decline at different rates. He concludes that the rate of decline in the output price is a weighted average of the different input costs' rates of decrease.

[12] The October 1998 conference on real options held at the Columbia Institute for Tele-Information, from which this volume was drawn, is one example.

[13] Hausman suggests that the effect of uncertainty on economic cost applies mainly to sunk assets; other investments can be redeployed in the face demand uncertainty. For example, while some of the plant needed to provide access lines to customers in a certain area cannot be reused if the expected demand fails to materialize, switching facilities are more fungible between areas.

[14] Hausman credits Dixit and Pindyck for the formula that produces the markup. Dixit A. and R. Pindyck. 1994. *Investment Under Uncertainty*, Princeton, NJ: Princeton University Press, pp. 279-80 and p. 369.

[15] MacDonald, Robert and Daniel Siegel. 1986. "The Value of Waiting to Invest," *Quarterly Journal of Economics*, Vol. 101, pp. 707-728.

[16] Dixit and Pindyck, op. cit.,·p. 153.

[17] Federal Communications Commission, *Implementation of the Local Competition Provisions of the Telecommunications Act of 1996*, CC Docket No. 96-98, *Interconnection between Local Exchange Carriers and Commercial Mobile Radio Service Providers*, CC Docket No. 95-185, August 8, 1996, p. 687. Although the FCC correctly concluded that term contracts mitigate risk, it did not require competitors to enter such contracts as a condition for receiving low prices.

[18] With a long-term contract, the seller does not need to respond to a decline in output price generated by input price decreases and competition because the buyer has committed to purchase at the pre-determined price. Therefore, the pattern of prices over the life of the contract is not a crucial detail from an economic perspective.

[19] Testimony of Jerry A. Hausman before the California Public Utilities Commission, on behalf of Pacific Bell, April 8, 1998.

[20] Emmerson, Richard D. 1999. "Cost Models: Comporting with Principles," in this volume. Emmerson characterizes such adjustments as "crude but useful."

12 The Effect of Sunk Costs in Telecommunications Regulation

Jerry Hausman
Massachusetts Institute of Technology[1]

Abstract - Under the Telecommunications Act of 1996, the FCC mandated forward looking cost-based prices for competitors to use unbundled local exchange company (LEC) facilities. The FCC does not permit any markup over cost to allow for the risk associated with investment in sunk assets; instead, it uses a total service long-run incremental cost (TSLRIC) type approach that attempts to estimate TSLRIC on a forward looking basis. TSLRIC allows for the recovery of the cost of investment and variable costs of providing the service over the economic lifetime of the investment. However, TSLRIC makes no allowance for the sunk and irreversible nature of telecommunications investment, so that it adopts the perfect contestability standard. This standard provides incorrect economic incentives for efficient investment once technological and economic uncertainty exist along with sunk investments. Equivalently, FCC regulation requires incumbent LECs to give a free option on the use of their sunk investment in network facilities to new entrants. Thus, the FCC has chosen the incorrect standard for setting regulated prices, which will be below the correct economic cost of the network investments. TSLRIC will lead to less innovation and decreased investment below economically efficient levels. Decreased consumer welfare will be the result of the FCC's policy.

1. CURRENT FCC APPROACH TO REGULATION OF UNBUNDLED ELEMENTS

The U.S. Congress passed the Telecommunications Act of 1996, which was the first basic change in the regulatory framework for telecommunications since 1934. The Congressional legislation called for less regulation, more competition, and the most modern, up-to-date telecommunications infrastructure: "[T]o provide for a pro-competitive, de-regulatory national policy framework designed to accelerate rapidly private sector deployment of advanced telecommunications and information technologies and services to all Americans by opening all telecommunications markets to competition."[2] The Federal Communications Commission (FCC) has instituted numerous regulatory rulemakings to implement the 1996 Telecommunications Act. The most important regulation so far has been the Local Competition and Interconnection Order of August 1996.[3] If implemented in its current form, this order will likely have serious negative effects on innovation and new investment in the local telephone network.[4]

This paper first considers the proper goal of regulation-set prices in telecommunications. Most economists agree that regulation should be used only when significant market power can lead to unregulated prices that are well above competitive levels.[5] The goal of regulators is then to set prices at "competitive levels." However, economists are much less explicit about how these competitive price levels can be estimated. Most economists would agree that perfect competition cannot yield the appropriate standard since prices set at marginal cost will not allow a privately owned utility to earn a return on capital that is sufficient to survive. The large fixed costs of telecommunications networks thus do not allow the price-equal marginal cost standard of perfect competition to be used.[6]

An alternative competitive standard has been proposed by William Baumol and his co-author, known as the "perfect contestability" standard. Baumol has proposed that regulators should require firms to set prices as if "the competitive pressures generated by fully unimpeded and costless entry and exit, contrary to fact, were to prevail."[7] However, costless entry and exit presumes that no sunk costs exist (i.e., costs that cannot be recovered upon exit by a firm). This assumption of no sunk costs is extremely far from economic and technological reality in telecommunications, where the essence of most investments is an extremely high proportion of sunk costs.

Consider the investment by an incumbent local exchange carrier (ILEC) in a new local fiber optic network that can provide new broadband services and high-speed internet access to residential customers. Most of the investment is sunk because if the broadband network does not succeed, the investment cannot be recovered. Thus, when either technological or economic uncertainty exists, "perfect contestability as a generalization of perfect competition" cannot provide the correct competitive standard.

In a perfectly contestable market, if the return to an investment decreases below the competitive return, the investment is immediately removed from the market and used elsewhere. This costless exit strategy is always available in a perfectly contestable market. However, the actual economics of telecommunications investment could not be further from such a perfectly contestable market.[8] When fiber optic networks are constructed, they are in large part sunk investments.[9] If their economic return falls below competitive levels, the firm cannot shift them to other uses because of their sunk and irreversible nature.[10] Thus, the use of a perfectly contestable market standard fails to recognize the important feature of sunk and irreversible investments: they eliminate costless exit. Because of its failure to take into account the sunk and irreversible nature of much telecommunications investment, the contestable market model has nothing of interest to say about competition in telecommunications.[11] An industry cannot be expected to behave in a manner that is fundamentally inconsistent with its underlying technological and economic characteristics.

One way to consider the problem is the situation of a new investment by an ILEC. Suppose a competitor wants to buy the unbundled elements associated with the investment. The ILEC could offer the new competitor a contract for the economic life of the investment - say ten years for investment in the local loop. The price of the unbundled element would be the total investment cost plus the operating costs each year for the unbundled element. If demand did not materialize or prices fell, the new entrant would bear the economic risk of this outcome.[12] However, regulation by total-service long-run incremental cost (TSLRIC) typically allows the new entrant to buy the use of the unbundled element on a month-by-month basis. Thus, if demand does not materialize or prices fall, the ILEC must bear the risk for the business case of the new competitor. Thus, the ILEC has been required by regulation to give a free option to the new entrant, where an option is the right, but not the obligation, to purchase the use of the unbundled elements.[13] The monthly price of the unbundled element should be significantly higher than the ten-year price of the element to reflect the risk inherent in the sunk investments, or equivalently, the value of the option given to the new entrant.[14] Regulators to date have not incorporated the value of the option, which arises from the sunk cost nature of much telecommunications investment, into their price setting.

Another way to consider the problem of regulation-set prices is to allow for the existence of the (all-knowing) social planner. Suppose a social planner is considering a new investment in a telecommunications network where the features of sunk and irreversible investments are important. The social planner wants to maximize the value of the social welfare integral over time subject to uncertainty. However, the investment is subject to both technological and economic uncertainty so that the cost of the investment may (randomly) decrease in the future. Thus, because of demand uncertainty, the social planner does not know whether the investment will be economically efficient. In making an optimal decision the social planner will take into account the sunk and irreversible nature of the investment because if the new service fails, the investment cannot be shifted to another use. Thus, assuming that sunk costs do not exist (which is the perfect contestability standard), when they are actually an extremely important part of the economic problem will lead to incorrect decisions and decreased economic efficiency. The economy will not reach its production possibility frontier.

2. REGULATION-SET PRICES FOR UNBUNDLED ELEMENTS

Under the Telecommunications Act of 1996, the FCC mandated forward looking cost-based prices for competitors to use unbundled LEC facilities.[15] The Commission did not permit any markup over cost to allow for the risk associated with investment in sunk assets; instead, it used a total service long-run incremental cost (TSLRIC) type approach that attempts to estimate the TSLRIC on a forward looking basis.[16] TSLRIC attempts to solve the perfect competition problem that price cannot equal marginal cost by allowing for the fixed costs of a given service to be recovered. TSLRIC allows for the recovery of the cost of investment and the variable costs of providing the service over the economic lifetime of the investment. However, TSLRIC makes no allowance for the sunk and irreversible nature of telecommunications investment, so that it adopts the perfect contestability standard. The perfect contestability standard provides the incorrect economic incentives for efficient investment once technological and economic uncertainty exist. The FCC has chosen the incorrect standard for setting regulated prices. TSLRIC will lead to less innovation and decreased investment below economically efficient levels.[17]

2.1 The TSLRIC Standard and R&D and Investment in New Services

The first and easiest example to consider is R&D and investment in new services. Many new telecommunications services do not succeed; recent failures include Picturephone services (AT&T and MCI within the past eight years) and the information service gateway services offered by many ILECs. These new gateway services required substantial sunk costs of development for the creation of large data bases to provide information service gateways. Now if a new service is successful, under TSLRIC regulation, an ILEC competitor can buy the service at TSLRIC. Thus, for a successful new service, the ILEC recovers at most its costs. For unsuccessful services, the ILEC recovers nothing and loses its sunk investment. Thus, the TSLRIC regulation is the analogue of a rule that would require pharmaceutical companies to sell their successful products to their generic competitors at incremental cost and would allow the pharmaceutical companies to recover their R&D and production costs on their successful new drugs, but to recover nothing on their unsuccessful attempts.

This truncation of returns where a successful new telecommunications service recovers its cost (but no more), and unsuccessful new services recover nothing decreases economic incentives for innovative new services from regulated telecommunications companies. By eliminating the right tail of the distribution of returns as demonstrated in Figure 1, TSLRIC regulation decreases the mean of the expected return of a new project. For example, consider a project with returns, y, which follow a normal distribution with mean μ and standard deviation σ. The expected value of the return when it is truncated at cost c is:

$$E(y|y<c) = \mu - \sigma M(c) \tag{1}$$

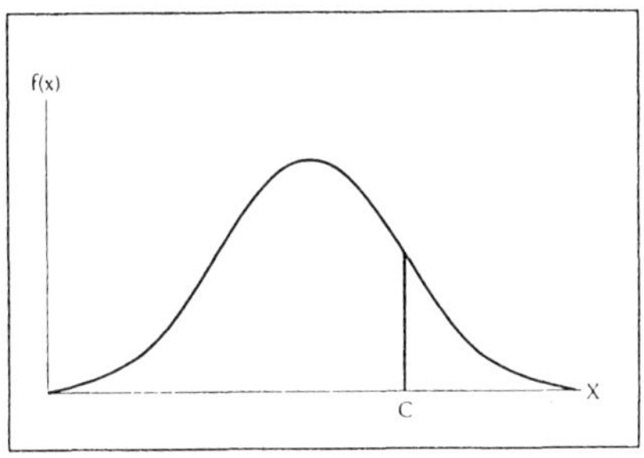

Figure 1

where M(c) is the inverse Mills ratio evaluated at c.[18] The tighter the cost standard, the lower the incentives to innovate, as expected. More importantly, as the returns to the innovation become more uncertain, the expected return and the incentives to innovate also decrease. Thus, even in the absence of sunk and irreversible investments, a TSLRIC pricing policy will decrease the economic incentives for investment in innovative services, and may eliminate these economic incentives to invest altogether.

Regulators could allow for something similar to patent protection for new services to provide economic incentives for ILECs to innovate.[19] However, this policy option is a recipe to delay new telecommunications services for ten years or more and bring enormous consumer welfare losses as occurred with voice messaging and cellular telephone.[20] Currently, it takes the U.S. Patent Office, on average, over two years to grant a patent (longer time periods are not uncommon). However, no opponent of the patent is allowed to be part of the process. In a regulatory setting where competitors would attempt to delay the introduction of new services, as happened with both voice messaging and cellular telephones, as discussed in Hausman (1997), one would expect much longer delays. Thus, the patent approach will not solve the problem.

A better approach would be not to regulate new services. Given the large welfare gains from new services and price cap regulation for existing services, ILECs should be permitted to offer new services with no prior approval or price regulation. The gains in consumer welfare from successful new services would lead to significant gains for consumers. Attempting to "fine tune" prices of new services through cost-based regulation will lead to overall consumer losses. However, regulators find it extremely difficult not to regulate any new service of a regulated company.[21]

2.2 The Effect of Sunk and Irreversible Investments [22]

TSLRIC assumes that all capital invested now will be used over the entire economic life of the new investment and that prices for the capital goods or the service being offered will not decrease over time. With changing demand conditions, changing prices, or changing technology, these assumptions are not necessarily true. Thus, TSLRIC assumes a world of certainty where the actual world is one of uncertainty in the future. Significant economic effects can arise from the effects that the sunk nature of investment has on the calculation of TSLRIC.

Consider the value of a project under no demand uncertainty with a risk-adjusted discount rate of r and an assumed known exponential economic depreciation at rate α. This assumption on depreciation can be thought of as the price of the capital decreasing over time at this rate due to technological progress. Assume that price, net of the effect of economic depreciation of the capital goods, is expected to decrease with growth rate $-\alpha$.[23] The initial price of output is P. The value of the project is:

$$V(P) = \int_0^\infty \lambda \exp(-\lambda t)\, P \, \frac{1 - \exp(-\delta t)}{\delta} dt = P/(\lambda + \delta) \qquad (2)$$

where $\lambda = r + \alpha$. Note that δ is added to the expression to account for the decreasing price of capital goods. This term, omitted from TSLRIC calculations, accounts for technological progress in equipment prices, which is one economic factor that leads to lower prices over time. Suppose that the cost of the investment is I. The rule for a competitive firm is to invest if $V(P) > I$. Equivalently, from equation (2), $P > (\lambda + \delta)\, I$. The economic interpretation of this expression is that the price (or price minus variable cost) must exceed the cost of capital, which includes the change in the price of the capital good to make the investment worthwhile.[24] Note that the net change in the output price and the price of the capital good both enter the efficient investment rule that a firm invests when $V(P) > I$. TSLRIC calculations ignore the basic economic fact that when technological change is present, (quality adjusted) capital goods prices tend to decline over time. This economic factor needs to be taken into account or economic inefficiency will result.

A simplified example demonstrates the potential importance of changing capital goods prices when competition exists. Suppose a new investment is considered that uses computer technology in a significant manner. Because computer technology is advancing rapidly, the price of the capital good used in the investment will decrease over time. Consider the following example where a competitive firm priced according to equation (2), but did not take account of changing prices of capital goods due to technological progress (i.e., $\delta = 0$ is assumed). A company "New Telecom" decides to enter the Internet access business. The company goes and buys a switch (router) that costs \$10,000. It expects to serve 100 customers each year with variable costs at \$500 per year. The firm's cost of capital is 10 percent and it expects to use the router for five years, at which time the resale (scrap) value of the router will be zero.[25] The discounted cost of the project over five years is \$11,895, which is the TSLRIC. On a per-customer basis, the cost is \$118.95 so that if the price were set at \$31.38 per year, the net present value (NPV) of the project is zero. Thus, the price based on TSLRIC is \$31.38 per year. Unfortunately, the company will lose money at this price and so the investment will never be made. There is a reason for this conclusion.

The price of routers, switches, fiber optic electronics, and other telecommunications equipment is decreasing with technological progress, e.g., Groves' law for microprocessors. Assume that the price of the router declines by \$1000 each year, but all other costs remain the same. For a market entrant in year 2, the TSLRIC calculation would lead to a discounted cost of \$10,895 (exactly \$1000 less if no further price reductions occurred) so that the TSLRIC-set price will be \$28.74 per year. Now the initial entrant, New Telecom, will be forced to decrease its price by \$2.64 and it will lose money on each customer (taking the original cost of capital into account). Indeed, as expected, New Telecom will lose \$760 on the project. The story will continue the next year when the router price falls to \$8000. Thus, TSLRIC-based prices cause the initial entrant to lose money even in a world of complete certainty because of decreasing capital costs. Instead of charging \$31.38 for each year as TSLRIC implies, New Telecom must charge decreasing prices of (\$36.65, \$33.75, \$30.85, \$27.95, and \$25.04) due to competition. Where does TSLRIC go wrong?[26]

TSLRIC fails to recognize that the change in the price of the equipment needs to be included in the cost of capital, which has been recognized by economic theory for many years. Indeed, the competitive price would not be the TSLRIC answer of \$31.38. The correct answer is that New Telecom must charge \$36.65 the first year and then decrease its price to \$33.75 the next year, and so on, because of the decreased price of the router. Thus, the TSLRIC-set price is too low by about 17 percent for the first year because it ignores the falling price of capital goods.

Now, the usual TSLRIC calculation does not include δ, but it instead assumes that both the prices of capital goods and output do not change over time. This assumption is extremely inaccurate. Take a Class 5 Central Office Switch (COS), for example. Ten years ago an AT&T Class 5 switch (5-ESS) was sold to an ILEC for approximately \$200 per line.[27] Today, the price of AT&T 5-ESS switches and similar NTI switches are in the \$70 per line or lower range. A TSLRIC calculation would be based on the \$70 price. An ILEC who paid \$200 per line made the efficient investment decision when it purchased its COS. But TSLRIC, by omitting economic depreciation due to technological progress, leads to a systematically downward-biased estimate of costs. Indeed, the economic depreciation of central office switches has been near 8% per year over the past five years, while the cost of fiber optic carrier systems has decreased at approximately 7 percent per year over the same period.[28] The omitted economic factor δ can be quite large relative to r for telecommunications switching or transmission equipment due to technological progress.

TSLRIC calculations make the following further assumptions: 1) the investment is always used at full capacity, 2) the demand curve does not shift inwards over time, and 3) a new or improved technology does not appear that leads to lower costs of production. Of course, these conditions are unlikely to hold true over the life of the sunk investment. Thus, uncertainty needs to be added to the calculation because of the sunk nature of the investment.

It is possible to account for the sunk nature of the investment and its interaction with fundamental economic and technological uncertainty.[29] Given the fundamental uncertainty and the sunk nature of the investment, a "reward for waiting" occurs because over time, some uncertainty is resolved. The uncertainty can arise from at least four factors: 1) demand uncertainty, 2) price uncertainty, 3) technological progress (input price) uncertainty, and 4) interest rate uncertainty.[30] Now the fundamental decision rule for investment changes to:

$$P^{s} > \frac{\beta_1}{\beta_1 - 1}(\delta + \lambda)I \tag{3}$$

where $\beta_1 > 1$ so that $m = \beta_1/(\beta_1 - 1) > 1$. The parameter β_1 takes into account the sunk cost nature of the investment coupled with inherent economic uncertainty.[31] Parameter m is the markup factor required to account for the effect of uncertain economic factors on the cost of sunk and irreversible investments. Thus, the critical cutoff point for investment is $P^S > P$ from equation (2).

To see how important this consideration of sunk costs can be, the markup factor m can be evaluated. The parameters β_1 and m depend on a number of economic factors. It can be demonstrated that as uncertainty increases (i.e., the variance of the underlying stochastic process), β_1 decreases and the m factor increases.[32] Also, as δ increases, β_1 increases, which means that the m factor decreases. As r increases, β_1 decreases so that the m factor increases. MacDonald and Siegel (1986) and Dixit and Pindyck (1994, p.153) calculate m = 2 so that, for instance, $V^S = 2I$. A TSLRIC calculation that ignores the sunk cost feature of telecommunications network investments would thus be off by a factor of two.

Using parameters for ILECs and taking account of the decrease in capital prices due to technological progress (which Dixit and Pindyck assume to be zero in their calculation) and because the expected change in (real) prices of most telecommunications services is also negative given the decreasing capital prices, the value of m can be calculated to be around 3.2 to 3.4.[33] Thus, a markup factor must be applied to the investment cost component of TSLRIC to account for the interaction of uncertainty with sunk and irreversible costs of investment.[34] Depending on the ratio of sunk costs to fixed and variable costs, the overall markup on TSLRIC will vary, but the markup will be significant given the importance of sunk costs in most telecommunications investments. Note that this same markup over TSLRIC would be used by the hypothetical social planner to choose optimal investment in a telecommunications network since the social planner would face the same inherent economic and technological uncertainty over future demand and cost factors.

Now when the markup for sunk and irreversible investment is applied, it should only be used for assets that are sunk (e.g., potentially stranded). Other investments that are fixed, but not sunk, would not have the markup. This methodology can be applied to transport links and ports, which are treated as unbundled elements by U.S. regulation. The proportion of sunk costs for links is 0.59 so that the markup factor for the overall investment using a markup factor of m = 3.3 is approximately 2.35 times TSLRIC. By contrast, the proportion of sunk costs for ports is about 0.10, so that the markup factor becomes 1.23 times TSLRIC. The markup over TSLRIC that takes account of sunk costs and uncertainty is the value of the free option that regulators force incumbent providers to grant to new entrants (in this case, 1.35 times TSLRIC for links and 0.23 times TSLRIC for ports). Thus, the proportion of sunk costs has an important effect on the correct value of regulated prices when sunk costs are taken into account.

Regulators, by failing to apply a markup to TSLRIC, will set too low a regulated price for telecommunications services from new investment. The result will be to decrease new investment in telecommunications below economically efficient levels, contrary to the stated purpose of the Telecommunications Act of 1996 in the United States and enabling legislation in other countries. Thus, through its focus on static cost efficiency considerations in setting regulated prices equal to TSLRIC, regulators will miss the negative effect on dynamic efficiency that TSLRIC-based prices will cause. Because the examples of voice messaging, cellular telephone, and the Internet demonstrate that the dynamic efficiency effects are quite large in telecommunications, the use of TSLRIC to set regulated prices will likely cause substantial welfare losses to consumers similar to past FCC regulatory policy in the United States.

3. CONCLUSIONS

The cost-based regulation of telecommunications (e.g., rate-of-return regulation in the United States) had significant negative effects on innovation while it was claimed that it led to excessive capital investment. Most economists conclude that cost-based regulation led to significant consumer harm. During the 1980s price cap regulation was implemented instead of cost-based regulation in most countries when telephone companies and other utilities were privatized. In the majority of U.S. states, rate-of-return regulation has been replaced by price cap regulation. Price cap regulation has important economic incentive attributes for innovation and investment in networks by the incumbent firms in telecommunications.

During the 1990s cost-based regulation has reappeared because of the necessity to set prices for unbundled network elements sold by incumbent firms to their competitors. Unfortunately, the adoption of TSLRIC as a cost basis to set the prices for unbundled elements has negative economic incentive effects for innovation and for new investment in telecommunications networks.

Regulators' failure to recognize the sunk cost character of much network investment leads to the grant of a free option to the competitors of the incumbent. Causing the shareholders of the incumbent firm to fund the free option for the competition will lead to underinvestment. Given the amount of uncertainty in a dynamic industry with rapidly changing technology and economics, this misguided regulatory policy can have an especially large effect on investment incentives because the value of the option is high. The losers will be consumers and businesses who will not have access to the most up-to-date service that would be provided if regulators did not create disincentives to new investment.

NOTES

1 Presented at a conference at Columbia University, October 2, 1998. I thank Nick Hausman and Dr. My Cahouy for research assistance. Parts of this paper have appeared previously in J. Hausman. 1997. "Valuation and the Effect of Regulation on New Services in Telecommunications," *Brookings Papers on Economic Activity: Microeconomics*. Further discussion of the effects of regulation on innovation can be found in that paper.

2 Conference Report to the Telecommunications Act of 1996, Pub. L. No. 104–104, 110 Stat. 56.

3 FCC, "First Report and Order, CC docket No. 96-98 and 95-185," August 1, 1996.

4 The FCC is being challenged by the incumbent local exchange carriers (ILECs) in Federal Court. The U.S. Supreme Court reversed and remanded for further consideration the FCC's regulatory approach in January 1999. See AT&T Corp. *v.* Iowa Utils. Bd., 119 S. Ct. 721 (1999). The key issue remanded to the FCC is what network elements should be unbundled. Justice Breyer, in his separate opinion, discussed the effect of the FCC approach on prices of unbundled elements and the likely negative effect on new investment and innovation in local networks, which is the subject of this paper.

5 In considering the regulation of unbundled elements, the FCC has failed to consider whether, in the absence of regulation, market power could be exercised by the ILECs. Instead, the FCC has adopted a "competitor welfare standard," which is inconsistent with the economic analysis of competition and the modern antitrust law. In contrast, Canadian regulators have taken competitive considerations into account in their decision on which elements should be unbundled. Hausman and Tardiff (1995) discuss competitive considerations in unbundling.

6 Economists have long agreed on this point. See, e.g., Kahn (1988) for a discussion.

7 W. J. Baumol and J. Gregory Sidak (1994), p. 28. and pp. 31 ff.

8 To the extent that some network elements are fixed, but not sunk, investments should not be unbundled by regulators because new entrants can enter and exit markets using these elements without undergoing sunk investments, which can create entry (and exit) barriers.

9 The electronics used in the networks need not be sunk, but much of the actual dark fiber will be a sunk investment.

10 This feature of sunk and irreversible investment has been widely recognized by economic research for over a decade. See MacDonald and Siegel (1986) and for a recent comprehensive textbook treatment, see Dixit and Pindyck (1994).

11 The contestable model of competition has been highly criticized as relating to real-world situations. Previous criticisms of its attempted application to telecommunications include Armstrong and Vickers (1995), "In fact, of course, the industry does not remotely resemble a contestable market..."

12 The contract (or regulation) could allow the new entrant to sell the use of the unbundled element to another firm if it decided to exit the business.

13 The use of real options analysis extends far beyond the evaluation of sunk and irreversible investments. See, e.g., Treigeorgis (1996) and his paper in this volume.

14 In contracts between unregulated telecommunications companies (e.g., long distance carriers) and their customers, significant discounts are given for multi-year contracts.

15 The FCC decision is currently under remand by the FCC. In the FCC proceeding the author provided testimony on behalf of the ILECs.

16 The FCC chose a variant of TSLRIC, called TELRIC for total element LRIC. However, the essential economic problem of TSLRIC also exists in TELRIC. The FCC is currently constructing a TELRIC model to be used in future regulatory proceedings.

[17] TSLRIC would provide the correct approach in a world with no uncertainty, so long as economic depreciation was done correctly. However, given the dynamic technological advances in telecommunications, considerable uncertainty exists, especially over the long economic lifetimes of much investment in telecommunications.

[18] The inverse Mills ratio is the ratio of the density function and distribution function of the standard normal distribution evaluated at $(c - \mu)/\sigma$. The inverse Mills ratio M(C) increases monotonically as c decreases for given μ and σ, e.g., Greene (1990), p. 718.

[19] The FCC chief economist, Joseph Farrell (1997) considered this option.

[20] See Hausman (1997) for a discussion on consumer losses from this policy.

[21] The FCC, remarkably enough, has proposed to regulate new services under TSLRIC-type regulation, even when the FCC itself has found that significant competition currently exists for these services. See Deployment of Wireline Services Offering Advanced Telecommunications Capability, Memorandum Opinion and Order and Notice of Proposed Rulemaking, CC Dkt. Nos. 98–147, 98-11, 98-26, 98-32, 98-15, 98-78, 98-91, 13 F.C.C. Rcd. 24,011, 24,055-59 and Inquiry Concerning the Deployment of Advanced Telecommunications Capability to All Americans in a Reasonable and Timely Fashion, and Possible Steps to Accelerate Such Deployment Pursuant to Section 706 of the Telecommunications Act of 1996, Report, CC Dkt. No. 98-146, (released Feb. 2, 1999). The FCC is proposing to regulate new services even when no regulation is required since no market failure exists. This unnecessary regulation is potentially extremely harmful to consumers (the "public interest") as I discuss in Hausman (1997), where previous FCC regulation of new services led to billions of dollars in consumer harm. See Hausman (1998) and Hausman and Shelanski (1999) for a discussion of why regulation should consider consumer welfare to be the primary factor in "public interest" regulation, not the "competitor welfare" standard that the FCC has adopted.

[22] This discussion follows Hausman (1996). See also Laffont and Tirole (1996).

[23] This factor arises due to changes in demand and changes in total factor productivity.

[24] For simplicity, this calculation assumes only capital costs and no variable costs. Variable costs can be included by reinterpreting P to be price minus variable costs, which will lead to the same solution.

[25] The terminal value assumption can be changed with no change in the conclusions to the analysis.

[26] TSLRIC-type formulae can be corrected by using equation (2) with δ not equal to zero to account for decreasing capital prices. However, to the best of my knowledge, these corrections have not been undertaken by regulators.

[27] Hausman and Kohlberg (1989), p. 204.

[28] Testimony of Prof. Jerry Hausman before the CPUC, April 1998.

[29] Salinger (1998) attempts to generalize the approach of equation (2) to allow for uncertainty by appending various ad hoc assumptions on randomness to the equation. However, his approach has severe limitations, of which only two are mentioned here. First, he assumes away the effect of lumpy investment by assuming that investment occurs continuously, while the technological nature of much investment in telecommunications depends on its lumpiness. Second, he assumes that regulators update their depreciation formulae in continuous time so that the option value discussed in this paper decreases in importance. These assumptions bear a similarity to the contestability assumptions (instantaneous free entry and exit) which, as discussed above, bear no relationship to the actual technology of much investment in telecommunications networks.

[30] The FCC incorrectly assumed that taking account of *expected* price changes in capital goods and economic depreciation is sufficient to estimate the effect of changing technology and demand conditions; see the FCC "First Report and Order," para. 686. Thus, the FCC implicitly assumed that the variances of the stochastic processes that determine the uncertainty are zero, i.e., that no uncertainty exists. Under the FCC approach, the values of all traded options should be zero (contrary to stock market fact), since the expected price change of the underlying stock does not enter the option value formula. It is the uncertainty related to the stochastic process as well as the time to expiration that gives value to the

option as all option pricing formulae demonstrate (e.g., the Black-Scholes formula). See, for example, (Hull) 1997 for a discussion of the value of options.

[31] This equation is the solution to a differential equation. For a derivation see, for example, Dixit and Pindyck (1994), pp. 254-256, pp. 279-280, and p. 369. The parameter β_1 depends on the expected risk-adjusted discount rate of r, expected exponential economic depreciation δ, the net expected price $-\alpha$, and the amount of uncertainty in the underlying stochastic process. Note that this result holds under imperfect competition and other types of market structure, not just under monopoly, as some critics have claimed incorrectly. See, for example, Dixit and Pindyck (1994), Ch. 8, "Dynamic Equilibrium in a Competitive Industry." Imperfect competition is the expected competitive outcome in telecommunications because of the significant fixed and common costs that exist.

[32] See, for example, Dixit and Pindyck (1994), p.153.

[33] Because of the expected decrease in the price of capital goods, even if the standard deviation of the underlying stochastic process were 0.25 as high as a typical stock, the markup factor would still be 2.1. For a standard deviation 0.5 as high, the markup factor is 2.4. I have also explored the effect of the finite expected economic lifetimes of the capital investments in telecommunications infrastructure. Using expected lifetimes of 10-15 years leads to only small changes in the option value formulas, e.g., for a project with a 12-year economic life, the markup factor of 2.0 changes to 1.9.

[34] It is the advent of competition which requires correct regulatory policy to apply the markup. Previously, when regulatory policy did not allow for competition, regulators could (incorrectly) set prices based on historic capital costs. Given the onset of competition arising from the Telecommunications Act of 1996 and the regulatory removal of barriers to competition, regulators must now account for changes in prices over time. Otherwise, ILECs will decrease their investment below economically-efficient levels because their expected returns, adjusted for risk, will be too low to justify the new investment.

REFERENCES

Armstrong M. and J. Vickers. 1995. "Regulation in Telecommunications," in M. Bishop, J. Kay, and C. Meyer eds., *The Regulatory Challenge*. Oxford, UK: Oxford University Press.

Baumol W. J. and J. G. Sidak. 1994. *Toward Competition in Local Telephony*. Cambridge, MA: MIT Press.

Dixit, A. and R. Pindyck. 1994. *Investment Under Uncertainty*. Princeton, NJ: Princeton Univ. Press.

Farrell, J. 1997. "Competition, Innovation and Deregulation," mimeo.

Greene, W.H. 1990. *Econometric Analysis*. New York: Macmillan Publishing Co.

Hausman, J. July 1996. "Reply Affidavit of Prof. Jerry Hausman," FCC CC Docket No. 96-98, mimeo.

Hausman, J. 1997. "Valuation and the Effect of Regulation on New Services in Telecommunications." *Brookings Papers on Economic Activity: Microeconomics*.

Hausman, J. 1998. "Taxation by Telecommunications Regulation," *Tax Policy and the Economy*, no. 12.

Hausman, J. 1998. "Telecommunications: Building the Infrastructure for Value Creation," in S. Bradley and R. Nolan eds., *Sense and Respond.* Boston, MA: Harvard Business School Press.

Hausman J. and W. E. Kohlberg. 1989. "The Evolution of the Central Office Switch Industry," in S. Bradley and J. Hausman eds., *Future Competition in Telecommunications.* Boston, MA: Harvard Business School Press.

Hausman J. and H. Shelanski. 1999. "Economic Welfare and Telecommunications Welfare: The E-Rate Policy for Universal Service Subsidies," *Yale Journal on Regulation,* no. 16.

Hausman, J. and T. Tardiff. 1995. "Efficient Local Exchange Competition," *Antitrust Bulletin.*

Hull, John C. 1997. *Option, Futures and Other Derivatives,* 3rd ed. London: Prentice Hall International.

Kahn, A.E. 1988. *The Economics of Regulation.* Cambridge, MA: MIT Press.

Laffont, J.J. and J. Tirole. Nov. 1996. "Competition in Telecommunications," mimeo.

MacDonald R. and D. Siegel. 1986. "The Value of Waiting to Invest," *Quarterly Journal of Economics,* 101, 707-728.

Salinger, M. 1998. "Regulating Prices to Equal Forward-Looking Costs," *Journal of Regulatory Economics,* 14, 149-163.

Trigeorgis L. 1996. *Real Options.* Cambridge MA: MIT Press.

Real Options:
Evaluations

13 Real Options and the Costs of the Local Telecommunications Network

Nicholas Economides
School of Business, New York University

Abstract - The Telecommunications Act of 1996 invites entry in the local telecommunications networks whereby entrants will lease parts of the network ("unbundled network elements") from incumbents "at cost plus reasonable profit." A crucial question in the implementation of the Act is the appropriate measure of cost. This paper examines the economic principles on which the cost calculation should be based. It concludes that the appropriate measure of cost (maximizing allocative, productive, and dynamic efficiency) is forward-looking economic cost and not the historical, accounting, or embedded cost of the incumbent's network. In calculating costs, demand and supply uncertainty, as well as the asymmetric position of incumbents and entrants, should be taken into account. A close examination of the issue of uncertainty in the local telecommunications network reveals that 1) for most unbundled network elements, there is little demand uncertainty, and 2) those elements that face significant uncertainty do not have sunk value. Thus, the incumbent does not face higher expected costs by investing. Moreover, the rewards to the incumbent can be higher because buyers prefer to buy services from the owner of the network. Finally, strategic considerations in oligopolistic interaction are likely to dominate any uncertainty considerations and will increase the incentive of incumbents to invest.

On February 1, 1996, President Clinton signed into law the Telecommunications Act of 1996 (1996 Act). This was the first major reform since the original 1934 Telecommunications Act. In passing the 1996 Act, Congress took radical steps toward a major restructuring of the U.S. telecommunications markets. These steps may result in very significant benefits to consumers of telecommunications services, telecommunications carriers, and telecommunications equipment manufacturers. But the degree of success of the 1996 Act depends crucially on its implementation through decisions of the Federal Communications Commission and state public utility commissions, as well as the outcomes of the various court challenges that these decisions, and the Act itself, face.

The Act attempts to introduce and enhance competition in all parts of the telecommunications network. It envisions a network of interconnected networks that are composed of complementary components and generally provide both competing and complementary services. The 1996 Act uses both structural and behavioral instruments to accomplish its goals. It attempts to reduce regulatory barriers to entry and competition. It also outlaws artificial barriers to entry in local exchange markets in its attempt to accomplish the maximum possible competition. The 1996 Act attempts to enhance competition in telecommunications markets wherever it exists and establish it where it does not. Before competition takes hold, the Act attempts to create conditions that imitate competition in the local exchange. To facilitate entry in the local exchange, the Act mandates the interconnection of telecommunications networks, unbundling, non-discrimination, number portability, and cost-based pricing of leased parts of the network, so that competitors can enter easily and compete component by component as well as service by service.

1. COST PRINCIPLES FOR LEASING OF UNBUNDLED NETWORK ELEMENTS IN IMPLEMENTING THE 1996 ACT

Currently, the "last mile" of the telecommunications network that is closest to the consumer (the "local loop") remains a bottleneck controlled by an incumbent local exchange carrier (ILEC), a Regional Bell Operating Company, GTE, or a smaller independent. The 1996 Act boldly attempts to introduce competition in this last bottleneck, and in all parts of the local exchange market, while preserving the effective competition that has developed in the long distance market.

To facilitate entry in the local exchange, the Act imposes mandatory interconnection, unbundling, and number portability. In particular, Section 251(c)(2) mandates:

> "*interconnection*,
> (B) at any technically feasible point
> (C) that is at least equal in quality to that provided by the local exchange carrier to itself or to any subsidiary, affiliate, or any other party to which the carrier provides interconnection; and
> (D) on rates, terms, and conditions that are just, reasonable, and nondiscriminatory, in accordance with the terms and conditions of the agreement and the requirements of this section and section 252."

Section 251(c)(3) mandates unbundling, that is, offering for sale network elements at "rates, terms, and conditions that are just, reasonable, and nondiscriminatory." The 1996 Act allows for entry in the local exchange through the leasing of unbundled network elements from the ILEC.

Entry through leasing unbundled network elements would be uneconomical unless prices for the leased elements were set appropriately to imitate competitive prices. The 1996 Act orders that the pricing of interconnection or unbundled network elements [252(d)(1)]:

> "(A) shall be
> (i) based on the cost (determined without reference to a rate-of-return or other rate-based proceeding) of providing the interconnection or network element (whichever is applicable), and
> (ii) nondiscriminatory, and
> (B) may include a reasonable profit."

The measure of cost has been the subject of considerable controversy. The Federal Communications Commission (FCC) and state public utilities commissions (PUCs) have ruled that the word "cost" in Section 252(d)(1) should

(1) be a forward-looking economic cost
(2) be the least cost to provide the service
(3) be a long-run cost
(4) be an incremental cost corresponding to the particular network element
(5) include a competitive return on capital
(6) exclude monopoly rents
(7) exclude cross-subsidies of any kind
(8) in general, should reflect cost differences among geographic regions.

Moreover, any cost calculation of unbundled network elements (UNEs) should be based on cost-causation: only costs caused by the production of an element should be included in the calculation of UNE cost.

Total element long-run incremental cost (TELRIC) is the sum of minimized costs paid for all inputs required to supply the unbundled network element. TELRIC conforms to the eight principles above.

Using TELRIC as the basis for prices performs several functions which, in combination, guarantee economic efficiency. First, it gives the right signal to consumers in making purchasing decisions among goods, because then these decisions are made on the basis of what society must give up to supply these goods. In other words, it achieves allocative efficiency. Second, such a price directs production to the most efficient, least-cost suppliers, because these producers can offer the lowest prices. Thus, it achieves productive efficiency. Third, it gives the appropriate signal to firms in decisions on investment, entry, and exit, because firms make these decisions purely on the basis of forward-looking costs. In other words, it achieves dynamic efficiency.

It is incorrect to use embedded, historical, or book costs. True common (firm-wide) costs are minimal. A percentage of common costs "attributable" to an element may be added to the TELRIC of an element. Any significant deviation of prices above TELRIC creates efficiency losses.

The interpretation of the Act by the FCC and the PUCs does not allow unbundled network elements to be leased at a price equal to private opportunity cost, since private opportunity cost

- is based on the final price of the service for which the element is used
- typically includes the supernormal profits of the incumbent
- may include past inefficiencies reflected in higher than efficient costs.

Therefore, the Act does not allow UNEs to be leased at prices based on the "efficient component pricing rule" (ECPR) or its variant (M-ECPR).

2. ON DEPRECIATION, COST OF CAPITAL, AND REAL OPTIONS

The cost of capital calculation accepted by most regulatory commissions has been challenged by Professor Hausman in two ways.[1] The first is that variable rates of depreciation are not employed in the typical models and state PUC orders that assume straight-line depreciation. But, because the calculation of TSLRIC can accommodate variable-rate (not straight-line) depreciation, any criticism of this sort can be easily accommodated. In such a setup, one can have higher depreciation in the early years and lower depreciation in the later years.

Professor Hausman's second challenge to the way depreciation is employed in the typical models and PUC orders is more substantial. He claims that the ILEC, by investing in a network element that an entrant is going to lease, loses the option value of not investing, say, in the case when demand would drop. Professor Hausman concludes that the incorrect capital cost is used in the TELRIC of some network elements.

In order for Professor Hausman's proposed argument to have a chance at being correct, it must meet two requirements:

1. The network element for which the real options issue could apply needs to have significantly lower resale value, i.e., its cost needs to be sunk to a significant extent.

2. The ILEC must face significant uncertainty about the network elements of zero resale value.

It is very unlikely that both of these requirements can be fulfilled for any network element of the telecommunications network. To start, many of these network elements, such as electronics, can be moved and/or resold at almost full value, or can be used for other functions. Because such elements do not have zero resale value, they fail the first requirement. Applying real options theory will not increase their cost estimates. Moreover, many network elements fail the second criterion because there is no significant uncertainty about their demand. For example, the ILEC rarely faces much uncertainty about local loops that are arguably the most likely to be purchased by competitive local exchange carriers (CLECs). In the absence of demand uncertainty, the application of real options theory will not increase the cost estimates of such elements.

There is also a fundamental criticism of the basic assumptions under which real options theory has been developed in contrast with the conditions that now prevail and are expected to prevail in the telecommunications industry in the United States. Real options theory assumes that the ILEC will remain a monopolist and has the luxury of putting off investment (because it faces no competitors). Real options theory is based on Dixit and Pindyck (1994), who do not consider or prove results for conditions of oligopolistic interaction.[2]

Intuition suggests that, in oligopoly, contrary to the monopoly results of Dixit and Pindyck, firms may invest much more aggressively because of strategic reasons - so that the investing firm is the one to control and lease its network, rather than leasing it from others. Because most of the investments in ILEC equipment for which costs need to be estimated were made in the 1990s, when competition was anticipated, it is absurd to assume that investment occurred with the anticipation that the ILEC would remain a monopolist. In the current oligopolistic environment with anticipation of competition, firms invest looking forward to competition and cannot afford to wait; the value to an ILEC of waiting to invest may well be negative. Finally, it is a well known fact that large customers of telecommunications services are willing to pay more for services provided by an integrated provider than for resold services. For these reasons, contrary to Professor Hausman's claim, the application of real options theory to the conditions of the telecommunications market may well imply a lower cost for the affected unbundled network elements than if real options theory was not applied.

3. CONCLUDING REMARKS

The Telecommunications Act of 1996 attempts to introduce and enhance competition in all parts of the telecommunications network. To facilitate entry in the local exchange, the Act imposes mandatory interconnection, unbundling, and number portability. The Act mandates that ILECs lease, at cost, parts of their network (unbundled network elements) to potential entrants. The FCC and state PUCs have ruled that the appropriate cost is forward-looking least economic cost. In calculating the cost of the UNEs, it is important to define correctly the cost of capital.

Based on the theory of real options, Professor Hausman claims that the cost of capital to be used in these calculations should be very significantly higher because, in investing, the incumbent faces risks that the entrant/buyer does not. However, a closer examination of the conditions in the U.S. telecommunications market as well as the assumptions of real options theory reveals that it is very unlikely that a higher cost of capital should apply to any unbundled network elements, and in fact, it could possibly result in a lower cost for the affected unbundled network elements.

First, there are no real options theory results under conditions of oligopoly where the investing firm may have a strategic advantage over a reseller. Second, large customers prefer to buy from an owner rather than a reseller. Thus, the value of a network is higher for the investing firm than a reseller. Third, according to real options theory, the cost of capital for a UNE may be higher only if two requirements are met: the network element has zero resale value (i.e., its cost is sunk) and there is significant uncertainty about the network elements of zero resale value. These conditions are very difficult for most unbundled network elements to meet. For example, many network elements of the telecommunications network, such as electronics, can be moved and/or resold at almost full value, or can be used for other functions, and therefore their costs are not sunk. Moreover, ILECs face no significant uncertainty in the demand for network elements such as the loop that are the most likely to be purchased by CLECs, and therefore the issue of real options does not arise for them. Thus, applications of real options theory to the conditions of the telecommunications market may well imply a lower cost for the affected unbundled network elements than if real options theory were not applied.

NOTES

[1] See Hausman (1998).

[2] Examinations of the same problem by Trigeorgis (1996) and Economides and Trigeorgis (1999) reveal that the logic of Dixit and Pindyck does not necessarily hold in oligopoly.

REFERENCES

Dixit, A.K., and R.S. Pindyck. 1994. *Investment under Uncertainty.* Princeton NJ: Princeton University Press.

Economides, N., and L. Trigeorgis. 1999. "Real Options in Oligopolistic Interaction," forthcoming.

Hausman, J. 1998. "Testimony before the California Public Service Commission," April 7.

Trigeorgis, L. 1996. *Real Options: Management Flexibility and Strategy in Resource Allocation.* Cambridge, MA: MIT Press.

14 Option Value Analysis and Telephone Access Charges

William J. Baumol
C.V. Starr Center for Applied Economics, New York University, and a consultant for AT&T

Abstract - This paper explores the policy implications of the recent options value analysis for telecommunications. It shows that application requires very great care because otherwise, the actions taken, while they appear to follow the analysis, can actually go in the opposite direction. This is demonstrated by access fees for interexchange carriers' use of the local loop. Because options analysis shows that the true cost of an investment, including future opportunity cost, is greater than it appears to be, the access charges should apparently be raised accordingly to discourage excessive investment in facilities. But here, raising access fees, rather than discouraging investment, is likely to increase it. Increasing the cost of entry through the use of currently extant facilities will lead to increased facilities-based entry. This will thereby exacerbate any excessive investment rather than reduce it.

1. THE ISSUE

The very illuminating new analysis stemming from the work of Dixit and Pindyck has profound implications for both theory and practice. The theory is deep and may sometimes entail complex and subtle reasoning. In contrast, its practical consequences may seem straightforward and even easy. This paper, however, employs a very current and urgent issue to show that, even by using the new analysis to deal with applications, matters are not always as straightforward as they can appear to be.

In short, one can characterize the pertinent part of the new analysis as follows. It tells us that investment decisions typically have a cost component that has usually been overlooked, so that the total costs of such decisions (and, hence, their appropriate price) is normally underestimated. The overlooked cost component is the narrowing of future choices that a current investment commitment entails. By making such a commitment, the decisionmakers forego some of their future options. The decisions preclude choices the decisionmakers *may* prefer to change as the passage of time increases the information available to them. But such changes are no longer open to them because of their investment commitment.

Dixit and Pindyck note that this is obviously a real cost that can be avoided only by postponing the investment decision. They also demonstrate that using the net present values of the expected future revenues and costs as the decision criterion to choose between immediate investment and the postponement of the decision can lead to erroneous choices. Neglecting the value of the foregone options biases the decision in favor of current investment over decision postponement. The error cannot be cured without including the value of the foregone options as part of the cost of an immediate or early commitment. Thus, the true total costs of the investment are higher than they usually are calculated to be.

Moreover, the true *marginal* cost of increased investment can also be expected to be higher than it is usually estimated to be. So it seems plausible that there should be a concomitant enhancement of the efficient price of access to the resulting facility as well as that of any product using the facility as input. From the point of view of economic welfare, the role of such a price enhancement is the prevention of inefficient overinvestment by the market. That is, by reducing the quantities demanded, the enhanced prices will prevent the expansion of current investment commitments beyond the point called for by expected revenues and true costs, including foregone option costs.

This, in considerably oversimplified form, is the basic story, and it is, of course, fundamentally valid. However, the use of this reasoning for practical application, without careful consideration of the pertinent relationships, can lead to indefensible and inefficient decisions. This is demonstrated by relating the analysis to a hotly debated current issue – the appropriate level of the access fees that the local exchange carriers (LECs) should charge the interexchange carriers (IXCs) for access to the former's local-loop facilities.

2. APPEARANCE AND REALITY OF OPTION VALUE COSTS IN ACCESS CHARGES

The obvious interpretation of the options value scenario to the LECs' access fees seems straightforward enough. The appearance of the matter, which is very different from the reality, is the following. In order to enter the local telecommunications market, the IXCs desire to rent access to the LECs' facilities because it is likely to be less expensive for the IXCs than building duplicative facilities of their own. The resulting increase in demand for the facilities may therefore require the LECs to enlarge the capacity of those facilities – an investment commitment that entails foregone future choices for the LECs. Everyone seems to agree that the appropriate access fees should be based on costs (even though there is heated dispute over which costs these should be). The apparent conclusion is that the access charges should be higher than they would be if the foregone option value were ignored in the calculation.

However, this all-too-easy conclusion ignores two vital considerations. First, the grant to the IXCs of access to the LECs' facilities is likely to require little, if any, expanded investment commitment. Second, an increase in access charges is likely to speed up and increase IXCs' commitment to facilities-based entry into the local markets. That is, it will provide an incentive for investment commitments *by the IXCs*, which themselves have a cost in terms of foregone option value. Indeed, it is plausible that this is the type of investment most in danger of being driven to excessive levels in terms of economic efficiency. Below, these two contentions are discussed in turn.

First, if IXC entry into the local telecommunications markets is successful, it will mean that the LECs will lose some of their local business to the new entrants (presumably made up for by LEC entry into the interexchange arena). In terms of local traffic, the transfer of some traffic from the LECs to the IXCs will reduce the LECs' use of their own facilities, leaving unused capacity available for rental to the IXCs. Thus, the entry should result in little, if any, need to expand capacity and investment. More than that – in the debates over the proper access charges before the many regulatory agencies involved in the process, *the LECs have repeatedly contended that entry will leave them with substantial stranded assets.* But this is tantamount to saying that, far from having to *expand* capacity, the LECs expect to have considerable excess capacity left on their hands. They patently cannot have it both ways – they cannot legitimately claim at the same time that entry will force them to make substantial new investment commitments with high option-value costs, and that entry will leave them with a significant burden of excess capacity.

Second, entry can lead not just to one but to two different types of investment decisions, either of which is in danger of being carried to levels that are excessive in terms of economic efficiency. And here it must be emphasized once more that efficiency in investment decisions is the central point of the new options value analysis. It has just been demonstrated that access prices that disregard the cost of foreclosed choices can conceivably lead to overinvestment by the LECs, although it was shown to be unlikely. *But the level of access charges can also result in overinvestment by the IXCs.* If those charges are too high but entry into the local telecommunications market promises to be profitable, the IXCs may feel compelled to build duplicative facilities, even in cases where substantial excess capacity already exists on the LEC's local loop. It is at least plausible that this sort of overinvestment – the natural extension of uneconomic bypass – is the more likely possibility. And it can indeed occur when some of the option values most likely to be relevant are overlooked.

This, then, is the important point: foregone option value is a very real cost of a current commitment to invest. The failure to recognize and incorporate this fact into pricing decisions can, indeed, lead to an inefficient overallocation of resources to investment. But the implication for pricing is not always as straightforward as it may appear, which has been demonstrated here for telecommunications access charges because they should be set to avoid the inefficient overcomitment of resources by the IXCs and not only by the LECs. Thus, quite plausibly, option value analysis may well call for an access price that is *lower* than the one that would otherwise be adopted, rather than the higher price that a superficial consideration of the matter would recommend.

15 Rethinking the Implications of "Real Options" Theory for the U.S. Local Telephone Industry

Richard N. Clarke
AT&T[1]

Abstract - Real options theories are an important advance in analyzing the value of various business arrangements. Because incumbent exchange carriers' business arrangements with their new competitors are at the center of regulators' efforts to demonopolize the U.S. local telephone industry pursuant to the Telecommunications Act, it is natural that these new arrangements should be inspected to determine whether they correctly reflect the import of real options' costs. Investors and regulators have recognized these considerations, and to the extent that certain real options models do not reach the same conclusion, it is because they have not been parameterized to reflect accurately the market conditions facing the U.S. local telephone industry.

Accounting for the option value of an investment is not new. Although appropriate mathematical formulations for option values have only been developed within the last twenty-five years, markets, investors and regulatory commissions have long incorporated options effects in valuing and pricing regulated services.[2] It is thus useful to evaluate whether more recent developments in "real options" theory have uncovered effects and considerations not previously known to or accounted for by markets, investors and regulators.[3] Certain analyses by real options proponents have suggested that lack of attention to these considerations in U.S. local telephone markets may possibly have caused prices for some regulated telecommunications services to incorporate less than half of their truly required return.[4] Given the potential significance of these claims to an industry with over $100 billion in commerce annually, it is important that the underlying analyses be examined to determine whether:

(a) Real options theories are simply invalid[5] or

(b) Real options theories are valid and have been parameterized by their proponents to model the local telephone industry accurately – with the foreboding implication that the incumbent local exchange companies incumbent local exchange carriers (ILECs) may be on the brink of financial ruin or

(c) Real options theories are valid, but have not been parameterized to model the local telephone industry accurately.

This paper examines the validity of each of these possible conclusions about real options. Conclusion (c) is the most compelling. When real options models are parameterized to represent the local telephone industry accurately, these models affirm that investors and regulators have incorporated appropriate real options considerations into their investment evaluations and ratemaking decisions for ILEC local telecommunications services.

1. MIGHT THE ENTIRE THEORY BE INVALID?

While it is possible that the entire theory of real options is in error, this seems unlikely. First, this theory is not especially new, and due to its notoriety it has been exposed to substantial scrutiny from professional economists. If the theory is simply wrong, its deficiencies should already have been revealed in the literature. A second reason to doubt the invalidity of real options theory is that when these models are parameterized realistically, they appear to generate predictions that comport with current conditions and expectations. Thus, it seems unlikely that conclusion (a) is correct.

2. MIGHT THE THEORY AND ITS CURRENT PARAMETERIZATIONS BE CORRECT?

If proponents of real options theory such as Hausman have correctly parameterized their models of real options to reflect accurately the conditions of the local telephone industry, the implications are profound. These parameterizations suggest that rather than enjoying rather high and relatively riskless returns, ILECs are actually in grave financial danger; and to ameliorate this, their returns on services incorporating significant options value may need to double, or more.[6] Thus, given that return and income tax components constitute 30 percent of a typical ILEC's total revenue and depreciation constitutes an additional 22 percent, the return and/or depreciation inadequacies suggested by these real options parameterizations could be as large as half of the affected services' current revenues. Correcting this would require that regulators quickly grant ILEC rate increases of up to 50 percent for these services.

This foreboding view of the current ILEC financials, however, does not appear to be shared by investors, regulators, or by the ILECs themselves. In particular, even recent forward-looking determinations of the major ILECs' cost of capital using standard discounted cash flow or capital asset pricing model methods confirm that based on current investor expectations, the weighted average cost of capital to the ILECs is in the 9 percent range - and certainly not in the 20 percent to 30 percent range as speculated by certain of the real options models using their proposed parameterizations.[7] Indeed, if the ILECs' "true" cost of capital is in this elevated range and a substantial portion of their services is subject to real options effects, it is remarkable that ILEC bond ratings remain at the highest investment levels, and that none of the over 1300 ILECs has gone bankrupt in recent memory.[8]

Equally telling is the fact that the ILECs themselves also appear not to believe that their proper cost of capital is in the 20 percent to 30 percent range. In comments they have made to the Federal Communications Commission concerning their authorized rate of return, none suggested that their return should be set at such levels.[9] Furthermore, no ILEC appears to have pointed toward real options theory as a justification for any increased return level.

Thus, because none of these groups, which have significant interest in the financial status of the ILECs, appears to believe that current returns are inadequate to provide ILECs with a profitable, sustainable financial future, it appears unlikely that conclusion (b) is correct.[10]

3. MIGHT THE THEORY BE CORRECT, BUT ITS PARAMETERIZATION BE WRONG?

It is not a necessary feature of real options theories that they should project overall ILEC rates of return to be inadequate. This projection is critically sensitive to the parameterization of the real options model in question. Among the parameter values that appear to be necessary to support a conclusion that current ILEC returns are inadequate are:

- Most ILEC investment is sunk and irreversible, and regulator-set price and sales conditions are irreversible, too.
- The effect of technical progress is always to devalue earlier investments.
- There is a competitive gain to "waiting" before deciding to make investments and enter the product market.
- The terms and conditions that the Telecommunications Act specifies for the provision of network elements and interconnection are fundamentally different and less favorable to the ILECs than the terms and conditions under which the ILECs currently market local and access services.[11]

A closer examination will reveal that each of these suppositions is inaccurate.

3.1 Irreversibility?

The vast majority of ILEC investments are not sunk and/or irreversible. In the event of a local demand insufficiency, a large portion of telecommunications equipment can be physically moved to locations where market conditions are more favorable. Furthermore, even outside-plant facilities that cannot be physically moved can be transferred to buyers who find these facilities more valuable than the ILEC. Indeed, the ILECs have transferred several million customer lines from one to another over the last five years.[12] That such transfers may still be infrequent should not be construed as evidence that these investments are irreversible. Rather, they reflect both the facts that telecommunications demand has uniformly been growing at a substantial rate throughout the country (with this growth projected to continue, if not accelerate), and that the depreciation lifespans of most telecommunications equipment have been relatively brief.[13] Indeed, ILECs have refused to dispose of even what they claim are their least-profitable investments.[14] But if ILEC investments are reversible from a financial perspective, they do not incorporate significant real options value.

Any analysis of the effects of reversibility on options value and risk would be incomplete if it focused solely on the physical reversibility of investments. Many important financial aspects of the provision and sale of regulated monopoly network elements and interconnection are more reversible than comparable aspects of unregulated competitive markets. For example, regulators frequently allow their decisions about prices or permitted uses for a network element to reverse equally earnest earlier decisions. The risks generated by such reversibility commonly have a chilling effect on the likelihood that a new entrant local carrier will be able to assemble the capital required for successful market entry. Examples of these effects of reversibility include public utility commissions abrogating contractually agreed-to prices for unbundled loops in favor of higher prices supported by their own cost "studies," or permitting ILECs to renege on supplying special-access transport services for resold Centrex lines after it became apparent that this permitted new-entrant carriers profitable and efficient use opportunities.[15] Thus, it is by no means clear whether the overall effects from the reversibility or irreversibility of investment and regulatory decisions favor or disfavor the ILECs.

3.2 Technological Progress?

While it is true that technological progress may have devalued certain earlier ILEC investments in central-office switching and interoffice transmission, this is not a representative example. Only about 20 percent of all forward-looking ILEC investment is for these network elements, whereas 60 percent to 70 percent of their investments are in outside-plant facilities. Because of increased congestion and urbanization, outside-plant investments commonly have appreciated in value, not depreciated.

In addition, technologies may arise that make "old" investments appreciate in value. A useful example is xDSL, or digital subscriber line. In the early 1990s, the received wisdom was that copper loop distribution plant in local telephone networks was economically obsolete. Because it would not support the high-speed services that customers were beginning to demand, no more of it would be installed, and the installed base would be replaced rapidly by fiber optic or coaxial distribution cables. Instead, these latter distribution technologies have turned out to be much more expensive than previously anticipated, and xDSL technologies have arisen that allow the embedded copper loop distribution cables to be used efficiently to provide high-bandwidth services. Thus, because of the great cost of replacing these cables, they are now more valuable than when they were initially installed.

3.3 Gains from Waiting?

Another key parameter in real options models is whether there are gains from waiting to invest.[16] If such gains are assumed to exist, then ILEC prices for network elements and interconnection may yield insufficient returns because they fail to incorporate the value of the "free option" of waiting to invest that they offer purchasers. But in the telecommunications industry, gains typically do not flow to those who wait, but rather are reaped by those who can become "first movers."[17] Even if investment costs are expected to decline in the future, it is typically more profitable to enter a market quickly, accumulate customers and experience, and then, because of the flexibility inherent in telecommunications networks, transition these customers to the newer, lower-cost technologies that may have been developed subsequently.

3.4 Different Terms and Conditions?

Many of the real options analyses suggesting that new unbundled network elements or interconnection prices may be set too low to allow ILECs to earn adequate returns appear to assume that the terms and conditions under which the ILECs must sell these items are more disadvantageous to the ILECs than the terms and conditions under which they sell their current local or access services. As an example, it is alleged that purchasers of network elements or interconnection will receive a unique options advantage because they may discontinue their purchases.

However, the requirement to offer services on a month-to-month basis is typical for all services offered by the ILECs. Thus, purchasers receive no distinct options value from new interconnection services vis à vis purchasers of traditional ILEC access services. Indeed, because the sale of new interconnection services pursuant to the Telecommunications Act permits the use of negotiated contractual arrangements, the ILEC likely has more ability to appropriate the value of the real options aspects of these sales than sales of its traditional local and access services. This is because the latter type of services frequently can only be offered pursuant to regulator-approved tariffs incorporating specific terms and conditions.[18]

4. CONCLUSIONS

Real options theories are an important advance in analyzing the value of various business arrangements. Because ILEC business arrangements with their new competitors are at the center of regulators' efforts to demonopolize the U.S. local telephone industry pursuant to the Telecommunications Act, it is natural that these new arrangements should be inspected to determine whether they correctly reflect the import of real options' costs. This report finds generally that investors and regulators have recognized these considerations, and to the extent that certain real options models do not reach the same conclusion, it is because they have not been parameterized to reflect accurately the market conditions facing the U.S. local telephone industry.

NOTES

1 The opinions expressed here are solely the author's, and do not necessarily represent those of AT&T.

2 The first rigorous development of the mathematical theory of financial option values was provided in Black, F. and M. Scholes. 1993. "The Pricing of Options and Corporate Liabilities," *Journal of Political Economy*, No. 81, pp. 637-659.

3 Major contributions to real options theory include: Dixit, A. and R. Pindyck. 1994. *Investment Under Uncertainty*, Princeton University Press. McDonald, R. and D. Siegel. "Investment and the Valuation of Firms When There is an Option to Shut Down," *International Economic Review*, Vol. 28, No. 2, pp. 331-349; Pindyck, R. "Irreversible Investment, Capacity Choice and the Value of the Firm, *American Economic Review*, Vol. 78, No. 5, pp. 969-985. Hubbard, R.G. "Investment Under Uncertainty: Keeping One's Options Open," *Journal of Economic Literature*, Vol. 32, pp. 1816-1832, provides a useful summary.

4 See, for example, Jerry Hausman, "The Effect of Sunk Costs in Telecommunications Regulation," in this volume, which states, "A ... calculation which ignores the sunk cost feature of telecommunications network investments would thus be off by a factor of two."

5 If these theories are invalid, it makes no difference whether they have been parameterized accurately – their results are simply irrelevant.

6 Hausman, op. cit.

[7] See, *Direct Case of the General Services Administration* ("GSA calculates the weighted cost of capital as 9.27 percent"), filed January 19, 1999 in Federal Communications Commission CC Docket No. 98-166; or *Responsive Submission of AT&T Corp.* with its accompanying *Affidavit of Bradford Cornell and John I. Hirshleifer* ("applying established financial economics principles to the market data on the publicly-traded firms that operate local telephone networks yields a weighted average cost of capital range of no higher than 8.5% to 9.5%"), filed March 16, 1999 in the same proceeding.

[8] The absence of bankruptcy among such a large group of industry members is unprecedented. Rather than revealing an industry in a precarious financial position, it suggests that the earnings currently available to ILEC monopolies are both high and stable – or that few ILEC services are subject to significant real options effects.

[9] See, for example the *Comments of GTE* ("there is no basis to alter the current prescribed authorized rate of return of 11.25%"), filed January 19, 1999 in Federal Communications Commission CC Docket No. 98-166; or the *Comments of Bell Atlantic* ("the Commission should not adjust the prescribed rate of return") filed in the same proceeding.

[10] Indeed, if conclusion (b) is correct and a significant portion of ILEC services is affected, then the people privy to these real options analyses and their import should be shorting ILEC stocks in anticipation that once this information is assimilated by the larger financial markets, there will be a significant drop in ILEC stock prices.

[11] This note focuses only on the terms and conditions that are explicit in the Telecommunications Act and that are relevant to real options issues. It does not address ancillary complaints that are sometimes included in presentations on real options that claim, incorrectly, that the Telecommunications Act somehow requires regulators to blind themselves to economic factors such as risk or technological obsolescence in the setting of appropriate prices or depreciation rates.

[12] While many of these sold lines were in rural exchanges owned by large ILECs and sold to smaller ILECs, many also were transfers between large ILECs, e.g., Sprint/Centel to Ameritech, GTE both to and from Alltel.

[13] The average depreciation life for telecommunications equipment is just over 14 years. In contrast, electric power generating and transmission equipment may frequently have lifespans of 30 years and more. See U.S. Department of Energy, Energy Information Administration, Form EIA-412, "Annual Report of Public Electric Utilities," demonstrating that in 1997, the average life of electrical plant was 32.5 years.

[14] As an example, in the early 1990s, NYNEX claimed that only its midtown and downtown Manhattan exchanges were profitable, and that its other New York City exchanges generally "lost" money. But when Teleport then offered to purchase any of these "unprofitable" exchanges at their net book value, NYNEX refused to sell. See "The Local Call Goes Up for Grabs," *New York Times*, December 29, 1991, Section 3, p. 1.

[15] See "In the matter of U S West Tariff F.C.C. Nos. 3 and 5," FCC Common Carrier Bureau *Order on Transmittal 629*, September 28, 1995.

[16] In addition to gains from waiting to invest, there may be other advantages in managerial flexibility that incorporate real options value. See L. Trigeorgis. 1996. *Real Options: Managerial Flexibility and Strategy in Resource Allocation*, MIT Press.

[17] Witness the first mover value of "1-800-COLLECT" in MCI's establishment of the dial-around market, or "Digital One Rate" in AT&T's establishment of the seamless wireless services market. In contrast, it is difficult even to identify the secondary entrants such as AT&T's "1-800-OPERATOR" or Bell Atlantic's "DigitalChoice SingleRate USA" or Sprint PCS' "Free and Clear" offerings.

[18] For example, local service tariffs often prohibit offering volume or term discounts.

16 Application of Real Options Theory to TELRIC Models: Real Trouble or Red Herring

Michael D. Pelcovits
MCI WorldCom

Abstract - Since the inception of policy debates on opening local markets to competition, the incumbent local exchange carriers (ILECs) have argued against any costing methodology that would erode their monopoly level of revenue and profits. Real options issues were introduced to this debate at a time when the FCC was considering adopting TELRIC models to set rates for interconnection to the local exchange. The ILECs' goal was to use these real options issues to undermine the credibility of the TELRIC methodology, leaving the FCC with no choice but to rely on embedded costs.

Although the theoretical issues raised by real options are legitimate and intriguing, they do not apply to the case at hand. The competitors' use of the local network does not expose the ILECs to more risk than the typical customer. Customers of the ILECs have always had the option to use or not use the ILECs' network, and the ILECs have never imposed a premium for option values on those customers. Indeed, the customers that imposed the greatest risk on the ILECs - the Centrex customers - frequently paid the lowest rates.

An attempt to measure the upper bound of the option value effect also shows that the ILECs will be fully compensated for the use of their network when prices are set at the levels estimated by the TELRIC models. The risk to the ILECs of a failure to recover the costs of sunk investments is greatest for portions of the local loop plant. Yet, this plant is shown to exhibit very large economies of scale, and the ILECs' option to build a smaller-scale network is essentially valueless. The conditions that would render the real options theory as a killer critique of the use of the TELRIC models simply do not exist.

It is important to understand the policy context of this conference. The topic chosen – the application of real options theory to telecommunications pricing – has been the subject of recent filings at the FCC in its landmark proceeding to implement the Telecommunications Act of 1996.[1] In response to the Commission's proposal to use forward looking economic prices for unbundled network elements

(UNEs), the incumbent local exchange carriers (ILECs) sponsored an affidavit by Professor Jerry Hausman in which he argued that the use of "a TSLRIC calculation which ignores sunk costs for networks is systematically downward biased by a factor of at least 2, and the factor probably exceeds 3."[2] Although this argument was eventually rejected by the FCC in its order adopting TELRIC (total element long-run incremental cost), the debate has not ended.

The debate over the validity of TELRIC (and hence the importance of these challenges to TELRIC) can be traced to fundamental conflicts between the incumbent local exchange carriers and the competitive local exchange carriers (CLECs) over ratemaking policies that will have a profound influence on the telecommunications market. Specifically, the ILECs argue for full recovery of their embedded accounting costs, even if competitors succeed in capturing customers and market share. The CLECs insist that interconnection and UNE prices should not be saddled with make-whole costs reflecting accounting or embedded costs, but rather should be set at forward looking cost. In response to the CLECs' proposed use of forward looking costing methods and models, the ILECs launched a full-scale attack on the TELRIC models, designed to eliminate this significant challenge to their "right" to recover all of their embedded costs.[3] Thus, although the focus of the conference is on real options theory, at the root of the debate lie fundamental conflicts about the direction that public policy should be taking at this crossroads regarding competition in telecommunications markets. This calls for a more complete understanding of the policy context.

The ILEC position on how competition should affect pricing and costing policies is well illustrated by a paper of Monson and Rohlfs of Strategic Policy Research (SPR), released by the United States Telephone Association (USTA) in July 1993.[4] The paper entitled "The $20 Billion Impact of Local Competition in Telecommunications," claimed that competition threatened the ability of the ILECs to recover the "contribution" to universal service from the customers of services priced above cost – especially toll and access services. According to USTA, this "contribution is an integral part of the regulatory fabric that has maintained universal service through subsidized rates for rural areas and residential customers."[5] The thesis of the Monson and Rohlfs paper was that the policy goal of providing universal service was inextricably linked to the ILECs' ability to recover their embedded costs.[6] Furthermore, the size of the universal service subsidy did not need to be measured directly by estimating the costs of providing local telephone service to the subsidized customer groups (e.g., rural customers), but could be measured by the excess of rates over costs from the "contributing" services. In other words, according to USTA, there was a simple duality theorem: *All revenues collected from services priced above cost are used to subsidize the provision of services to beneficiary customer groups at rates below cost.* Therefore, any shortfall of contribution caused by competition would need to be made up by increases in universal service subsidies, lest these rates increase and universal service be threatened.

MCI opposed USTA's position, arguing that while local competition might threaten the ILECs' profits, it did not have to threaten universal service. MCI proposed that universal service subsidies be made explicit, and then the ILECs' rates could be driven to forward looking cost by competition, without sacrificing universal service. In MCI's view, the size of the universal service subsidy (both then and in the future) should be estimated directly, as the difference between the direct costs of providing service to targeted customer groups (e.g., rural customers) and the revenues received from those customers.[7] The size of the "contribution" from overpriced services was irrelevant to that measurement, in MCI's view, because these overcharges could be explained by many factors other than "contributions" to universal service, such as cross-subsidies to competitive services, inefficiencies, or excess profits.

To prove that universal service subsidies could be measured directly by looking at the costs of serving rural customers from the "bottom up," rather than from the "top down" (i.e., embedded costs), MCI commissioned Hatfield Associates Inc. (which was later renamed HAI) to construct a stylized model of the costs of providing local telephone service as a function of the density of population.[8] This model showed that the size of the subsidy to basic local telephone services from other services was $3.7 billion per year.[9]

The sizeable gap between the HAI model estimate and the SPR estimate – between $14 and $16 billion – received much attention at the time and to this day provides a powerful insight into the debate between the ILEC-sponsored and CLEC-sponsored economists on the issues of the validity of TELRIC and the relevance of real options theory to the pricing of UNEs. This is not a debate of abstract economic theory, but rather part of a major public policy dispute between warring corporations.

The Telecommunications Act of 1996 included two major provisions that moved forward looking cost models to the forefront. First, the Act required that universal service subsidies be converted from an implicit to an explicit mechanism. This meant that the size of the required subsidy had to be determined directly – rather than using the USTA/SPR "duality" approach, which measured the $20 billion contribution from above-cost services. Second, the Act required the ILECs to provide access to network elements on an unbundled basis at cost-based prices "determined without reference to a rate-of-return or other rate-based proceeding."[10] The passage of the Act and its implementation at the FCC and the state commissions caused the potential new entrants into the local market (especially MCI and AT&T) to launch major efforts to turn the initial stylized HAI model into a highly sophisticated engineering-economic cost model of local telephone networks.[11]

The latest version of the HAI model includes sophisticated engineering algorithms that compute the amount of telephone plant required to serve customers in all parts of the continental United States. The inputs on customer locations, telephone line counts, and numerous geographical factors are highly detailed and disaggregated, and enable the model to estimate costs separately for each Census Block. Because the model contains separate modules for each category of telephone plant, it yields cost estimates for each network element as well as the cost of the bundle of services encompassed by the FCC's definition of the basic universal service.

Two features of the HAI model are particularly noteworthy. First, the model is completely open to inspection and dissection by outside parties. It is written in Microsoft Excel and all of the data and algorithms are provided to the public on a CD-ROM. Second, many of the model's formulas and inputs can be varied to test sensitivities. For example, the cost of copper wire or the fill factors (the percent of telephone cables actually in use) can be varied at the will of the user. This stands in marked contrast to the "black box" cost models provided by the ILECs in the past (both those based on embedded and incremental cost). Among the major differences between the TELRIC models and the traditional ILEC-sponsored models are:

- TELRIC models are open and transparent
- TELRIC models can be tested for sensitivities to hundreds of inputs and assumptions.
- Consistent TELRIC models can be used for all ILECs.
- TELRIC models develop costs for each major element of the network from the ground up, which minimizes the complex and controversial allocations necessary when using embedded costs.

Clearly, the use of costing methods outside the control of the ILECs was a major change to historic practice and created a significant threat to the ILECs at a crucial juncture in the history of regulation.

Recently, the FCC adopted a model "platform" that it plans to use to size the universal service fund for the large ILECs beginning in January 2000.[12] The model is a synthesis of three models, including the HAI model. It shares much of the HAI approach to modeling described above, differing primarily in the methods used for "clustering" customers into local serving areas and to calculate distribution plant requirements. Because the FCC model platform is still being tested and has not been on stage for long, one must surmise that it will receive much of the same criticism that the ILECs leveled at the HAI model over the past five years. Thus, the debate between the ILEC-sponsored critics and the TELRIC proponents will undoubtedly be repeated as the FCC synthesis model moves into the limelight.

The HAI model has been vigorously, and unceasingly, attacked since its first incarnation in 1994. USTA and SPR claimed that the first HAI model's assumption that the telephone plant was built from scratch on a "greenfield" was only appropriate for costing telephone service in Kuwait or Bosnia.[13] The ILEC attack has focused on the theme that HAI models a "fantasy" network. Soon after the passage of the Telecommunications Act, and the interexchange carries' proposal to use the model as the basis for pricing the unbundled network element as well as for universal service, USTA sponsored an attack that focused on the claim that the model failed to account for growth in demand, but instead assumed that the ILEC "invests at a single point in time to serve instantaneously the entire market."[14] Jerry Hausman's FCC filing on real options theory returns to the same theme, claiming "the HAI model assumes a 'start from scratch' world where technology has never changed, no uncertainty exists, and no firm ever made an investment without correctly predicting how technology would change."[15]

It is beyond the scope of this paper to address all of the attacks on the TELRIC models made over the last several years. Nevertheless, it is important to put this debate in perspective. All models by their nature involve simplification; the alternative is the construction of a parallel universe. So the question is not whether the assumptions of the model are correct (indeed all simplifying assumptions are technically "incorrect"), but whether use of the model creates substantial irremediable error, which some other feasible alternative does not.[16]

What the ILECs really want is for the TELRIC modeling process to be discredited, so that the FCC would be forced to rely on some embedded cost basis for setting rates paid by the CLECs.[17] In the ongoing universal service debates, USTA recently filed a new plan at the FCC based on embedded cost.[18] USTA estimates the size of the universal service subsidy as the amount necessary to replace the intracompany implicit subsidies included in interstate access charges. According to USTA, "cost models can properly be used for non-rural carriers to implement the distribution of high cost funds, but should not be used to size the fund itself. Rather, the fund should be sized based on the need to support universal service and on the need to replace other sources of support."[19] USTA cites SPR's 1993 estimate of the $20 billion support contributed from access and toll services, noting the estimate was recently updated to nearly $24 billion annually. Interestingly, in this age of rapidly declining prices in telecommunications services, the cost of universal service is higher than ever before. Old habits die hard.

The purpose of presenting this historical overview to the policy issues at the heart of the debate in the conference is to emphasize that the goal of the attacks on TELRIC is to destroy, not to improve, the TELRIC models, and by doing so, force the FCC and the state commissions to rely only on embedded cost-based prices. Taken in this context, the test that the models must pass is not whether they are always "right" or whether they are even capable of solving all of the economic riddles posed by their opponents, but rather whether the models are reasonably accurate and provide a fair regulatory tool, *in comparison* to the embedded cost approach. The opponents of the models are clearly trying to show that the TELRIC models fail to meet a reasonableness standard. How else can one interpret Professor Hausman's attempt to claim that the TELRIC prices are biased downward by a factor of 2 or 3?

1. CAPITAL RECOVERY ISSUES IN TELRIC MODELS

Critics of the TELRIC models raise two issues concerning the models' treatment of capital recovery costs. First, they claim that the assumption of constant capital goods prices is at variance with an expected large decline in the price of switches and other electronic equipment over time.[20] Second, they argue that there is a substantial option value that should be included in the TELRIC-based prices paid by the CLECs. Each of these arguments is examined here in turn.

There are several reasons why the potential for declining capital goods prices should not undermine our confidence or reliance on the models. Three of these are stated briefly (and then discussed more fully below):

1. The most important network element, from the standpoint of both universal service and CLEC competition, is the loop. The loop is the most essential of all ILEC facilities and also accounts for about one-half of the typical ILEC's rate base. It is highly unlikely that the capitalized value of the loop plant is falling over time, and thus the critics' argument concerning the declining value of the ILECs' plant neglects a large portion of the plant, whose value is constant or even increasing.
2. It is difficult to postulate future changes in switch prices from historical trends. Moreover, the ILECs themselves have argued that productivity improvements in local telephony will not continue at historic levels.[21]

3. TELRIC models can be adjusted for accelerated depreciation, just as they are adjusted for hundreds of other variables. Plausible estimates of declines in capital goods prices would have a very small effect on TELRIC-based price.

The first point is that the unbundled network element that matters the most is the loop. The ILECs currently provide 168 million subscriber lines, while the CLECs provide only 5.6 million.[22] For the vast majority of customers, CLECs will be unable to duplicate the loop plant any time soon, so the only way they can offer service to the public at large is by leasing unbundled loops. This makes unbundled loops, and associated elements such as collocation, the linchpin of the Telecommunications Act of 1996. This point is realized by the industry and policymakers, and consequently the model developers and regulatory agencies have focused the greatest attention on the loop.

Rather than depreciating rapidly over time, much of the investment associated with loop plant – such as poles and conduit – retains a substantial percentage of its economic value over long periods of time.[23] Indeed, much of the supporting structure may actually increase in value over time, to the extent that replacement costs are highly labor-intensive and the costs of installation are much higher after an area is fully developed. Even the copper loop, which at one time was viewed as plummeting in value because fiber was considered a superior alternative, has recently become more attractive as a medium for carrying xDSL signals. With respect to loop plant, then, the depreciation concerns raised by the opponents of TELRIC are much ado about nothing.

With respect to the second point, Hausman cites the example of an AT&T Class 5 Central Office Switch to demonstrate a rapid decline in capital goods prices. He claims the price of the switch has fallen from about $200 per line in 1989 to $80 per line today.[24] Could this trend, if accurately measured, continue? There is some evidence that it will not,[25] and it is useful to explain why large declines in prices are unlikely to continue. As Professor Hausman points out, the Central Office switch includes a switch block and a computer. The price of chips used in the computer has declined rapidly in the past ten years, which is reflected in lower switch prices. The prices of other components, as well as of software that is capitalized in the purchase price, have not declined at similar rates. The price of labor used to engineer, furnish, and install the switch has likely increased over time. This implies that as chips become a smaller proportion of the total cost of the switch, even continued declines in chip prices would not cause as large a percentage drop in switch prices as they have in the past.

What have the ILECs said about the significance of the decline in capital goods prices on their overall costs? USTA has recently filed comments on access charges at the FCC in which they argue that the productivity improvements of the recent past will not be achievable in the future.[26] Central to their argument is that past productivity gains have been achieved by reductions in employment and a "dramatic operational restructuring," which cannot be replicated in the future. Further, USTA's expert economist claims that a longer-term downward trend in productivity has already begun, and that without future declines in employment, productivity improvements will be even smaller.[27] USTA's arguments on productivity, and the notable lack of any recognition of a "dramatic" decline in capital goods prices, is in stark conflict with the position taken by their experts critiquing TELRIC.

The final, and most important, point to make about the depreciation issue is that the TELRIC models *can be adjusted for accelerated depreciation,* just as they are adjusted for thousands of other variables.

Although the model has not yet been modified to allow for accelerated depreciation, the author has conducted several runs of the model to estimate the impact of different depreciation rates on estimated UNE costs.[28] Table 1 shows the sensitivities of the cost of "basic universal service" to reductions in the projected lives of three categories of equipment: digital switching, computers, and digital circuit equipment for New York Telephone (the reporting area for Bell Atlantic in the State of New York). It is evident that even large reductions in depreciation lives do not cause large-scale increases in the total costs of the UNEs or of local exchange service. For example, even if the service lives of *all three major categories* of electronic equipment were cut in half, the cost of universal service (the loop, the switch port, and local usage) would increase by only 11percent: from $13.66/month to $15.14/month.[29] This extreme example, where all of the electronic equipment in the ILECs' network is assumed to be worthless in half its normal lifetime – as opposed to being worth less, as the critics posit – demonstrates how the rhetoric of the ILEC advocates goes beyond any reasonable interpretation of the reality of modern telecommunications networks.

Table 1. Depreciation Scenarios

Scenario	Total Loop (Unit Cost)	% Change	End Office Switching Line Port	% Change	End Office Switching Non-Line Port	% Change	Total Switched Network Elements (w/o Public)	% Change
	per month		per month		per minute		per month	
HAI Model Default Inputs	9.34		0.98		0.00173		13.66	
One Half Depreciation Life								
Digital Switching	9.24	-1.1%	1.17	19.4%	0.00206	19.1%	14.22	4.1%
Computers	9.38	0.4%	0.98	0.0%	0.00174	0.6%	13.76	0.7%
Digital Circuit Equip.	10.02	7.3%	0.99	1.0%	0.00175	1.2%	14.49	6.1%
All three categories	9.97	6.7%	1.18	20.4%	0.00208	20.2%	15.14	10.8%

2. OPTION VALUES AND TELRIC

Hausman argues that "competitive firms use a 'hurdle rate' for investments far beyond their estimated cost of capital."[30] He cites Summers' survey of firms to back up his claim that hurdle rates "exceed the cost of capital by a factor of between 2 and 10."[31] A closer examination of Summers' evidence shows, however, that it does not back up Hausman's claim, and that Summers' survey is consistent with conventional capital asset pricing model (CAPM) cost of capital estimates, as well as with the cost of capital used by the FCC.

The mean hurdle rate of 17percent reported by Summers can be compared to the CAPM cost of capital.[32] The CAPM cost of capital for a company of average risk (beta equals one) is simply the risk-free rate plus the equity premium. The real riskless rate has averaged 1.0 percent for the last sixty years. The equity risk premium for large companies such as those surveyed by Summers has averaged 7.4 percent, for a total average real return of 8.4 percent.[33] To compare this real return to Summers' nominal hurdle rate, it is necessary to adjust for inflation. The expected inflation at the time of the Summers' survey can be estimated by taking the ten-year government bond rate in 1985, which was 10.62 percent, and subtracting the average real return on such bonds of 2 percent, to yield expected inflation of

8.6 percent (which coincidentally was the approximate inflation rate over the decade prior to 1985).[34] Subtracting 8.6 percent from Summers' mean nominal hurdle rate of 17 percent gives a real hurdle rate of 8.4 percent, *which is identical to the CAPM cost of capital* for a firm of average risk.

This real hurdle rate of 8.4 percent is somewhat below the 11.25 percent rate of return currently prescribed by the FCC.[35] With current expectations of inflation running around 2.0 percent, the nominal hurdle rate consistent with Summers would be approximately 10.4 percent.[36] Interestingly, recent estimates of the ILECs' cost of equity using the CAPM model also yield estimates in the range of 9.96 to 10.22 percent.[37]

The literature on option values is relatively new and it cannot be proven that CAPM or other conventional cost of capital estimates always capture these effects. Nevertheless, there is little evidence to suggest that required rates of return deviate significantly from CAPM estimates.[38] For example, in U.S. industries generally, Caballero and Pindyck find that doubling industry-wide uncertainty raises the required rate of return on new capital by about 20 percent.[39]

Although the author does not agree that the ILECs' cost of capital is understated by the traditional measurements relied on by the FCC, an upper bound to the potential effect of uncertainty on the costs estimated by the TELRIC model has been estimated here by running the HAI model with a 15 percent cost of equity. The basis for this estimate is the recent filing of the ILECs at the FCC, which discusses the marketplace uncertainties faced by the ILECs as the major reason for their claim that their cost of capital has increased significantly to a range of 13.95 percent to 14.15 percent, from the 11.25 percent rate of return set in 1991.[40] It is an interesting coincidence that the increase proposed by the ILECs is close to the 20 percent suggested by Caballero and Pindyck for the impact of a doubling of uncertainty. Changing this input yields an increase in the average TELRIC cost for basic exchange service by 8 percent compared to the default run of 11.9 percent cost of equity – an upper bound well below the one suggested by Hausman.[41]

The final factor to consider is whether the CLECs' use of the network exposes the ILEC to more risk than the typical customer. ILEC customers have always had the option to use or not use the ILECs' network. The uncertainty in demand faced by the ILECs can be ascribed to a number of factors, including: Centrex (which is discussed in greater detail below), demand for second lines, substitution of different forms of access (special vs. switched) that require different mixtures of facilities, and competition. For many years the ILECs have argued that competition (of one form another) has been a major factor causing substantial financial risk. Thus, there is no reason to believe, *a priori*, that the risk to the ILECs from leasing UNEs is different than these other risks. Indeed, it is reasonable to presume that the CLECs' use of UNEs will reduce ILECs' risk, because it means that a loss of customers to a competitor will not result in a lower utilization of the network.

Regulators are unlikely to have the information available to quantify the differences in uncertainty across different users of the ILECs' network. Perhaps this explains the apparent goal of the ILECs to sow doubt and confusion on this issue. Faced with an inability to scope out the size of a problem, the regulator could reject a methodology (i.e., TELRIC) that is perceived to be highly sensitive to factors that are difficult to quantify. This concern can be dispelled by analyzing the possible impact of the CLEC demand for UNEs on the ILECs' investment costs.

The first step in this analysis is to look at the major elements of a local exchange network and consider what investments are sunk. The ILEC network has three major components: the local loop, the local switch, and interoffice transport.[42] Of these, only the local loop involves substantial sunk costs. Switching has become more modular over the last several years. Capacity can be added by installing additional line cards, switching modules, and in some cases, processor capacity. Relatively large variations in demand can be accommodated by installing or removing these different components, which can then be reinstalled at other locations. The capacity of interoffice transport facilities, which consist mainly of fiber optic links between wire centers, can be easily augmented or reduced (a rare occurrence) by substituting for the electronics at each end of the fiber.

The local loop portion of the network includes both significant sunk and non-sunk costs. Sunk costs include structure costs (poles, conduits), trenching, serving area interface construction costs, and the costs of placing the cable (copper or fiber) on the structure. Non-sunk costs include the electronics installed at the serving area interface (such as digital loop carrier equipment) and terminating equipment at the central office (e.g., fiber terminating equipment, distribution frames).

The next step in the analysis is to attempt to measure the ILECs' exposure to the risk that the CLECs will use loops for only a short period of time, after which the plant is "stranded." Making the best possible case for the ILEC side of this argument, one could measure the ILECs' exposure to this risk as the difference between the investment cost to serve 100 percent of the market versus the investment cost of serving something less than 100 percent of the market, i.e., the situation where the ILEC does not stand ready to offer UNEs to the CLECs.[43] It is then possible to answer the question of whether the ILECs will receive adequate compensation for this risk when UNEs are priced at TELRIC.

The analysis is based on the conservative assumption that the CLECs' use of UNEs would strand 10 percent of the existing number of subscriber loops. Since the ILECs' plant would be stranded only if the decline in CLEC demand is not offset by the growth in the market, this analysis allows for far greater than 10 percent market penetration by the CLECs using UNEs. To estimate the investment cost of different sized loop networks, the HAI Model 5.0a for New York Telephone was run at three levels of demand: 100 percent, 90 percent and 10 percent of current demand. Table 2 shows the results, which demonstrate significant economies of scale in the production of subscriber loops: a change in demand from 90 percent to 100 percent of the existing market requires only a 4 percent increase in investment, while the per-unit cost of serving 10 percent of the market is 5.7 times higher than the per-unit cost of serving 100 percent of the market. The presence of such large economies of scale implies that the ILECs should have a strong incentive, absent any anticompetitive strategy, to lease capacity at prices well below the CLECs' cost of constructing their own loops.

Table 2. Investment Costs by Quantity Demanded

	100 percent	90 percent	10 percent
Copper feeder cable (u/g)	274,272,241	251,740,976	55,826,874
Copper feeder cable (buried)	32,487,105	30,009,074	7,771,892
Copper feeder cable (aerial)	36,175,145	33,404,872	8,620,244
Fiber feeder cable (u/g)	24,349,087	24,119,864	23,157,448
Fiber feeder cable (buried)	63,996,012	63,246,234	55,849,239
Fiber feeder cable (aerial)	35,048,947	34,611,657	30,610,292
Feeder conduit	33,613,018	33,276,368	30,916,862
Feeder manholes	150,538,172	150,571,749	150,717,899
Copper feeder u/g placement	436,932,943	436,972,541	437,218,243
Fiber feeder u/g placement	454,238,241	454,136,879	452,549,981
Copper feeder buried placement	12,741,689	12,746,758	12,760,470
Fiber feeder buried placement	61,859,281	61,715,172	59,185,419
Feeder pole inv	50,028,698	49,943,163	48,345,673
Distribution cable (u/g)	17,216,717	15,891,511	3,879,548
Distribution cable (buried)	640,778,401	588,524,892	133,358,001
Distribution cable (aerial)	353,290,848	325,453,835	75,707,322
Distribution conduit	4,388,020	4,233,079	2,432,575
Distribution conduit placement	190,237,578	185,450,195	110,507,589
Distribution buried placement	645,979,763	616,998,556	306,282,915
Distribution poles	212,452,228	203,186,086	102,863,175
TOTAL	3,730,624,135	3,576,233,460	2,108,561,663
Per Unit Cost	37,306,241	39,735,927	210,856,166

To determine the return necessary to compensate the ILEC for making investments, it is necessary to consider the choices it faces prior to making irrevocable commitments. The ILEC has two choices. Either it can invest to have the capacity to serve 100 percent of the market, or it can invest to have the capacity to serve 90 percent of the market, maintaining the option to make an investment in the future period to serve the additional 10 percent of the market. An investment to serve 100 percent of the market involves no real option calculation, because management has no flexibility (or interest) in adding to the capacity or withdrawing that capacity in the future.[44] An investment in the first period to serve 90 percent of the market gives the ILEC the option to add to its plant in the second period, and that option must be valued.

Using the formula from Trigeorgis,[45] the value of the option to invest more in period 2 can be calculated as:

$$C = \frac{pC^{+} + (1-p)C^{-}}{1+r}$$

where C^{+} equals the value of the option if demand materializes in period 2 and C^{-} equals the value of the option if demand does not materialize in period 2. As shown in Table 2, however, the cost of the incremental investment in period 2 is 5.7 times the TELRIC cost of serving 100 percent of the market. At that per-unit cost, the incremental investment would have a negative NPV, unless for some bizarre reason the regulator allowed the ILEC to set a UNE price 5.7 times higher than its retail rates and then CLECs actually purchased the UNEs at that price – both of which are remote possibilities. Therefore, under either possible market condition, the incremental investment is not worth making. This means C^{+} and C^{-} are zero and the value of the option is zero.

Having shown that managerial flexibility is not a factor in the investment decision, it is possible to compare the cost of the investment in 100 percent versus 90 percent of market capacity to determine whether TELRIC will compensate the ILEC for making the additional investment in the first period.

If one considers the ILEC's *a priori* choice of whether to sink the investment necessary to serve this demand, the expected revenue from this investment will be a function of the probability that the CLEC uses the capacity over the life of the plant. If probable revenue (net of variable cost) equals or exceeds the cost of building the extra capacity, the ILEC will be better off building the capacity. This is expressed as:

$$\sum_{i} P_{TEL} * Q_i \lambda_i \geq (I_{100\%} - I_{90\%})$$

where PTEL is the TELRIC price (net of variable cost), Q is quantity demanded, l is the probability of demand, and I_x percent is the cost of building capacity to satisfy a demand equal to x percent of the existing market.

The analysis above indicates that the incremental investment per unit for the last 10 percent of the loops is approximately 40 percent of the average investment per loop for the entirety of the loop plant (precisely 11.1 percent additional loops are built for an additional 4.1 percent of investment, which yields a ratio of 36.9 percent). This allows the simplification of the equation above to:

$$\lambda_i \geq 0.4$$

This implies that the ILEC would build capacity to serve the CLEC at TELRIC prices, if it anticipates a 40 percent or greater probability (each year, adjusted to yield the present discounted value) that the CLEC will use the capacity over its lifetime.

This appears to be an easy condition to satisfy for a number of reasons. First, the CLECs are unlikely to build loop plant in most areas, because they will be unable to realize economies of scale equal to those of the ILECs. Second, any decline in demand by CLECs for loop UNEs may well be offset by growth in the overall demand for telephone service (e.g., second residential lines), in which case, the loop plant will not be "stranded." Third, the ILECs' tolerance for the risk of abandoned loop plant appears to be very high, based on their revealed preferences. Let history be our guide.

Over the past several decades, the ILECs have served other large customers who expose them to significant risks of decreased utilization of loop plant. Centrex has been a major competitive offering of the ILECs for decades and the ILECs have built vast amounts of additional loop plant (often concentrated in small geographic areas) to provide customers with the option to buy Centrex. Centrex service requires a dedicated loop for each station at a customer's premises. The competitive alternative to Centrex, which is a PBX at the customer premise, requires a loop only to trunk traffic between the PBX and the central office. Each individual station is linked to the PBX with inside wire and then shares the PBX trunks (i.e., the local loops) with all of the other stations at the customer premises. The ratio of the loops needed for Centrex compared to a PBX is approximately 10 to 1. Thus, the Centrex customer receives the option value of the investment made in the additional nine loops needed to provide the service. Yet the ILECs have traditionally priced Centrex service aggressively, well below the TELRIC-based rates considered as a usable proxy by the FCC in its 1996 interconnection order. The ILECs have revealed their tolerance for risk in the many Centrex tariffs filed over the past twenty years.[46] It appears that their tolerance for risk adjusts depending on the case that needs to be made to the regulator.

3. CONCLUSION

The real options issue is simply the latest in a series of arguments raised by the ILECs in an attempt to forestall competition for large segments of the local exchange market. The thesis that the ILECs are not being compensated for use of the network by the ILECs is a thinly veiled attempt to destroy any costing method or pricing rule that would deviate from guaranteeing the ILECs full recovery of embedded costs. The ILECs have, and will summon, a host of equity arguments to support their case for full recovery of embedded cost. They undoubtedly will have their day in court to argue equity, but this attempt to cloak equity in the garb of efficiency should not be given any credibility in the public policy arena.

The best way to encourage CLECs to use UNEs for a long period of time and thereby reduce the ILECs' risk of stranded plant is for the ILECs to provide high-quality service at a low price. Cooperation on the ordering, testing, and provisioning of UNEs is essential to the commercial success of the CLECs and the willingness of the CLECs to continue to use the UNEs over the long run. Thus, the greatest danger of adopting the ILEC view of the real options theory is that it will lead to greater stranded plant. That this will be accompanied by a slower introduction of competition may be in the ILECs' interests, but it is not in the public interest.

NOTES

1. Telecommunications Act of 1996, Pub. L. No. 104-104, 110 Stat. 56 (1996), amending the Communications Act of 1934, 47 U.S.C. §§ 151 et. seq.; and"Joint Board on Universal Service" and "Forward-Looking Mechanism for High-Cost Support for Non-Rural LECs," Further Notice of Proposed Rulemaking, CC Docket Nos. 96-45 and 97-160 (May 28, 1999).
2. J. Hausman, "Reply Affidavit of Professor Jerry A. Hausman," Before the Federal Communications Commission, CC Docket No. 96-98 (May 29, 1996), 1. It is difficult to sort out what Professor Hausman is referring to when he states that a "TSLRIC calculation" is biased by a factor of at least 2 and probably in excess of 3. Is he referring to the results of a TSLRIC model, or to some component in the model? The FCC's rejection of Hausman's thesis seemed to interpret his claim as referring to the "forward looking methodologies" per se (see FCC Order p. 688). This also comports with my recollection of the way in which the debate was conducted at the time. It is possible, however, that Professor Hausman's statement was misinterpreted. In a later filed affidavit, he seems to have clarified his position that the bias only refers to the sunk portion of the investment (see Testimony of Jerry Hausman, April 7, 1998, before the California PSC).

3 Although the thrust of Jerry Hausman's remarks at this conference and in his affidavits was not to defend embedded cost pricing by the ILECs, it strains credulity to believe that the goal of his attack on TELRIC costing is not part of an overall effort mounted by the ILECs to secure this result. In his first affidavit submitted in the Interconnection proceeding at the FCC, Professor Hausman states that "Numerous regulatory distortions and other economic factors weigh strongly against applying long-run incremental pricing to interconnection and network elements." (Affidavit of Professor Jerry A. Hausman, FCC CC Docket No. 96-98, filed on May 16, 1996). Further, the actual comments filed by USTA to which Professor Hausman's affidavit on real options was attached, call specifically for the recovery of embedded costs and vehemently reject the use of TSLRIC to set prices, stating that "TSLRIC-plus should still not be used as a rigid pricing formula" (see Reply Comments of United States Telephone Association, FCC CC Docket No. 96-98, filed on May 30, 1996, at 19). Further discussion of this point can be found later in this paper.

4 Monson. C. and J. Rohlfs. July 16, 1993. *The $20 Billion Impact of Local Competition in Telecommunications*, Strategic Policy Research, Inc.

5 USTA Press Release. July 1993. "Potential Impact of Competition on Residential and Rural Telephone Service," at 1.

6 The term "embedded" is an odd appellation, because its usual connotation is that the ILECs would recover the net book value of their investments *plus* their recorded operating expenses. There is nothing embedded about expenses that reflect day-to-day operational decisions by the ILECs. These expenses are not fixed costs, and there is even less legitimacy to the ILECs' argument that their rates should be set prospectively to compensate them for these costs.

7 "Defining and Funding Basic Universal Service: A Proposal of MCI Communications Corporation," July 1994.

8 Hatfield Associates, Inc. July 1994. *The Cost of Basic Universal Service.*

9 The $3.7 billion subsidy is estimated by subtracting the total cost of serving residential customers nationwide from total basic local revenues collected from these customers. This calculation yields a measure of the subsidy going to local service from other services (e.g., toll, access). There is an additional flow of subsidy going from low-cost to high-cost residential customers, which is not included in the $3.7 billlion figure. The total of both types of subsidies is approximately $6.4 billion, according to this version of the Hatfield model.

10 Section 252(d)(1).

11 Parallel to, and at times in conjunction with, the Hatfield modeling efforts, several of the ILECs developed the Benchmark Cost Proxy Model. Although this model yielded different results than Hatfield, these differences can be traced almost entirely to different input assumptions. Structurally these models were quite similar, and indeed the ILECs' participation in the BCPM process helped enhance the credibility of the TELRIC modeling efforts.

12 Fifth Report and Order, CC Docket No. 96-45 and CC Docket No. 97-160, Adopted October 22, 1998.

13 This leads to an interesting possibility, that according to USTA, the only way to get low-priced telephone service is to move to Kuwait or Bosnia.

14 Taylor, William E. October 16, 1996. *Not the Real McCoy: A Compendium of Problems with the Hatfield Model*, National Economic Research Associates, Inc. Prepared for United States Telephone Association, Ex Parte Filing at the FCC, CC Docket No. 96-45.

15 Hausman, Reply Affidavit, p. 18.

16 The ILECs' criticism of the TELRIC modeling process is at odds with their own use of LRIC models in numerous cases in the past.

17 In his first-round affidavit at the FCC, Professor Hausman supported the use of proxy rates in place of TSLRIC-based rates. He states "measurement of costs, no matter how defined, is in my experience labor intensive, time consuming, and contentious. The NPRM raises the possibility of using proxy

variables to set rates (p. 134). The idea provides significant potential benefits because transactions costs are likely to be much lower if the Commission provides a safe harbor that both parties know is acceptable." He goes on to propose the use of current access rates for interconnection charges. These rates are based on embedded costs (see Hausman, Affidavit, p.17). Similarly, the USTA filing to which the Hausman affidavit on real options was attached states that "It would be an administrative nightmare – indeed an impossibility – for the Commission itself to attempt to calculate reasonable TSLRICs for network elements" (USTA Reply comments, at 26).

[18] United States Telephone Association, Ex Parte Notice, CC Docket Nos. 96-45 and 96-262, September, 18, 1998.

[19] Id.

[20] Hausman, Reply Affidavit, at 4, argues that the assumption of constant prices for capital goods is "extremely inaccurate."

[21] See CC Docket Nos. 96-262, 94-1, 97-250, RM 9210, Comments of The United States Telephone Association, October 26, 1998.

[22] FCC. May 1999. "Preliminary Statistics of Communications Common Carriers, and New Paradigm Resources Group." *1999 CLEC Report*, 10th ed.

[23] Digital Loop Carrier equipment is the only electronic component of the subscriber loop plant, and even in a forward looking network, this equipment accounts for less than 15 percent of the total investment in the loop plant. For example, for Bell Atlantic in the State of New York, DLC costs (inclusive of the site costs) are 14.9 percent of total loop costs. Excluding the site costs, which has not been done here, would lower this percentage.

[24] Hausman, Reply Affidavit, p. 4.

[25] Northern Business Information. January 1996. *The U.S. Central Office Equipment Market,* Northern Business Information.

[26] CC Docket Nos. 96-262, 94-1, 97-250, RM 9210, Comments of The United States Telephone Association, October 26, 1998.

[27] Gollop, Frank. October 22, 1998. "Attachment D to Comments of USTA," *Technical Report: Replication and Update of the X-Factor Constructed Under the FCC Rules.* Gollop, Frank. November 5, 1998. "Attachment D to USTA Reply Comments," *Sensitivity Analysis of the FCC X-Factor to Changes in Economic Variables.*

[28] For a given expected useful life, accelerating depreciation will not change the total depreciation, but will shift the recovery schedule to earlier years. The example given in this paper of the increased costs resulting from shorter depreciation lives is a rough estimate of this effect during the early life of the equipment. Later in its life, depreciation expenses would be lower and the TELRIC prices would have to be reduced to account for the lower value of the equipment and the lower depreciation expenses.

[29] It might seem odd that loop costs fall as a result of a decrease in the life of digital switches. The reason for this is that the model spreads some categories of common cost to the elements in proportion to their annual capital costs. Hence, the increase in digital switching costs causes a decline in the *relative* costs of loops and a decreased assessment of common costs to the loop.

[30] Hausman, Reply Affidavit. p. 1.

[31] Id. ftn. 10. The reference cited by Hausman is: Lawrence Summers, "Investment Incentives and the Discounting of Depreciation Allowances." 1987. *The Effects of Taxation on Capital Accumulation,* Martin Feldstein, ed. Chicago: University of Chicago Press.

[32] This discussion was originally presented in "Depreciation and Capital Recovery Issues: A Response to Professor Hausman," Kenneth C. Baseman, Fredrick R. Warren-Boulton, and Susan Woodward, filed at the FCC in CC Docket 96-98 on July 24, 1996.

[33] See, Ibbotson Associates, *Stocks Bonds Bills and Inflation,* 1995 Yearbook, Table B-1 at 157.

[34] *Economic Report of the President,* 1993, Table B-69 at 428.

[35] The cost of equity component of the 11.25 percent cost of capital is approximately 14.0 percent, because the debt comprises approximately 43 percent of their capital and the cost of debt according to FCC methods is 7.35 percent.

[36] A measure of inflation expectations is the differential between the yield on 10-year treasury bonds and 10-year inflation adjusted treasury bonds, which is currently running at 2.0 percent (*Wall Street Journal,* 6/24/99).

[37] AT&T. March 16, 1999. *Affidavit of Bradford Cornell and John I. Hirshleifer,* FCC CC Docket 98-166.

[38] Another paper finds that price uncertainty does not affect investment in any but the most unconcentrated markets. See Goshal, Vivek and Prakash Loungani. June 1996. "Product Market Competition and the Impact of Price Uncertainty on Investment: Some Evidence from U.S. Manufacturing Industries," *Journal of Industrial Economics.*

[39] Caballero, Ricardo and Robert S. Pindyck. September 1995. "Uncertainty, Investment, and Industry Evolution," Discussion Paper, M.I.T.

[40] Comments of Dr. Randall S. Billingsley CFA, FCC CC Docket 98-166, Filed on behalf of USTA et al., March 16, 1999.

[41] The default run of the HAI model uses a cost of equity of 11.9 percent and a cost of debt of 7.7 percent, for a weighted average cost of capital of 10.0 percent, well below the current prescribed rate of return of 11.25 percent.

[42] The FCC has identified four other network elements: network interface, signaling network, operations support systems, and directory assistance and/or operator services. These account for a very small portion of the total costs of the ILECs.

[43] This test is not appropriate for measuring the short-term static efficiency benefits of requiring the ILECs to offer loop facilities at TELRIC, because the loop investments have already been made, and the return needed to maintain and operate the plant will be much lower than what it would earn at TELRIC prices.

[44] Clearly, there are other strategic considerations that the ILEC faces that will give it flexibility in the future. But for purposes of the analysis of whether prices set at TELRIC are compensatory, it is reasonable to assume that these considerations are not significant when comparing the choice between investing to serve 100 percent versus 90 percent of the market. The strategic benefit of retarding entry is explicitly excluded here because the regulator, in setting compensatory prices for UNEs, would not set prices that compensate the ILEC for foregoing entry deterring behavior.

[45] Trigeorgis, Lenos. 1996. *Real Options, Managerial Flexibility and Strategy in Resource Allocation.* Cambridge Massachusetts: The MIT Press, at 348.

[46] Another aspect of Centrex service is also instructive for the UNE debate. Centrex tariffs generally offer a lower price if the customer is willing to commit to a term of service (usually three years). This is one way of introducing the option value into the pricing process, and should be considered as an option for UNE prices. Of course, this does not mean that the month-to-month tariffs should be raised above current TELRIC estimates (just as the month-to-month Centrex tariffs were still low compared to TELRIC or other retail rates for identical network elements), but rather that discounts should be offered to CLECs that are willing to absorb more of the risk than the typical ILEC customer.

17 Discussion: A View from Outside the Industry

Lenos Trigeorgis
University of Cyprus

Because my expertise is not the telecommunications industry, I will approach the issues generically. From what I understand, the intention is to enhance competition and explicitly capture the value of any subsidies by allowing some parties to use part of the infrastructure facilities of others. If there is no explicit limitation on how long this phase will last, then there might be an incentive to delay if there are no strategic considerations. That's because if you can lease facilities in the short term versus sinking a large investment to create your own infrastructure (given the uncertainty - technological and otherwise - in the environment), it may create a bias to delay, to benefit from a "wait-and-see" approach.

If we want to encourage further investment, it should be made clear that this delay is only a temporary phase. The intention is that at the end (of this phase), we're going to move to a more competitive environment. We should thus make explicit the expiration of the option that is being provided. If the expiration of this option is limited, then other strategic considerations may arise that create incentives to invest earlier on. This is because competing firms could become worried about whether they are being positioned strategically by investing in infrastructure and obtaining benefits in order to keep up with the next generation, become a technological leader, derive benefits from spin-off applications, and so forth. Thus, there are important strategic dimensions that should be factored into this equation as we move into a more competitive environment.

In the meantime, there is an option value here, and it is only fair that it is explicitly priced in the market. One way to provide a market value to it, perhaps, would be to allow tradability in options to use these leasing rights for different time horizons (create flexibility as to whether somebody may want to use a one-year leasing option or a five-year option) and allow the marketplace to decide what the market value of these options should be, just like options traded in the environmental protection area. There are options to pollute, and there is a market for them that works quite well. In that case, the factors that determine option values, such as uncertainty, maturity, and others parameters, would have to be reflected in the traded option price.

There is also the issue of whether real options value is driven by irreversibility and whether the investment is sunk or not. I do not know enough about the telecommunications industry to judge to what degree investment is sunk. It seems that parts of the infrastructure (e.g., loops) are more irreversible and sunk than other components (like PCs and electronics circuits, which may be more reversible and may be repositioned into other uses).

In a more general environment, it would seem that part of a generic investment in a general context is reversible. We can sell assets in second-hand markets. Companies that take over other firms in order to acquire the usage of certain facilities are paying a premium for the use of those assets (the premium is embedded in the market price). We can reposition assets; and, in general, there is some salvage value, some market value for used assets, facilities and equipment. The degree of economic depreciation becomes relevant; the expected value of the asset at the end is relevant. Also, the degree of uncertainty in that value is relevant in the real options framework. And the degree of correlation of the value of that asset in an alternative use versus its value in the current use also becomes relevant.

But we need to find some way to put a fair value on the options component here. There is a premium attached to the option value. If a firm or an industry has an option to reposition assets (or some form of an abandonment option) rather than finding some useful alternative use, then the presence of this option would reduce the premium that should be paid in the absence of this option. And the exact amount of the reduction in the premium is not clear. It is not a linear relationship; there is interaction. For example, consider two options. The first is an option to delay investment or an option to expand production – this is a call-type of option in the sense that you benefit on the upside if things go well. The second is an option to abandon a project, sell it for salvage or reposition its assets in some other use – that is a put-type option, a kind of insurance that benefits one on the downside. If one has both types of options, the value of the combination is not the sum of the parts. If you first expand, you can later abandon; but if you first abandon, you cannot later expand. The values are not additive, and so determining the right premium is not straightforward.

Investment in a general context is not necessarily irreversible. It is partly reversible and flexible. And, if by investing earlier you can create a set of other related options, or there are benefits that might be derived in terms of either coming up with spin-off applications or being in a better position to come up with improved generations of the product, or if one can influence competitors' behavior through preemption or otherwise, there may be strategic benefits deriving from investing earlier. And the more and faster we move to a competitive environment, the more clear (and perhaps dominant) these strategic benefits would become, offsetting the bias of delaying rather than investing earlier. So there are many other sources of competitive advantage that may lead to a positive-NPV project or an incentive to invest early. But to get there, we must clearly see the current phase as a temporary one and put incentives in place to move to a competitive environment (that may likely put more value on infrastructure investments) as quickly as possible.

18 Rejoinder

Jerry Hausman
Massachusetts Institute of Technology

The FCC is spending hundreds of thousands, or perhaps even millions, of dollars, on constructing a computer model to set regulatory prices for the ILECs (incumbent local exchange companies). However, the economic foundation of the model is mis-specified and inappropriate because it does not take account of sunk and irreversible investments in telecommunications networks. The use of this incorrect regulatory approach is likely to cost consumers and businesses billions of dollars in lost consumer welfare due to decreased innovation and incorrect price signals. This outcome is the message of my paper, which seems to have received wide agreement from the conference participants, several of whom are cited here.

Professor William Baumol's contribution to this volume recognizes that sunk costs must be considered in a proper regulatory approach owing to the "profound implications for both theory and practice." Because Professor Baumol was an inventor of TSLRIC (which mutated into the TELRIC approach currently in use at the FCC) and supported the use of TSLRIC and TELRIC when the FCC decided on its current form of regulation in 1996, his paper is especially welcome.[1] Professor Baumol states that a cost component in the investment decision has been overlooked, so that the total costs of such decisions, and hence their appropriate prices, are normally underestimated. Professor Baumol brings in investment considerations of the IXCs (interexchange carriers), which he claims will attenuate the effect. However; I disagree with his conclusion because residential access lines cannot typically be reused for other customers. Nevertheless, we both agree that the options value of investment is a real cost that regulators must take into account if they are to make the correct decisions.

Dr. Richard Clarke similarly concludes in this volume that the application of real options theory is a valid approach in the current situation. He does not agree with my parameters for the model, but I leave this disagreement to future regulatory hearings where I would fully expect AT&T to argue for the lowest rates possible.

In his note, Professor Economides disagrees with Professor Baumol, his senior and august colleague, when he claims that the use of TELRIC guarantees economic efficiency. As Professor Baumol and I agree, TELRIC misses a cost that arises from the sunk and irreversible nature of much telecommunications network investment (whether by an ILEC or IXC). Thus, its use cannot guarantee economic efficiency. Professor Economides asserts that sunk costs are not important in ILECs' investment decisions. This assertion is in direct contradiction to Professor Baumol's previous testimony for AT&T before the FCC that sunk costs are extremely important in investment decisions in telecommunications networks. Last, Professor Economides claims that the real options approach assumes a decision-making context by a monopolist; I disagree and provide references in my paper (footnote 31). So long as imperfect competition and sunk costs exist together, the option to wait will still have value.[2] Dr. Pelcovits interprets the use of the theory as "simply the latest in a series of arguments raised by the ILECs in an attempt to forestall competition for large segments of the local exchange market." Conspiracy arguments are looked upon much more favorably within the Beltway than in academia.

Professor Baumol, Dr. Clarke, and I agree that the application of real options theory to the regulation of ILECs is potentially important, given the presence of sunk and irreversible investments. The FCC should take note of these considerations because its current approach assumes that sunk and irreversible investments are not present. Otherwise, the FCC will be an example of Lord Keynes' observation, as quoted in Professor Samuelson's textbook, that:

> The ideas of economists and political philosophers, both when they are right and when they are wrong, are more powerful than is commonly understood. Indeed the world is ruled by little else. Practical men, who believe themselves to be quite exempt from any intellectual influences, are usually the slaves of some defunct economist.[3]

In addition, the FCC is basing its regulation of ILECs on contestability theory, which does not take account of the effect of sunk and irreversible investments.[4] However, Keynes ended on an optimistic note:

> But, soon or late, it is ideas, not vested interests, which are dangerous for good or evil.[5]

Hopefully, the FCC will realize the mistake that is making sooner, rather than later.

NOTES

[1] See Affidavit of W. Baumol, J. Ordover, and R. Willig on behalf of AT&T in FCC CC Docket No. 96-98, July 1996. Also see Baumol, William J. and J. Gregory Sidak. 1994. *Toward Competition in Local Telephony.* Washington, DC: The American Enterprise Institute for Public Policy Research.

[2] While this discussion revolves around the application of real options methodology to sunk and irreversible costs, the methodology does not rely solely on this, but more generally can be applied in any situation in which management has flexibility. See Trigeorgis 1994 and 1996 and the references cited therein.

[3] Samuelson, P.A. and W.D. Nordhaus. 1986. *Economics.* Boston: McGraw Hill, 12th ed., p. 12, quoting from Keynes, J.M. 1936. *The General Theory of Employment, Interest and Money.* London: Macmillan.

[4] Indeed, contestibility assumes away sunk costs – a contestable market is one in which entry and exit are costless, hardly a representation of the telecommunications industry.

[5] Ibid.

Summary/Conclusions

19 Real Options, False Choices: A Final Word

Eli M. Noam
Columbia University

The articles in this book have been fascinating, and for several reasons. The first is the authors – their quality, diversity, readability, and engaging combativeness. The articles contained here were written by some of the most creative thinkers on the subject of the economics of telecommunications, theorists with a practical bent and practitioners at home with economic thinking.

The second owes to the book's approach: real options is fairly new as theory, and even newer as an application in telecommunications. To the best of the editor's knowledge, this is the first book to apply the new theory to the important and dynamic area of telecommunications.

But perhaps the most interesting aspect of these discussions is what they reveal about the process of knowledge creation and dissemination – how ideas are created and why, and how some ideas achieve prominence, while others meet indifference or generate ferocious opposition.

On one level, the creation and rapid prominence of real options theory tells us something about the new pecking order of the economics profession. For many years, finance theory did not enjoy great prestige. Its discounted cash flow models were boring, slow changing, and derivative. And its subject matter was narrow, materialistic, and applied. But now, as the ascendance of real option theory demonstrates, the flow of ideas has reversed its course.

Today, finance theory is exporting new tools to mainstream economics, such as to the valuation of physical assets and projects. One can speculate why finance theory has become so prominent. It is partly owing to the resources of Wall Street, which richly reward those who can provide the reality – or hope – of giving investors even the minutest of edges. The popularity of MBA programs that provide a solid institutional base is another factor. Yet another is the growing mathematical irrelevance of standard microeconomic theory. Whatever the reason, finance theory is hot, and with it real options theory.

This book demonstrates that another discipline is to be taken seriously: engineering. Once the theory needs to be supplemented with real numbers about cost –

something one would think economists are good at – they pass the buck to engineers and their network models, never minding that the underlying assumptions on prices would not pass muster at a graduate seminar. Thus, we have lawyers – the decisionmakers in the regulatory sphere – leaning on economists, and economists leaning on engineers, and engineers taking the lawyers' and economists' decisions as exogenous, each bootstrapping its validation from the other.

On a second level, the vigorous discussions in this book show that while ideas matter to the world, the world matters even more to ideas. This is not to denigrate the importance of real options theory if one suggests that it would not have achieved the same visibility if it had been primarily useful to a coterie of academic theorists. But as it happens, the idea of real options has implications, and these implications have value as powerful arguments in high-stakes debates. In telecommunications, these ideas could materially affect the interconnection charges paid by some companies to others. For some long distance companies, these payments used to account for about 40 percent of their overall expenditures; and for the local exchange companies, the receipts were over 20 percent of their revenues.

Similarly, real options theory relates directly to the payments that various companies make towards the financing of universal service in the United States, a redistributive system whose magnitude has been estimated, depending on definition, methodology, and interest, to be anywhere between about $4 and $20 billion. Given those stakes, it is not surprising that supportive ideas are in demand by both sides, and that they receive wide play by their proponents.

Unsurprisingly, different economic models lead to different conclusions. An "efficient component pricing rule" (ECPR) has been advocated by several distinguished economists. This rule is advantageous to the incumbent local exchange companies charging high prices, and has received more attention from regulators and judges than it might otherwise merit. Other pricing models result in low interconnection prices, and are therefore favored by new entrants. Forward looking long-run incremental cost (TSLRIC) is such an approach, and it, too, is supported by equally distinguished scholars. It is supplemented by planned-economy style, engineering-based proxy cost models that are advanced by the staunchest advocates of free markets. Various experts are lining up before the regulatory decision-makers, brandishing competing theories with well-compensated passion.

Who is right? Obviously, it often depends on the assumptions. But in a larger sense, it makes no difference which theory is "correct." It all depends on the policy goals. Regulators do not really care about theory, but about outcomes, along the lines determined by the political system. Interconnection prices are the tool and economic theorists provide the rationale.

Thus, when the policy goal is to expand basic telephone service or to keep basic telephone prices low, regulators will be supportive of the incumbents, as long as they recycle their gains into wide and affordable connectivity. In that situation, the cost models selected will tend to be along the lines of the "*efficient component pricing rule*" or "*distributed cost.*" Where large customers are to be favored, "*Ramsey pricing*" provides an efficiency rationale, but where consumer interests are promoted, "*network externalities*" are being factored in. More recently, as the policy goal has shifted to local competition, regulators have adopted "*long-run marginal cost*" models, whose fundamental advantage to entrants is that they are lower in price by reducing or postponing their contribution to fixed costs. And when regulators have tried to accelerate the pace of entry into local competition, they extended this approach into cost that is *"forward looking."* That phrase – as deceptively positive-sounding as "efficient components" was before it – means that the costs of a network are based on present and future prices, which tend to be lower than the "historical" ones, given the price trends of anything electronic. There are some strong theoretical arguments for such a methodology, but it is doubtful that this approach would have been chosen if the price would not trend conveniently down, but were instead going up, thus slowing down entry.

There is nothing wrong with regulators aggressively promoting their basic policies through the levers they control, such as interconnection prices. Competition had positive impacts on the telecommunications industry's performance in countries that have adopted it, and to reach such a market structure may require a temporary squeeze of entrenched incumbents to prime the pump. Yet the existence of an outcome-determined pricing model is not being openly acknowledged. Instead, regulators cloak their choices in a pseudo-scientific garb, using economics and engineering as rationalizations for what they wish to do anyway, while pretending to be led by the evidence.

This, of course, happens in regulation all the time, and everyone – except some of the economists involved – seems to understand it. Yet there is a deferred price to labeling policy preferences as economic truth because policies are temporary, shifting with circumstances. For example, once market structures have become more competitive, other pricing policies will be appropriate. It is difficult enough to wean any infant industry from regulatory protection. But if the previous model has been presented as truth rather than preference, it will be still more difficult to change.

Real options shakes up the debate with new arguments. Its proponents argue that sunk costs, depreciation, and the option value of investments should be considered in a way that would tend to raise the prices for interconnection and universal service contribution. Clearly, the incumbent LECs, having lost the previous rounds, like anything that reopens the debate. New ideas that challenge that status quo in their direction will therefore find their favor.

It would thus be easy to conclude that the new carriers of ideas are the champions of the old carriers of transmission. Yet if we measure new concepts only by the cynical yardstick of *cui bono*, debates over ideas would be pointless. One hopes that out of thesis and antithesis, however motivated, a higher form of understanding emerges. This is fundamental to scientific discourse, and no cynicism should obscure the effectiveness and success of this process.

And this forward and upward movement seems to have happened already in this project. Even several of the forceful critics of the approach largely concede its basic theoretical validity and argue against a specific application: incorrect assumptions of irreversibility, missing symmetry in both directions, lower sunk cost, management flexibility, etc. In other words, they are forging a new synthesis, against which other views can array themselves.

The next generation of discussion will inevitably challenge and improve the real options model. The truth is that the very applicability of finance-derived models to physical assets is far from settled. For securities, certain assumptions are made within the context, e.g., of the Black-Scholes model, and these are then adapted to different circumstances. Yet once this approach is taken for non-securities, the approximations may become quite distant, the noise/information ratio changes dramatically, and the model might not be appropriate. Work on the interactivity of real options is only in its infancy, and might reach different conclusions.

Similarly, the proxy cost models are a vast improvement over the black box estimates of the past. Even so, they are not the end of the story. And how could they? Huge revenue flows are directed by vast computer-based engineering models of valuation, which are based on assumptions that economists rarely support in other contexts. It should be possible to engage in this debate without working for any side or planning to do so.

In the process of intellectual discovery, the models will become more refined, more realistic, and more complex. Economists and regulators will justifiably take pride in them. In time, they might actually resemble the outcomes of market forces. But if so, why not try the real thing, market forces? Let us understand that all of the heated discussion is about a transitional system of pricing, bridging the period between monopoly and competition. If the system of administrative pricing becomes permanent, we have failed. There is a real cost in trying too hard to be exact, and tying up the policy system in developing the most advanced models. Most likely, it is better to be quick, approximate, and flexible. In that sense, there is a real societal option cost to the search for the best regulation, even if economic theory benefits in the meantime from the attention.

Biographies

James Alleman is associate professor in the Interdisciplinary Telecommunications Program at the University of Colorado and a senior advisor with PHB Hagler Bailly. He was previously the director of the International Center for Telecommunications Management at the University of Nebraska at Omaha, director of policy research for GTE, and an economist for the International Telecommunication Union in Geneva, Switzerland. Dr. Alleman has conducted research in the area of telecommunications policy, with an emphasis on pricing, costing and regulation, as well as on international telephony settlements, telecommunications in the infrastructure, and related subjects. More recently, he has been researching the application of real options valuation techniques to cost modeling. Dr. Alleman founded Paragon Service International, Inc., a telecommunications call-back firm, and has been granted a patent (number 5,883,964) on the call-back process widely used by the industry. He holds BA and MA degrees from Indiana University, and a PhD in economics from the University of Colorado.

William Baumol is director, C.V. Starr Center for Applied Economics, New York University; senior research economist and professor emeritus at Princeton University; and a consultant for AT&T. His areas of specialization include productivity growth, downsizing, scale economies, trade, antitrust, industry economics, the economics of the arts, and the economics of the environment. Among his books are, with Alan S. Blinder, *Macroeconomics: Principles and Policy*, 7th ed. (Dryden Press); with Klaus Knorr, *What Price Economic Growth?* (Prentice-Hall); *Welfare Economics and the Theory of the State* (Harvard University Press); and *Entrepreneurship, Management, and the Structure of Payoffs* (MIT Press). His book *Superfairness: Applications and Theory*, was named best book in business, management and economics by the Association of American Publishers Dr. Baumol is a member of the National Academy of Sciences.

Sanjai Bhagat was College of Business Graduate Professor of the Year – 1998 at the University of Colorado at Boulder, where he teaches corporate finance and new venture finance. He has worked previously at the U.S. Securities and Exchange Commission, Princeton University, and the University of Chicago. Dr. Bhagat has published extensively in the leading academic journals of finance (*The Journal of Finance, The Journal of Financial Economics, Journal of Accounting and Economics, Journal of Business*) on valuation, capital budgeting, investment banking, mergers and takeovers, executive compensation, board structure, and corporate performance metrics. He is the associate editor for *The Journal of Financial and Quantitative Analysis, Journal of Financial Research,* and *Journal of Corporate Finance*. He is a board member of Integra Bio-Health, a venture-capital company.

Barbara A. Cherry is associate professor in the Department of Telecommunication and the associate director of the James H. and Mary B. Quello Center for Telecommunication Law and Management at Michigan State University. Dr. Cherry also has extensive industry experience. In 1998, she left Ameritech, after completing five years as director of public policy studies. She previously worked at AT&T for ten years, where, during most of that period, she held the position of regional attorney in state government affairs.

She is the author or co-author of numerous articles on telecommunications policy. Dr. Cherry has recently written *The Crisis in Telecommunications Carrier Liability* (Kluwer Academic Publishers, Inc., 1999) and co-edited *Making Universal Service Policy: Enhancing the Process through Multidisciplinary Evaluation* (Lawrence Erlbaum Associates, 1999). She holds a PhD from the Department of Communication Studies at Northwestern University, a JD from Harvard Law School, an MA in economics and law from Harvard University, and a BS in economics from the University of Michigan.

Richard N. Clarke brings both theoretical and practical experience to the study of telecommunications markets. While at Bell Labs in the 1980s, he modeled the likely competitive effects of early proposals to eliminate the RBOC line-of-business restrictions from the 1984 Modified Final Judgement. After joining AT&T in 1989, he became responsible for developing and advocating the company's regulatory policy on access charges, LEC price cap regulation and interconnection rules. More recently, he has assumed responsibility for economic policy related to the provision of local telephone services. He is responsible for AT&T's position on the efficient pricing of interconnection, unbundled network elements, and the costing of universal service. He has testified on efficient unbundling, interconnection and pricing in state proceedings. Dr. Clarke also directs AT&T's participation in the development of the HAI/Hatfield Model of forward looking economic costs for local exchange networks and services. Prior to joining AT&T Bell Labs, he was an assistant professor of economics at the University of Wisconsin-Madison, and worked as an economist with the Antitrust Division of the U.S. Department of Justice. Dr. Clarke holds a BA in mathematics and economics from the University of Michigan, and MA and PhD degrees in economics from Harvard University.

Nicholas Economides is professor of economics at the Stern School of Business of New York University. His fields of specialization and research include the economics of networks, especially of telecommunications, computers, and information, the economics of technical compatibility and standardization, industrial organization, and the structure and organization of financial markets. He has published widely in the areas of networks, telecommunications, oligopoly, antitrust, product positioning, and liquidity and the organization of financial markets and exchanges. He has previously taught at Columbia University (1981-1988) and Stanford University (1988-1990). Professor Economides is editor of the *International Journal of Industrial Organization* and of *Netnomics*. He has recently edited a special issue of the *International Journal of Industrial Organization* on Network Economics. His book, *The Telecommunications Act of 1996 and Its Impact*, is forthcoming from MIT Press and the American Enterprise Institute. Professor Economides holds PhD and MA degrees in economics from the University of California at Berkeley, as well as a BSc (First Class Honors) in mathematical economics from the London School of Economics.

Richard Emmerson is chairman and chief executive officer of INDETEC International. He has served as senior vice president and president of Criterion Incorporated and Econometric Research Associates, Inc., respectively. He was a member of the economics faculty at the University of California, San Diego throughout the 1970s. Today, Dr. Emmerson is known as one of the world's leading experts in managerial and telecommunications economics, specializing in the long-term consequences of management decisions. With more than 25 years of experience as an economic and management consultant, he has advised such leading telecommunications providers as AT&T, the Regional Bell Operating Companies (RBOCs), GTE, Hong Kong Telecom, and many others. He has been an instructor for the Bellcore Technical Education Center, the United States Telephone Association (USTA), and Lucent, and regularly consults with the officers and senior management of Fortune 100 companies on strategy, reorganization, resource allocation, and business planning. In addition, he has worked for many international clients. Dr. Emmerson holds BA and MA degrees in economics from Humbolt State, and a PhD in economics from the University of California at Santa Barbara.

Greg Hallman is a consultant with PHB-Hagler Bailly's Palo Alto, California office. Dr. Hallman specializes in consulting and litigation assignments, primarily dealing with issues in finance. His experience includes engagements in telecommunications, energy, intellectual property, business valuation, and statistical analysis. Dr. Hallman has taught courses in finance for the University of Texas at Austin and University of California Berkeley's extension program. He holds a PhD in finance from the University of Texas at Austin, an MBA in finance from Tulane University, and a BA in chemistry from the University of Virginia.

Jerry A. Hausman is the John and Jennie S. MacDonald professor of economics at the Massachusetts Institute of Technology and director of the MIT Telecommunications Economics Research Program. Professor Hausman received the Frisch Medal from the Econometric Society in 1980, and the John Bates Clark Award from the

American Economics Association in 1985. He has conducted academic research and been a consultant in telecommunications since 1974. Dr. Hausman has published numerous academic papers in telecommunications. He is the author and editor of *Future Competition in Telecommunications* (Harvard Business School Press, 1989), and *Globalization, Technology, and Competition: The Fusion of Computers and Telecommunication in the 1990s* (Harvard Business School Press, 1993). His recent academic papers in telecommunications include "Valuation and the Effect of Regulation on New Services in Telecommunications," *Brookings Papers on Economic Activity: Microeconomics*, 1997; "Taxation by Telecommunications Regulation," *Tax Policy and the Economy*, 1998; and "Economic Welfare and Telecommunications Welfare: The E-Rate Policy for Universal Service Subsidies," with H. Shelanski, *Yale Journal on Regulation*, 1999.

Mark Jamison is the director of telecommunications studies for the Public Utilities Research Center at the University of Florida (UF). His responsibilities include developing training programs and conducting research on telecommunications issues. He is also associate director for business and economic studies at the Center for International Business Education and Research, and is a research associate with the Center for Public Policy Research at UF. From February 1993 through June 1996, he was a manager of regulatory policy for Sprint, where he developed policies on pricing, costing, and market structure. Prior to joining Sprint, he spent nine years working for state commissions. From 1987 until 1993, he was with the Iowa Utilities Board as a telecommunications analyst and later as head of research. During this time, he served as chairperson of the NARUC Staff Subcommittee on Communications, as chairperson of the State Staff for the Federal/State Joint Conference on Open Network Architecture, and as a member of the State Staff for the Federal/State Joint Board on Separations. From 1984 through to 1987, he was the communications economist for the Kansas Corporation Commission. Mr. Jamison has served on the faculty of the NARUC Annual Regulatory Studies Program.

Randall B. Lowe is the executive vice president and chief legal officer of Prism Communication Services, Inc. and Of Counsel to the law firm of Piper & Marbury in its Telecommunications, Electronic Commerce and Intellectual Property Practice Group. Mr. Lowe began his career in telecommunications with AT&T in Washington, DC, where he was responsible for the company's corporate legal activities in a five-state area including the District of Columbia; later he represented AT&T's domestic and international operations on corporate, regulatory, and legislative matters from its New York office. He then assumed similar responsibilities at ITT, where he also became involved in the development and implementation of costing methodologies for telecommunications services including access to the local exchange. Mr. Lowe has served on the boards of advisors of the International

Center for Telecommunications Management and the Netherlands-American Amity Trust. He has represented the United States on communications issues before the Trans Atlantic Business Dialogue and is a member of the Federal Communications Bar Association as well as of the Bars of the District of Columbia, New York, Connecticut, and Illinois. Mr. Lowe graduated from the University of Rhode Island. He holds a JD degree from Washington University School of Law.

Christopher B. McClain, president and CEO of Vouchsafe, Inc., has experience in the telecommunications industry both as a consultant and an employee at Pacific Bell. As a manager of strategic planning at Pacific Bell, Mr. McClain was responsible for the pricing of resale and unbundled network elements in support of interconnection agreement negotiations. He also developed and recommended long- and short-term strategic plans, including pricing plans. As a management consultant at PHB Hagler Bailly, Mr. McClain worked with a wide variety of telecommunications firms in the wireless, long distance, local, and Internet marketplaces. Mr. McClain earned a BA in economics and history and an MBA from the University of California at Berkeley. He has also taken executive management coursework at the Kellogg Graduate School of Management at Northwestern University and at the Center for Creative Leadership in Greensboro, NC.

Eli M. Noam is professor of finance and economics at the Columbia University Graduate School of Business and director of the Columbia Institute for Tele-Information. He has also served as a public service commissioner engaged in the telecommunications and energy regulation of New York State. His publications include 18 books and about 300 articles on domestic and international telecommunications, television, Internet, and regulation subjects. He served as a board member for the federal government's FTS-2000 telephone network, of the IRS' computer modernization project, and of the National Computer Laboratory. He is a member of the Council on Foreign Relations. Professor Noam holds an AB (1970, Phi Beta Kappa), a PhD in economics (1975), and a JD (1975) from Harvard University. He is a member of the New York and Washington DC bars, a licensed radio amateur advanced class, and a commercially rated pilot.

Michael D. Pelcovits is chief economist at MCI WorldCom, where he is responsible for analysis and advocacy on domestic and international economic issues before federal and state government agencies, legislative bodies, and courts. Since joining MCI in 1988, he has held senior staff and management positions supervising economic and analytical submissions to regulatory and legislative bodies. Earlier, Dr. Pelcovits was a principal of the Washington, DC consulting firm of Cornell, Pelcovits and Brenner. Before entering the consulting practice, Dr. Pelcovits served as a senior economist in the Office of Plans and Policy at the Federal Communications Commission and in the Bureau of International Aviation at the Civil Aeronautics Board. Prior to that, he was an assistant professor of economics at the University of Maryland, College Park. Dr. Pelcovits graduated summa cum laude from the University of Rochester in 1972 and received his PhD in economics from the Massachusetts Institute of Technology in 1976, where he was a National Science Foundation Fellow.

William W. Sharkey is senior economist with the Common Carrier Bureau of the Federal Communications Commission in Washington, DC. Previously he was a visiting professor at the Institut d'Economie Industrielle in Toulouse, France and at the Ecole Polytechnique in Paris, and was a member of the economics research group at Bellcore and Bell Laboratories. While at the FCC he directed the development of a staff model of the cost of local exchange telecommunications. As a consultant to the World Bank he is also assisting in the development of cost models in developing countries. His research interests include the economics of regulation, the economics of telecommunications, cooperative game theory, cost allocation, and the economics of networks. Dr. Sharkey is the author of *Theory of Natural Monopoly* (1982, Cambridge University Press). He received a BS degree in mathematics from the University of Michigan in 1969 and a PhD in economics from the University of Chicago in 1973.

Todd Strauss is a principal with the consulting firm PHB Hagler Bailly. He specializes in the development and application of quantitative models for network industries such as electric power, natural gas, telecommunications, and transportation. He has taught statistics, program evaluation, and management in the energy industry at Yale University, where he was assistant professor of public policy and management science. Dr. Strauss was a regulatory fellow at the California Public Utilities Commission, and a Gilbert White fellow at Resources for the Future. He holds a PhD in operations research from the University of California at Berkeley, and an SB in mathematics from the Massachusetts Institute of Technology.

Timothy J. Tardiff is a vice president in the Cambridge office of National Economic Research Associates (NERA). At NERA since 1984, he evaluates pricing policies for competitive telecommunications markets, including incentive regulation plans and prices for access services to competitors; studies actual and potential competition for telecommunications services; and develops approaches for measuring the incremental costs of telecommunications. Most recently, he has participated in federal and state regulatory proceedings on the implementation of the Telecommunications Act of 1996, including pricing of unbundled elements, universal service reform, carrier access pricing reform, and interLATA entry. Dr. Tardiff received a BS in mathematics from California Institute of Technology and a PhD in social science from the University of California, Irvine.

Lenos Trigeorgis is professor of finance at the University of Cyprus, and recently has been a visiting professor of finance at the University of Chicago, Columbia University, and Bocconi University, Milan. He previously taught at Boston University and the University of Massachusetts. He has published in numerous journals on corporate finance, competition and strategy, and particularly on capital budgeting and real options. He is the author of *Real Options* (MIT Press, 1996), and has edited books with Praeger and Oxford University Press; he is also preparing a number of books with Princeton University Press, McGraw Hill, John Wiley and others. He serves on the editorials boards (associate editor) of the journals *Multinational Finance Journal* and *Economia*. He holds a PhD (DBA) from Harvard University (1986).

Index

Index

A

B

C

D

E

F

G

H

M

N

O

P

Q

R

U

V

W

X

Y